To Fill the Skies with Pilots

SMITHSONIAN HISTORY OF AVIATION
AND SPACEFLIGHT SERIES

Dominick A. Pisano and Allan A. Needell, Series Editors

Since the Wright brother's first flight, air and space technologies have been central in creating the modern world. Aviation and spaceflight have transformed our lives—our conceptions of time and distance, our daily routines, and the conduct of exploration, business, and war. The Smithsonian History of Aviation and Spaceflight Series publishes substantive works that further our understanding of these transformations in their social, cultural, political, and military contexts.

TO FILL THE SKIES WITH PILOTS

THE CIVILIAN PILOT TRAINING PROGRAM, 1939–1946

DOMINICK A. PISANO

SMITHSONIAN INSTITUTION PRESS
WASHINGTON AND LONDON

Library of Congresss Cataloging-in-Publication Data

Pisano, Dominick, 1943–
    To fill the skies with pilots : the civilian pilot
training program, 1939–1946 / Dominick A. Pisano
        p. cm.—(Smithsonian history of aviation and spaceflight series)
    Originally published: Urbana ; Chicago : University of Illinois Press, 1993.
    Includes bibliographical references and index.
    ISBN 1-56098-918-1 (alk. paper)
        1. Civilian Pilot Training Program (U.S.)—History. 2. Air pilots—Training of—
    United States—History. I. Title. II. Series.
    TL560.1 .P57 2001
    387.7'4044'097309043–dc21   00-044540

British Library Cataloguing-in-Publication data available

A Smithsonian reprint of the edition published by the University of Illinois Press
in 1993

Manufactured in the United States of America

07 06 05 04 03 02 01   5 4 3 2 1

⊗ The paper used in this publication meets the minimum requirements of the
American National Standard for Information Sciences—Permanence of Papers for
Printed Library Marerials Z39.48-1984.

To Diane

Contents

Illustrations follow page 110

Preface

Franklin Delano Roosevelt's tenure as president covered twelve epoch-making years, a period marked by the Great Depression and World War II. During that time, aviation grew at an unprecedented pace and emerged as a major industrial and technological force, becoming a key element in transportation and an essential weapon of war. However, aside from two institutional histories published by the Federal Aviation Administration in the late 1970s, a chapter in Arthur M. Schlesinger, Jr.'s *The Coming of the New Deal,* and a few scattered articles, historians have given little attention to aviation in the Roosevelt years, although virtually every other facet of the New Deal has been covered extensively.

This study attempts to fill that historical gap by examining one area of Roosevelt's aviation policy, the Civilian Pilot Training Program (CPTP). Extending over the critical years from 1939 to 1946, the CPTP was a dual-purpose governmental program conceived by the Civil Aeronautics Authority to serve as a New Deal economic panacea for a neglected segment of the aviation industry and as a bulwark in the national defense by providing trained pilots in the event of war. During its lifetime, the CPTP endured a curious, and sometimes turbulent, history, one of concrete achievements and concrete failures.

The CPTP is significant because it spans the New Deal, war preparedness and mobilization, and the years of postwar adjustment; it also illuminates aspects of the Roosevelt administration's essential posture toward aviation during that important period. Moreover, the CPTP reflects a pattern of federal involvement in aviation, civilian and military, that began before World War I and continues to the present.

This book will discuss the genesis of the CPTP in the prewar years and trace how World War II shaped and transformed the program. I have attempted to analyze the changing expectations placed on the

CPTP during its existence and arrive at some conclusions about what effect these changes would have on society after the war.

My interest in the Civilian Pilot Training Program grew out of my involvement in an exhibition at the Smithsonian Institution's National Air and Space Museum titled "Black Wings: The American Black in Aviation." Research for the exhibition showed that the CPTP had been instrumental in allowing blacks, who had faced the same kinds of restrictive Jim Crow practices in aviation as in other areas of their lives, to fly in greater numbers than ever before. As my research grew, I learned more about the CPTP and was impressed by how often it was cited for successfully producing pilots in a wartime emergency and by the claims an admiring Civil Aeronautics Administration made for it long after the program ended. My curiosity about the CPTP and its broader implications was piqued. Given the state of scholarship on aviation in the Roosevelt era, however, I was not surprised to find that aside from a cursory review published in the mid-1960s by the Federal Aviation Administration and many popular articles in the aviation press, no comprehensive historical analysis existed. No single source could tell me what I wanted to know about the CPTP.

During the course of this study, I, too, came to appreciate the Civilian Pilot Training Program and its various administrators, but not for the reasons so often given. Rather, my recognition comes from an understanding of how intricate the program was, how it encountered many political and administrative problems in a brief span of seven years, and, although at times falteringly, how tenaciously it continued to adapt to meet the challenge of war on an international scale.

To be sure, the Civilian Pilot Training Program had many failings and failures and was controversial, something that has been largely forgotten with the passage of time. Moreover, many of the program's nuances and ambiguities have not been discussed and, in some instances, may never be completely explained. I believe, however, that this analysis of the Civilian Pilot Training Program takes into account all these factors, explains its multifaceted character in a balanced, even-handed way, and contributes to the extant sparse body of literature. I hope that it will add to established scholarship on the latter stages of the New Deal and America's efforts to prepare and mobilize for World War II.

For making this study possible, I would like to thank Bernard M. Mergen, professor of American civilization, American Studies Department, George Washington University; Tom D. Crouch, chair, Department of Aeronautics, National Air and Space Museum,

Smithsonian Institution; and Von D. Hardesty, curator and former chair, Department of Aeronautics, National Air and Space Museum, Smithsonian Institution. All three men made timely comments, asked critical questions about context, and provided helpful suggestions for improving various drafts of the manuscript. Without their help, encouragement, and forbearance, I could not have completed this work. Von Hardesty was especially kind in reading and reviewing the final draft and allowing me to take a brief leave of absence from the Aeronautics Department of the National Air and Space Museum.

To my colleagues at the museum, I am grateful for various forms of assistance and support. Special thanks go to Joanne Gernstein, Peter Jakab, Don Lopez, Anita Mason, Bob van der Linden, Howard Wolko, Trish Graboske, Phil Edwards, Martin Smith, Dave Spencer, Larry Wilson, and Bob Dreesen.

Financial support for substantial parts of this study was provided by the Smithsonian Institution's Research Opportunities Fund, which enabled me to visit the Robert H. Hinckley Papers and the Robert H. Hinckley Institute of Politics at the University of Utah. For this help I would especially like to thank Martin Harwit, David Challinor, Robert Hoffman, and Ross Simons.

I would also like to thank Nancy V. Young, head of the Manuscripts Division, Marriott Library, University of Utah, and Bea Gardner, assistant director of the Robert Hinckley Institute of Politics, University of Utah, for making available much invaluable material on the Civilian Pilot Training Program and Robert Hinckley. Karen Hewitt of the University of Illinois Press offered kindness, patience, and unstinting help during the editorial process. Mary Giles painstakingly edited the manuscript.

Finally, I am grateful to Diane Oberlin for her criticism, help, support, and loyalty.

Introduction

The United States, which had taken pride in distancing itself from foreign entanglements for more than two decades after World War I, entered 1939 with an endangered commitment to neutrality. The threat of war hung over Europe, and the destructive potential of the German war machine was a troubling prospect as America attempted to maintain peace. Expectations that the United States would remain neutral through the burgeoning conflict began to grow dim. In his State of the Union address to Congress on January 4, President Roosevelt had turned away from the domestic problems that had so consumed his administration for nearly six years and focused on the inflamed international situation. "The world has grown so small," he said, "and weapons of attack so swift, that no nation can be safe. . . . There are methods short of war, but stronger and more effective than mere words, of bringing home to aggressor governments the aggregate sentiments of our own people."[1]

There was little doubt that when F.D.R. spoke of the swiftness of the "weapons of attack" he was referring to Germany's takeover of Austria and the Sudetenland the previous year and, at least indirectly, to the ominous threat of Hitler's Luftwaffe. Although his reference to "methods short of war" was intentionally ambiguous, the phrase signaled a turn away from the isolationist policy that the United States had pursued after World War I.

The direction of American foreign policy, however, had already begun to be subtly transformed some fifteen months earlier in October 1937. In an indirect response to Japanese aggression in China, the president had warned an audience in Chicago that if acts of war were allowed to go unchecked in other parts of the globe, "let no one imagine that America will escape, that it may expect mercy, that this Western Hemisphere will not be attacked, and that it will continue tranquilly and peacefully to carry on the ethics and the arts of civilization." As Robert Divine has pointed out, the Chicago speech "boldly and dramatically repudiated [Roosevelt's] earlier hope that the United States could remain aloof from foreign wars as a beacon of liberty."[2]

A little more than a year later, the international scene had worsened considerably, this time with Adolf Hitler's conquest of Austria and Czechoslovakia. As if to underscore the urgency of his 1939 State of the Union address, Roosevelt, on January 12, sent Congress a message on the national defense, urging the expenditure of $525 million, $300 million of which was to be earmarked for the construction of modern military aircraft that could match the "increased range, increased speed, increased capacity of airplanes abroad." In requesting such a huge expenditure, the president had begun to step over the fine line he had walked in preparing a largely unprepared country for the possibility of war.[3]

The president was also acknowledging that the administration perceived air power to be a critical component of a future war. The well-known financier Bernard M. Baruch had brought home this fact most vividly. After his return from a mission to Europe in 1938, Baruch confirmed what the army and Ambassador to Great Britain Joseph P. Kennedy had ascertained from intelligence sources: German production of synthetic oil and rubber had made that country impervious to blockade, and Britain was falling behind Germany in the production of arms.[4]

More important, Baruch reported that Britain's air power was no match for Germany, a fact later verified by the Military Intelligence Division of the General Staff. In *The Struggle for Survival,* his study of the problems that beset America's war mobilization, Eliot Janeway points out that "the Luftwaffe commanded five bombers to Britain's one, and eleven to our one. The General Staff report credited Germany with having 3,353 medium and heavy bombers. In the year of Munich, this was enough." Although Baruch's report may have been exaggerated to win support for air power, the perception that Germany had an insurmountable lead in military aviation was enough to persuade Roosevelt that isolationism was untenable. To make matters worse, Baruch's assessment was given credence by the use of German and Italian air power in the recently concluded Spanish Civil War, especially the bombardment of Guernica by the Condor Legion.[5]

It was in this gray area between the struggle for American economic recovery and the emerging threat of war that the Roosevelt administration began to search for ways to prepare for what was beginning to be the eventuality of war, especially for ways to shore up

America's sagging aerial capabilities. The interwar years had been especially stark for the Air Service and its successor the Army Air Corps, which had to struggle for recognition, greater autonomy within the structure of the army, and a larger share of its part of the army's budget to meet its personnel and equipment needs.

Because it had been forced to make do with a limited number of aircraft in the interwar years, the prospect of increased military aircraft production could only hearten the Air Corps. Nevertheless, procuring large numbers of additional aircraft presented several problems, not the least of which was the lack of the trained pilots who would be needed if the United States were to fight a full-scale war in the air. In July 1939, the Army Air Corps set its goal: a twenty-four-group force by June 30, 1941. To achieve this objective, the Air Corps would have to train 1,200 pilots a year. Before 1939, the Air Corps produced an average of two hundred flying cadet graduates annually. Approximately six times this number of pilots would have to be produced to meet the quota.[6]

It was partially in response to the need for more trained pilots that the Civilian Pilot Training Program, the first full-scale, federally funded aviation education program and one of the largest government-sponsored vocational education programs of its time, was born. The brainchild of Robert H. Hinckley, a quintessential New Deal administrator with ties to Harry Hopkins and the regional Works Progress Administration network, the CPTP was designed to use the classrooms of American colleges and universities and the facilities of local flying schools certified by the CAA, supported by government funds, to provide a pool of young civilian pilots who would be available for military service if war came.

Hinckley believed that the CPTP would also make American youth "air-minded" through flight instruction and school curricula, provide vocational training for future employment in the aviation industry, resuscitate a depressed lightplane industry, and give an economic boost to fixed-base operators (who provided services such as flying lessons, charter flights, aircraft sales and maintenance, and fuel and supplies) who found themselves in straitened circumstances as a result of the depression. Finally, the program would pave the way for a postwar boom in private flying by providing a ready-made source of pilots who would spur demand for recreational aircraft.

The timing of the CPTP, coming as it did in early 1939, might suggest that it was strictly a military preparedness program designed to train pilots for the armed forces. However, the program was originally structured so that military service was optional and its trainees would be motivated by patriotism to enlist. Moreover, the program's dimensions were distinctly New Deal in philosophy. By pumping money into the light aviation industry and small airport operations, the CPTP would realize the New Deal goal of providing economic aid to business enterprises affected by the depression. By "air conditioning" young Americans to the emerging air age and providing vocational education, the CPTP would fulfill the New Deal idea that government should provide vocational education subsidies for American youth. By boosting a postwar aviation economy, the CPTP would satisfy the New Deal strategy of long-range planning to prevent economic dislocation on the scale caused by the Great Depression.

The duality of the CPTP—civilian versus military goals—appears to be self-contradictory. In theory, at least, the CPTP's objectives were in harmony with broader New Deal ideas about how to solve the problems caused by the depression. One could argue, as has William E. Leuchtenburg, that the New Deal owes a debt to the rhetoric and goals of mobilization for World War I. In Leuchtenburg's estimation, the New Deal consisted of a series of peacetime programs conceived and promoted using a wartime metaphor and wartime experience. The Tennessee Valley Authority "grew out of the creation of a government-operated nitrate and electric-power project at Muscle Shoals during and after the war" and "was only one of a number of resources operations—from soil conservation to public power development—that employed war rhetoric or drew from World War I experience."[7]

In a sense, Leuchtenburg's thesis could apply equally well to the Civilian Pilot Training Program. Although the CPTP's origins did not lie in World War I mobilization, its civilian-military dimensions were thought to be in perfect accord; its rhetoric was couched in terms of a holy, warlike crusade for aviation; and its New Deal social cultural ideals were never entirely abandoned throughout its lifetime, despite the disruption of war. Thus, the idea that the CPTP could successfully bridge the gap from depression to war without giving up its basic civilian direction was compatible with broad New Deal thinking.

However, as Frank Freidel has pointed out, "waging a war on the depression was in some ways the reverse of waging one on a foreign foe." This was true of the Civilian Pilot Training Program. From the outset, the CPTP suffered from a split identity that interfered seriously with its effectiveness. The CPTP's dual purpose—economic recovery for the depressed light aviation industry and small airport operators and the prewar mobilization of civilian pilots—was suspect from the start and contributed to the program's problems during the war. At the outset, legislators, the military, and nearly all sectors of the aviation industry with whom the New Deal's aviation policies had tenuous credibility had to be convinced of the benefits of the CPTP before agreeing to support the legislation. Although they had been consulted beforehand and had given tentative approval, the army and the navy, which both would be affected directly by the legislation, were tacitly suspicious that the Civil Aeronautics Authority, a civilian agency, would have administrative control over the training of men who might eventually become military pilots. In addition, the CPTP came under fire from isolationists and noninterventionists who saw the program as a thinly veiled militarist plot to embroil the United States in the war in Europe.[8]

Even before the United States entered World War II, the program had been criticized (some would say unfairly) for its supposed ineffectiveness in channeling pilots to the military. When the United States entered the war, the program—enlarged in scope, changed in direction to help directly in the war effort, and largely stripped of its New Deal impetus—was the source of further conflict between the Army Air Forces and the Civil Aeronautics Authority. Finally, congressional attempts to perpetuate the CPTP after the war again ran into trouble with the military. The expectation, based on the program's "air-mindedness" aspect, that a renewed CPTP would bring about a hoped-for revolution in private aviation never materialized.

If the CPTP only partially lived up to its original multifaceted promise to train and make pilots available to the war effort, to give an economic boost to the lightplane industry and fixed-base operators, and to condition young Americans to the evolving air age, the blame cannot be placed entirely on the program or its administrators, who were, in all respects, capable, dedicated, and inventive. As a transitional New Deal, war-preparedness program, the CPTP was born divided in its aims. Later, when exigencies of global conflict forced it to change directions, the program became caught up in the drive to win the war and was fragmented and reshaped beyond its original purpose and identity. As a result, it was only partially successful in making the necessary transition from peace to war and back to peace.

Gerald D. Nash and David Brody's characterization of the immediate period before America's entry into World War II most aptly describes the New Deal's and, thus, the CPTP's dilemma. Nash points out that the pattern of the general preparedness program laid out by the Roosevelt administration between 1939 and 1941 was "piecemeal and experimental" in nature, "as was the New Deal from 1933 to 1935." The ad hoc character of a good many of these programs, Nash observes, "resulted in waste and duplication that hampered rearmament." Brody comments that "for more than two years after the German invasion of Poland, the United States stayed formally at peace. Roosevelt led a country still largely isolationist in sentiment and unwilling to go on a war footing. Always far ahead of the country on the need for American intervention, yet never daring to call the country to arms, Roosevelt had to follow a tortuous course, that as events permitted, involved the country by slow steps in the Allied cause and that brought about a sadly incomplete form of mobilization."[9]

Moreover, Eliot Janeway has observed that the irregular pattern that Roosevelt established before the war persisted well into World War II. "Any judgment upon Roosevelt's leadership of the home front must allow for the double standard by which he worked. Politically, Roosevelt's performance was professional; technically, it was amateurish. Again and again, his administrators disorganized the home front. But this neither alarmed Roosevelt nor upset him. . . . Roosevelt's critics have said—and say—that he mobilized the Washington echelon of the home front on a basis that he better than any knew would not work . . . that he reorganized and reorganized wartime Washington into a comptroller's hell, into a jungle of confusion and duplication and self-contradiction in which even he ended by feeling lost." Ironically, "this irresponsibility—disastrous on the face of it—did not culminate in disaster."[10]

The Civilian Pilot Training Program falls squarely into the category described by Nash, Brody, and Janeway. Not only was the CPTP inadequate as a hedge against the eventuality of war, but in many ways it also was inadequate as a wartime program. The CPTP is significant because it illustrates how programs conceived either in a New Deal, or transitional New Deal, war-preparedness atmosphere were later either forced to shift gears to accommodate to winning the war or be abandoned. The degree to which they were able to adapt to changing conditions on a global scale, their success in establishing harmonious relationships with the military, and the extent to which the war compromised their broad prewar objectives would be the ultimate measures of their success or failure.

Such programs as the National Youth Administration (NYA) or the Civilian Conservation Corps (CCC), conceived earlier than the CPTP but with similar goals for the training of youth, did change but could not survive. By 1940, for example, the NYA was providing vocational training that would lend itself to national defense. At about the same time, the CCC required that its enrollees take part in military drills, learn to read blueprints, and work on military reservations. Later, both programs were scrapped because the need for them had diminished and also because conservatives in Congress cut off their funding.[11]

The difference between the CPTP and these programs, however, was that the CPTP was designed specifically with economic recovery and war preparedness in mind. Unlike the NYA and CCC, the CPTP survived World War II, but eventually was denied the appropriation that would have allowed it to continue. What the creators of the CPTP could not have foreseen in 1939, when its civilian-military goals did not appear to be incompatible, was the program later becoming an arm of the military, a job that it was not entirely suited for given its original charter as a civilian-military entity.

What is perhaps lost sight of amid a welter of seemingly contradictory ideas about the CPTP's primary function is that, as part of its New Deal dimension before World War II, the CPTP produced greater numbers of privately licensed pilots than ever before. It also provided a limited economic stimulus to the lightplane industry. Later, the CPTP made good on explicit New Deal promises to foster "air age education" by producing textbook and curriculum materials that used aeronautics to teach children about science, geography, social studies, industrial arts, and other subjects. The CPTP also gave a scientific foundation to psychological testing and research into various aspects of pilot training and provided training for blacks and, until January 1942, women. Moreover, although its broader New Deal mandates were largely cast aside by wartime considerations, the CPTP did contribute significantly to the successful training of hundreds of thousands of military pilots who served with distinction in various flight specialties during World War II.

Thus, the Civilian Pilot Training Program—with its duality, vicissitudes, endless conflicts with the Army Air Forces, and many problems political and otherwise throughout its duration—fits the crazy-quilt pattern that the Roosevelt administration established in its attempt to make the transition from peace to war. How well the Civilian Pilot Training Program fulfilled its multifaceted charter as part of a New Deal-war preparedness plan, and how successfully the Roosevelt administration handled aviation policy and war preparedness mobilization, are the central questions explored in the following chapters.

CHAPTER 1

The CPTP, the New Deal, and War Preparedness

On August 8, 1938, presidential appointee Robert H. Hinckley took his oath of office and began to assume his duties as a member of the Roosevelt administration's newly created Civil Aeronautics Authority (CAA). At the time, he had little or no idea of the controversy he would engender because of what appeared to be a simple idea. Hinckley's plan would apply New Deal economics to the need for trained pilots in what he thought would be the perfect solution to the problems of a depressed private aviation industry and the lack of preparedness for war in the air.[1]

Hinckley, a Mormon, was born in Fillmore, Utah, on June 8, 1891. After graduating from Brigham Young University in 1916, he had, among other things, taught school, been a member of the Utah State House of Representatives, owned an automobile dealership, and operated Utah-Pacific Airways Aviation Company, a fixed-base operation in the industry's parlance, that offered flight lessons and a charter taxi service, sold aircraft, fuel, and supplies, and provided maintenance. In 1932, Hinckley turned his attention to welfare administration for the state of Utah, serving on Governor Henry H. Blood's Voluntary State Relief Commission. In 1933, he became director of the State Emergency Relief Administration, organized the Civilian Conservation Corps (CCC) in Utah, and directed the Federal Emergency Relief Administration (FERA) for Utah and six other western states. In 1934, he managed a water conservation and development program for the state of Utah. Shortly afterward, Hinckley became acquainted with Harry Hopkins, who took him under his wing and persuaded him to work for the federal government during Franklin D. Roosevelt's New Deal.[2]

Hinckley's first job in Washington was as assistant administrator for the Federal Emergency Relief Administration. In 1935, when

Hopkins became head of the Works Progress Administration (WPA), Hinckley was named assistant WPA administrator for the western region, with jurisdiction over eleven states. He oversaw airport, highway, reservoir, and water conservation construction projects, along with the Federal Arts Project, the Federal Writers Project, and various other WPA programs.[3]

Worn out after nearly five years of FERA and WPA work and re-covering from a serious automobile accident, Hinckley decided to return to Utah and tend to his private business interests, which he had neglected. The hiatus from government service would be short-lived. In 1938, after F.D.R. signed the Civil Aeronautics Act, Hopkins cajoled Hinckley into coming back to Washington to assume one of the five posts in the newly organized Civil Aviation Authority.[4]

In April 1939, when CAA chair Edward J. Noble moved to the Department of Commerce, Hinckley was named to take his place. Because the CAA had responsibility for technical oversight and ap-proval of all airport projects initiated by government work relief agencies, one of Hinckley's first official tasks was to supervise the construction of Washington's National Airport, which F.D.R. had ap-proved in September 1938. Amid strong congressional disapproval over Roosevelt's involvement, funding disputes, and jurisdictional clashes between the District of Columbia and the commonwealth of Virginia over land boundaries, Hinckley guided the building of the airport, which began operations on June 16, 1941.[5]

During his early days in the CAA, Hinckley had come up with the idea of a government-sponsored plan of flight instruction that eventually would be called the Civilian Pilot Training Program (CPTP). The idea had originated in 1938 out of a discussion he had with Noble and Hopkins on the state of defense preparedness. The CPTP would give young people flight training through universities, colleges, local fixed-base operators, and flight schools certified by the CAA. The universities and colleges would provide ground in-struction; the fixed-base operators and flight schools, flight instruc-tion.

Hinckley envisioned that such a program would fit appropriately into the New Deal policy of pump-priming by resuscitating the de-pressed economy of the private aviation industry. It also would pro-vide a standing reserve of trained pilots in a wartime emergency. As Hinckley pointed out, "civilian lightplane aviation was on dead cen-ter if not in full retreat. Small fields were closing down by the score, others had such a small margin of profit that only love of flying kept their operators in business, lightplane builders were even closer to the brink of bankruptcy, and the entire industry was faced with disaster." As part-owner of Utah Pacific Airways, which had failed during the depression, Hinckley knew firsthand the struggle for survival that these small companies had waged in the lean years after the economy collapsed.[6]

Unlike many professionals in the CAA's bureaucracy, most of whom were interested in the business, engineering, or legal aspects of aviation, Hinckley believed if America was to be in the forefront of the so-called air age, aviation should have both cultural and technological importance. Thus, the CPTP would be the showpiece of what Hinckley called "air conditioning," the notion that American youths must be introduced to the new air age by learning to fly and taking courses in the emerging science of aeronautics. The program fit the larger pattern of state-sponsored air training of youth that had begun in Europe in the interwar period and was especially popular in Germany, Italy, France, Great Britain, and the Soviet Union. Hinckley commented that Adolf Hitler was so dedicated to promoting "air-mindedness" in the German education system "from kindergarten through college" that he "put all possible emphasis on the importance of aviation to the German Nazi state."[7]

The CPTP was originated with the postwar aviation economy in mind, too. Hinckley expected that if the United States did go to war, the CPTP would help produce a postwar boom in private aviation. How it would help in bringing about this upsurge was not formally defined until late 1943, when John H. Geisse and Samuel C. Williams, two consultants to the Department of Commerce, reported on it formally in "Postwar Outlook for Private Flying." However, postwar prosperity in the industry was considered more reality than hypothesis. Hinckley emphasized that "aviation would get into the vocational training system, and fixed-base operators, who would sponsor flight training, would have a chance to make a little money" and thus "give first-aid to defense and a stimulus to postwar industry."[8]

In its role as a stimulant to the flagging private aviation economy, the CPTP fit the paradigm of New Deal programs of the period. As many historians of the Roosevelt era have pointed out, the series of programs commonly called the New Deal was complex and not easy to define, however, some generalizations can be made. Arthur Schlesinger, for example, has commented that the New Deal was typified by "quick and spectacular action"; an "enlarged conception of governmental responsibility; "persistent experimentation," as F.D.R. put it; and "cooperative business-government planning," in Raymond

Moley's terms.[9] The CPTP met all these qualifications. The program was conceived in rapid and decisive fashion, involved the payment of generous government subsidies to bring a segment of the aviation economy back to life, was a cooperative government-business effort, and was experimental in that nothing on this scale of governmental assistance to private aviation had ever before been contemplated.

The CPTP was also typical of the era between the New Deal and the period of early, and often clandestine, war preparedness. During this period, Richard Polenberg obseves, "New Deal bureaucrats commonly justified their programs on the grounds of their contribution to preparedness." The Tennessee Valley Authority, National Youth Administration, and Civilian Conservation Corps, for example, justified continuing their programs for reasons of national defense. "The turn in this direction reflected not only a genuine belief that such projects would do the most good but a recognition that they were likely to receive funding from a stingy Congress."[10]

This was also true of the CPTP. Although ostensibly it was a civilian program, of necessity it became part of the larger effort of war preparedness that global events thrust upon the second Roosevelt administration. Despite his role as head of the peacetime Works Progress Administration, Harry Hopkins's interest in mobilization was no accident. According to Polenberg, "In 1938, officials of the Works Progress Administration became deeply involved in a planned expansion of aircraft construction, in part because Roosevelt mistakenly assumed that the government would have to build and operate a number of plants and would therefore be putting jobless men to work."[11]

Polenberg's observation aptly summarizes the duality of the CPTP. Hopkins and Hinckley saw the program as a way of accomplishing both New Deal and war-preparedness objectives. Hinckley convinced Hopkins that such a program would work, Hopkins gave his blessing to the enterprise, and Hinckley began to move to make the program a reality. In so doing, however, Hinckley faced many obstacles. Congress, the military, the aviation industry, and the aeronautical community at large were suspicious of the New Deal's attitude toward aviation and skeptical of the CPTP.[12]

If, on the one hand, the New Deal symbolized action, increased government responsibility, and cooperation between the private and federal sectors, it was also characterized by a haphazard quality and lack of coherent planning. Albert U. Romasco has commented that "there was neither unity nor meaning to Roosevelt's economic eclecticism in his improvisation of the New Deal, if these policies are analyzed and judged from an economic standpoint. His objectives, from first to last, were political, and Roosevelt's performance in pursuit of his political purposes was nothing less than masterful."[13]

This haphazardness and incoherence were especially evident in the administration's attitudes toward aviation. How it handled several key policy matters—the Black Committee hearings on the aviation "trust," the so-called airmail crisis and Eugene Vidal's $700 Airplane for Everyman program in 1934, the TWA crash that killed Senator Bronson Cutting in 1935, and the bitter disagreement over the Civil Aeronautics Act of 1938—demonstrates a lack of direction and a penchant for politically expedient measures. If one is to understand the CPTP, it is necessary to place it in a proper political context by examing events that preceded it.

High Hopes for a New Deal for Aviation

After twelve years of laissez-faire Republican attitudes toward aviation, the New Deal came as a shock to members of Congress who supported aviation, the military aviation community, and the aviation industry. As Nick Komons, a historian of the Federal Aviation Administration, aptly points out, whatever else the Coolidge administration may have done, it helped usher aviation into the mainstream of transportation in the United States. With the help of Dwight Morrow, Coolidge created the Air Commerce Act, the "legislative cornerstone," as Komons describes it, "on which to erect a commercial air transport system." This was "the only genuine legislative achievement of the Coolidge presidency." In providing for aircraft registration and certification, certification of pilots, and the regulation of air traffic, the Air Commerce Act untangled the mess that had characterized American aviation in the period immediately after World War I.

Similarly, Coolidge's successor, Herbert Hoover, through the efforts of Postmaster General Walter Folger Brown, could take credit for restructuring the U.S. airline map, correcting the wasteful and irrational airways that had been in place, and making a nationwide system of air-passenger routes possible. Throughout the period, especially from 1927 to 1929 when the value of aviation stocks climbed to $1 billion on the New York Stock Exchange, the Coolidge and Hoover administrations took a hands-off attitude toward widespread manipulation of aviation securities and the creation of monopolies. From 1927 to 1933, two major companies, United Aircraft and Transport Corporation and Curtiss-Wright, controlled aircraft and engine sales, with 81 percent of the market. As in other areas of American economic life, big business appeared to dominate aviation under approving Republican eyes.[14]

However, not everyone connected with the aviation industry was content with how the Republicans handled aviation policy. Despite Republican accomplishments in fostering civil aviation and the fact that the depression had no significant effect on the air transport industry, some segments of the aviation community—the military and private aviation—felt neglected because they had not been given as much support as had commercial aviation. As Roosevelt swept into office, these forgotten segments of the aeronautical world anticipated what they hoped would also be a New Deal for aviation.

The Black Committee Hearings

Subsequent events dispelled the unanimous favorable attitude toward F.D.R. in the aviation community. On January 17, 1934, Senator Hugo Black (D.-Ala.), a strong supporter of Roosevelt and the New Deal, began to hear testimony before his Special Committee on the Investigation of Air and Ocean Mail Contracts. Black had received a tip from correspondent Fulton Lewis of the Hearst newspaper chain that former Postmaster General Brown had conspired to award lucrative airmail contracts to selected air transport companies, disregarding the established method of competitive bidding. As Arthur Schlesinger, Jr., describes it, "a dismally familiar picture emerged—immense salaries, bonuses, and speculative profits; dubious relations between the industry and the government officials who dealt with it; the avoidance of competitive bidding; the covert destruction of official records—all in all, an exceptionally blatant case, it seemed, of an industry using government to exploit the public."[15]

The Black Committee focused on Brown's actions after Herbert Hoover had signed the McNary-Watres airmail legislation into law. In April 1930, shortly after the new act had gone into effect, Brown invited representatives from several airlines to Washington for a series of meetings and asked them to arrive at an agreement about how the airmail contracts would be distributed. Brown was interested particularly in who would be awarded the transcontinental airmail contracts. Because no agreement was forthcoming, he decided to take matters into his own hands. In what would later become famous as the "Spoils Conferences," the airline operators, according to an eyewitness, "agreed unanimously that the postmaster general should act as umpire in settling and working out such voluntary rearrangements as might be necessary, to the end that the . . . transcontinental lines be established."[16]

The upshot of the Spoils Conferences was that Brown awarded two transcontinental airmail contracts without competitive bidding. One went to American Airways, the other to Transcontinental and Western Air. Transcontinental and Western was the forerunner of Trans World Airlines, formed from the forced merger of Transcontinental Air Transport and Western Air Express—a merger Brown had mandated to accomplish his airline rationalization scheme. To shut out what he considered "wildcatters" (small, independent lines not tied to the huge airline conglomerates), Brown had written into the advertisement for bids a provision stipulating that a carrier must have flown a night route at least 250 miles in length over a period of six months in order to qualify for a contract. This provision blocked the efforts of small, independent companies to gain an airmail contract, and Brown later was blamed for discrimination in adding the stipulation.[17]

To Hugo Black, Brown's actions smacked of collusion and fraud. The Black Committee not only revealed Brown's role in the division of the spoils among those airline companies that he favored, but it also uncovered a pattern of what it considered abuses of government by previous Republican administrations on behalf of the aviation industry.

The committee's hearings were typical of the New Deal's antagonism toward big business and the trusts. Black was convinced that "the control of American aviation had been ruthlessly taken away from the men who could fly and bestowed upon bankers, brokers, promoters and politicians sitting in their inner offices allotting among themselves the taxpayer's money."[18] To the members of the aviation industry, however, Black's methods smacked not only of self-righteousness and inquisition but also constituted a threat to destroy what the industry had labored so long to build. *Business Week* echoed these sentiments by commenting that the Black investigation sought "to retard the aviation business, destroy its assets, weaken its credit, and shake public confidence in it."[19]

The Air Mail Contract Cancellations

The Black Committee hearings were enough to convince F.D.R. to cancel the airmail contracts and institute changes in mail delivery. On the morning of February 9, 1934, the day of the cancellation, Chief of the Army Air Corps Benjamin D. Foulois spoke with Second

Assistant Postmaster General Harllee Branch. Branch asked if the Air Corps could carry the airmail on an interim basis. Interpreting Branch's request as a direct order from Roosevelt, Foulois quickly assented, saying that the Air Corps could begin to fly the mail within ten days. Because of Foulois's reassurances, the president issued the order to void the contracts and directed the Army Air Corps to begin delivering the mail.[20]

The Air Corps, however, was ill-prepared and courted certain disaster by agreeing to take on what was under the best circumstances a difficult job. Besides having to operate obsolete aircraft that lacked the required radio and navigation devices for night and bad-weather flying over uncertain terrain, Air Corps pilots and crews were not properly trained for the task. To make matters worse, the winter of 1934 was one of the worst in recent memory throughout the country. Icy winds and heavy storms hit the West. Snow, rain, and heavy fog covered the Northeast from New England to Ohio, with similar conditions in the Midwest.[21] On February 16, three days before the first official mail deliveries, three Air Corps pilots died tragically in training accidents caused by the bad weather. By February 23, four days after the Air Corps had begun flying the mail, six pilots had died and one had been injured seriously.[22]

Predictably, members of the aviation industry were outraged by the cancellation and the deaths of the pilots. On February 11, two days after the president had given the order, Charles A. Lindbergh fired off a telegram to Roosevelt, charging that in canceling the contracts, the president had not discriminated "between innocence and guilt," and that he placed "no premium on honest business."[23]

The journalistic outcry against the cancellations was also vehement. The press blamed politics for the deaths of the military aviators and called for an immediate reinstatement of the civilian airmail service. The *New York Evening Journal* declared, "The senseless butchery of young Army aviators MUST STOP." The *Los Angeles Times* said it was "high time to halt [the] wanton slaughter" and claimed that the killing of army pilots was inevitable "when airplanes are put to uses for which they are not designed and pilots take up work in which they have no experience."[24]

By March 10, some three weeks after the army had assumed airmail delivery, four more Air Corps personnel had been killed. That same day, Roosevelt summoned Foulois and Army Chief of Staff General Douglas MacArthur to the White House and asked bluntly, "When are these airmail killings going to stop?" Foulois responded, "Only when airplanes stop flying, Mr. President." Roosevelt then unleashed a ten-minute tirade that Foulois later characterized as the worst tongue-lashing he had ever received.[25] Then, in a letter to Secretary of War George Dern, F.D.R. ordered a revised policy that the Air Corps was to put into immediate effect. The Air Corps would cease flying the mail "except on such routes, under such weather conditions and under such equipment and personnel conditions as will insure, as far as the utmost care can provide, against constant recurrence of fatal accidents."[26]

Because of the presidential order, the Army Air Corps began to retrench. It temporarily halted the airmail flights and took stock of the situation. It made safety rules more stringent, modified new equipment such as the technologically advanced Martin B-10 bomber to carry mail, and directed pilots and crew members to practice night and instrument-aided flight. Although another pilot was killed in a training flight near Cheyenne, Wyoming, after F.D.R. rescinded the order, the suspension had been a success. Roosevelt, convinced that he had no choice but to allow the airlines to recommence carrying the mail, decided to let temporary contracts for three months. The commercial airlines resumed flying the mail on May 7. On that day, after twelve deaths and sixty-six air accidents, the Air Corps made its final coast-to-coast mail run.[27]

Meanwhile, Roosevelt, worried that the airmail "fiasco" had darkened the reputation of his administration, ordered Postmaster General James A. Farley to look into the possibility of issuing new contracts. The resulting Black-McKellar Act of June 12, 1934, opened the airmail routes to competitive bidding, reduced postal rates, shortened the duration of contracts from ten years to one, and shifted the power to adjust rates from the Post Office Department to the Interstate Commerce Commission. The act also provided for a special presidential body, the Federal Aviation Commission, to investigate all aspects of American aviation and report its findings to Congress. Chaired by Clark Howell, the Federal Aviation Commission heard testimony from nearly two hundred witnesses and compiled some 4,500 pages of testimony. The commission called for sweeping changes and a restructuring of government regulation of aviation.[28]

Eugene Vidal and the $700 Airplane

During the Black Committee hearings and the airmail crisis, another tempest was brewing: F.D.R.'s selection of Eugene L. Vidal as director of the Aeronautics Branch of the Department of Commerce. The president's choice, a friend of F.D.R.'s son Elliott and Amelia Earhart, both of whom lobbied hard for his nomination, would further alienate the aviation industry from the New Deal.

The son-in-law of Senator Thomas P. Gore (D.-Okla.)—and father of the writer Gore Vidal—Vidal held a civil engineering degree from the University of South Dakota. In 1916, he entered the U.S. Military Academy at West Point, where he was a star athlete and an All-American halfback. In 1918, Vidal was commissioned into the Army Corps of Engineers. Two years later, he transferred to the Air Service, where he was a pilot until 1926. After his duty, Vidal was for a season a football coach at the University of Oregon. In 1928, after another brief period as a real estate salesman in Florida during the land boom there, he became assistant general manager of Transcontinental Air Transport (TAT).[29]

After leaving TAT, Vidal helped to organize Ludington Lines, a small commuter airline that flew from New York to Washington via Philadelphia. (Ironically, Walter Folger Brown had denied a contract to Ludington in favor of a larger company, Eastern Air Transport.) Early in 1933, Vidal was named assistant director of the Aeronautics Branch of the Department of Commerce and later that year was appointed director.[30]

Shortly after his appointment, Vidal began crusading for his own "New Deal for Aviation." In November 1933, he announced his intention to bolster the lightplane industry, which had suffered more than its share of economic downturns, by promoting the manufacture of a cheap, easy-to-fly private aircraft that would be sold to a mass market. This plan marked the New Deal's first attempt to shore up this long-neglected sector of the aviation industry. It would be accomplished, Vidal believed, through a government-subsidized aviation industry program to produce an all-metal aircraft to exact specifications, with built-in safety devices, for $700.[31]

Vidal's idea resulted from a Department of Commerce survey in November 1933 of thirty-four thousand licensed pilots, student pilots and aircraft mechanics throughout the United States. The survey asked respondents if they would be interested in a $700 all-metal, two-seat, low-wing monoplane with a top speed of a hundred miles per hour and flaps to decrease landing speed to a safe twenty-five miles per hour. The answer was overwhelmingly favorable, with 75 percent of those polled reacting positively to the idea.[32]

Vidal, convinced of a potential market, used the occasion of an April 1934 speech in Detroit to the Society of Automotive Engineers to explain his plan for the $700 airplane. "If there is such a thing as a New Deal for aviation," he said, "it is the recognition of the government's additional duty to aid in the development of a sound aviation industry, which means above all other things, the development of greater markets for the products of the industry."[33]

To oversee the Airplane for Everyman program, Vidal organized a development section within the Aeronautics Branch. Funding was to come from the Public Works Administration, which had promised $998,000, an amount later reduced to $500,000. In January 1934, a special committee was formed to explore ways in which the half-million dollar grant could be distributed to the aviation industry. The committee was made up of prominent persons in aviation, among them J. Carroll Cone of the Aeronautics Branch, George Lewis of the National Advisory Committee for Aeronautics, Edward P. Warner, editor of *Aviation,* Amelia Earhart, and Major Alford Williams.[34] In addition, three subcommittees were formed to supplement the special committee. The first worked out details of aircraft production with representatives of the aviation industry. The second and third focused on engine development and promotion of the project. Finally, a technical board of three Aeronautics Branch members advised the main committee on matters of engineering.[35]

Aviation, the most prestigious magazine in the aeronautical community, surveyed the industry to determine the consensus on Vidal's idea. According to its findings, 64 percent of the airframe manufacturers and more than 54 percent of the engine manufacturers opposed the $700 airplane project that pilots and mechanics had endorsed so enthusiastically. Seventy percent of those polled believed that their own business would suffer because prospective customers for light aircraft would delay purchasing until the $700 airplane appeared on the market. Whether these fears were well-founded is difficult to verify, however, the industry believed that they were.[36]

Nevertheless, with a half-million dollars in PWA money at stake, the industry was more than willing at least to put up a pretense of cooperation. In January 1934, twenty-two representatives of the Aeronautical Chamber of Commerce, the trade association of the industry, met in New York to give "wholehearted" endorsement to Vidal's project. Moreover, the chamber set up two industry committees to cooperate with the Aeronautics Branch. The first included representatives from the Taylor Aircraft Company, Curtiss-Wright, Waco, Stinson, and Consolidated. Their task was to develop airframe and engine performance specifications and iron out the technical details of the $700 airplane. The other committee, comprised of representatives from the Aeronautical Corporation of America (Aeronca),

Curtiss-Wright, North American, Fairchild, and United Aircraft and Transport, was responsible for determining the legal and economic feasibility of establishing a corporation within the aircraft industry to develop and manufacture the airplane.[37]

The industry's idea was to give the $500,000 PWA grant to a new corporation jointly owned by the other members of the industry and set up specifically to manufacture the $700 airplane. This company would in turn sell its stock to the other manufacturers. In this way, profits or losses could be evenly distributed throughout the industry, and no manufacturer would suffer unduly.[38]

When Roosevelt administration officials learned of the manufacturers' plans, they reacted negatively. Conferring with Roosevelt on January 24, 1934, Harold Ickes, chief of the Public Works Administration, expressed concern about rumors that suggested "collusion between men in the government and outside interests as a result of which this money will really be expended for the benefit of outside interests." The meeting of the Aeronautical Chamber of Commerce, which had taken place about a week before the Black Committee hearings were scheduled to begin, signaled to the administration that members of the industry might be conspiring again, as had been the case in the Spoils Conferences. On February 1, 1934, at a meeting of the Special Board for Public Works, Ickes informed Secretary of Commerce Daniel Roper, under whose jurisdiction the Aeronautics Branch came, that Roosevelt had decided not to approve the half-million-dollar grant.[39]

Rather than give up the idea of the $700 airplane entirely, Vidal decided to sponsor a design competition for a high-performance "safe" aircraft that would be used by Bureau of Air Commerce (the Aeronautics Branch had been renamed in July 1934) inspectors. Although the emphasis of the program had shifted from low cost to safety in design and thus ease of flying, Vidal hoped that the industry would be motivated by consumer pressure to produce an affordable aircraft for the private market. Such a plan would not only conform to Vidal's original goal of increased private aircraft sales but also meet administration demands that government contracts be bid competitively. When specifications for the safe aircraft were made public in July 1934, however, most of the established manufacturers, believing that the criteria were unrealistic and unacceptable, chose not to participate.[40]

Vidal's—and, by implication, the New Deal's—troubles with the industry and its congressional supporters continued for the remainder of his term as director of the Bureau of Air Commerce. In a June

1936 editorial, Cy Caldwell lambasted Vidal, calling him "the appointee who has been (and still is) clamoring for a 'safe' $700 airplane, and damning all our present airplanes as unsafe. Mr Vidal," Caldwell continued, "had demonstrated the very essence of bureaucratic ineptitude and pusillanimous poltroonery. The President once stated that if any of his experiments did not work, that he would admit it. The Vidal experiment has not worked."[41]

Although Vidal's plan failed, it had obvious ties to Robert Hinckley's later idea of a CPTP. Both were designed as remedies for a small segment of the industry—private aviation—which had been neglected in favor of a larger segment, air transportation. Vidal's $700 airplane had been viewed as an unwarranted government intrusion into the industry's affairs. Hinckley's scheme was designed to minimize government control, however, by placing pilot training in the hands of educational institutions and fixed-base operators, to whom federal subsidies would be paid to cover expenses. Moreover, in the CPTP the government would not, as in Vidal's plan, become involved in the lightplane manufacturing industry. Instead, the benefits would trickle down to manufacturers because the nationwide system of training pilots would theoretically increase the demand for light aircraft.

Vidal's plan for direct stimulation of the lightplane manufacturing industry might have worked had it been conceived in concert with a program like Hinckley's CPTP. However, the haphazardness of the New Deal, the fragmented nature of its policies toward aviation, and the fact that the CPTP probably would not have been so attractive had it not come at a time when pilots were seen as necessary for the national defense worked against such a cooperative effort in favor of private aviation.

The Cutting Crash

The plan to create Vidal's $700 airplane was not the last time the Roosevelt administration would be criticized over its handling of aviation matters. On Sunday May 5, 1935, at 4:00 P.M. Pacific Standard Time, TWA Flight No. 6, a Douglas DC-2 transport carrying ten passengers, set out from Los Angeles on its journey to New York, with scheduled stops in Albuquerque, Kansas City, Columbus, and Pittsburgh. At Kansas City, its crew was to have changed and a new pilot and copilot brought on board.[42]

About a hundred miles outside Kansas City, Flight No. 6 received a weather report that the airport's ceiling was six hundred feet, a hundred feet lower than the requirement. The pilot, Harvey Bolton, a TWA veteran, and the TWA dispatcher in Kansas City were faced with some crucial decisions. Should the flight proceed or be diverted to Wichita or Omaha, thus flying over the weather, and proceed to its next scheduled stop, Columbus? Or, should it land at an intermediate field in Burlington, Iowa, or Kirksville, Missouri? The situation was complicated further because the aircraft's radio was malfunctioning, and Bolton could not maintain contact with the ground. Fuel was running dangerously low. [43]

Bolton decided to continue with the flight and attempt to land in Kansas City. The weather there, however, was too inclement to allow a landing, and, after circling the field and expending precious fuel, Bolton made his way to Kirksville. A few minutes away from Kirksville, he descended below the clouds to establish visual contact. At times flying at tree-top level, Bolton encountered rolling terrain with little or no visibility. He flew about two miles, following a concrete highway until he lowered the aircraft down into a fog-filled gully and then abruptly attempted to pull up and turn to the left. Flying between a farmhouse and a barn, the aircraft's left wing caught the ground, and the aircraft lifted, went over the road, and plowed into a sixty-foot embankment. Three passengers, the pilot, and the co-pilot were dead.[44]

What made the crash so significant was that one of the casualties was Senator Bronson M. Cutting (R.-N. Mex.). Although a Republican, Cutting was a progressive in the Robert M. La Follette mold who had endorsed F.D.R. in the 1932 election. Later, he and the president had a falling out over the issue of veterans' benefits, and F.D.R. had supported Cutting's rival, Denis Chavez, in the 1934 senatorial race. Cutting managed to win the race by a narrow margin, but Chavez, backed by Roosevelt, disputed the election results. The contested election had been thrown into the Senate, and Cutting had been returning from Albuquerque with legal documents to support his case when he was killed.[45]

The progressive members of the Senate took the Cutting crash personally, and some even blamed F.D.R. for the senator's death, reasoning that had the president supported Cutting's reelection, he would not have been aboard the aircraft. The legislators were so grief-striken that when the other senator from New Mexico, Carl Hatch, announced Cutting's death, his colleagues George Norris (R.-Neb.) and William E. Borah (R.-Utah) could not hold back their tears. Robert M. La Follette, Jr. (D.-Wis.) was so distressed that he would not appear in the Senate chamber. When Chavez, eventually appointed to Cutting's Senate seat by the governor of New Mexico, appeared for his swearing in, Norris, La Follette, Hiram W. Johnson (R.-Calif.), Gerald P. Nye (R.-N.D.), and Henrik Shipstead (R.-Minn.) got up and walked out.[46]

Looking for a scapegoat, Senators Johnson and Hatch introduced a resolution on May 13, 1935, calling for an immediate investigation of the accident. Royal S. Copeland (D.-N.Y.), chair of the Senate Committee on Commerce, appointed a five-member subcommittee, which he would direct, to probe the causes of the crash. In addition to Copeland, other members of the committee included Johnson, Wallace H. White (R.-Maine), Bennett "Champ" Clark (D.-Mo.), and A. V. "Vic" Donahey (D.-Ohio).[47]

In an accident investigation report issued on June 4, 1935, the Department of Commerce placed blame on TWA and the pilot. The report claimed that TWA personnel in Albuquerque should not have given the pilot the go-ahead to continue the flight when they knew that the aircraft's radio was defective. TWA representatives at Kansas City should have rerouted the flight when they determined that it was impossible for it to land there. The pilot was also faulted for continuing the flight after it had become apparent that the radio was malfunctioning.[48]

Meanwhile, in a separate investigation of the crash, the Bureau of Air Commerce determined that TWA had committed several violations in handling the flight. This report claimed that the pilot and copilot of TWA Flight No. 6 had violated bureau regulations by not gaining prior approval for a regularly scheduled flight with which they had little or no familiarity. Flight crews were required to have flown a scheduled route for at least six months; neither pilot Harvey Bolton nor copilot Kenneth Greeson met the requirement. The report also stated that Bolton had not had his last required medical examination. Moreover, although TWA had obtained a waiver for Bolton to exceed the normal eight-hour flying stint (Los Angeles to Kansas City was eight hours and fifteen minutes), Greeson did not have the proper rating for a scheduled flight and thus, according to regulations, could not take over should Bolton become fatigued. Finally, the report was critical of Flight No. 6 because it failed to carry the required forty-five minutes of reserve fuel specified by safety standards, because its crew was flying on instruments without the required two-way radio communication, and because the flight had attempted to land at the Kansas City airport when the ceiling was below the minimum landing requirement there.[49]

TWA's president Jack Frye refused to admit negligence on his company's part. Frye, knowing that TWA could incur damaging lawsuits if it accepted the Bureau of Air Commerce's findings without question, took issue with the accident investigation report. In an open letter to William Randolph Hearst, Frye placed the blame squarely on the Bureau of Air Commerce for issuing erroneous information about the weather at Kirksville to the pilot of Flight No. 6.[50]

The evidence seemed to point unquestionably to negligence on TWA's part. The Copeland Committee and Copeland himself, however, were sympathetic to TWA and antagonistic to the Bureau of Air Commerce. By some perverse logic, Copeland held Franklin D. Roosevelt responsible for the death of his colleague. Moreover, Copeland had a political grudge against F.D.R., who had opposed his reelection in 1934, and delighted in making the Bureau of Air Commerce the scapegoat in the Cutting crash investigation.[51]

Despite the political mudslinging, the real issue was the Roosevelt administration's attitude toward aviation safety. Although responsible for safety in the air, the Bureau of Air Commerce could not carry out its job without sufficient funds. These had been reduced significantly in 1933 when F.D.R. first came into office and never restored. Before safety in the air could be maintained at what could be considered an optimal level, the airways had to be modernized.

The administration's tightfisted attitude toward improving the nation's airways pointed up its seeming lack of concern with airway modernization and, therefore, air safety. J. Monroe Johnson, the assistant secretary for transportation in the Department of Commerce, which administered the Bureau of Air Commerce, had gone to Secretary Daniel Roper with a $9 million airway modernization plan, which he turned down. Johnson cut the request to $5 million, but that, too, was rejected.[52]

Moreover, the bureau's stringent budget made its safety enforcement procedures difficult to administer. For example, in May 1936, J. Carroll Cone, the bureau's assistant director for air regulation, testified before the Copeland Committee, "I am ashamed to admit that at the present time only three inspectors are engaged in aircraft factory inspections. Any lack of inspection on the part of the Bureau is due wholly to the lack of sufficient personnel, or to facilities and funds for travel."[53] All this had a drastic effect on the bureau's safety record. During 1935, Director Vidal could boast that there were only 4.78 passenger fatalities per 100 million passenger-miles flown, an impressive record. By 1936, however, passenger fatalities had increased to 10.1 per 100 million passenger-miles, the largest number since 1932.[54]

The Copeland Committee strongly condemned the Bureau of Air Commerce (and, by inference, the Roosevelt administration) for neglecting to enforce air safety regulations. In a preliminary report issued on June 30, 1936, the committee blamed the bureau unfairly for three defective navigational aids that it said were primarily responsible for the Cutting crash. The aviation press, always eager to condemn the Roosevelt administration for what it considered blatant mishandling of aviation matters, endorsed the committee's findings.[55]

The Civil Aeronautics Act of 1938

The Black Committee hearings, the airmail contract cancellations, Eugene Vidal's $700 airplane, and the Bronson Cutting crash caused enough alarm among the aviation community and its political supporters to effect changes in the Roosevelt administration's air policies. Congressional advocates of aviation, in particular Congressman Clarence Lea (D.-Calif.) and Senator Patrick McCarran (D.-Nev.), who had had several disagreements with the White House about aviation, began early in 1935 to formulate legislation that they believed would solve many of the problems for which the Roosevelt administration, justly or unjustly, had been blamed.

Roosevelt, however, did nothing to support the McCarran-Lea proposals or the findings of the Federal Aviation Commission on which they were based. The commission had come out strongly for an independent body to regulate aviation and for airmail rate reform, and McCarran and Lea agreed that the commission's recommendations should be carried out. Roosevelt, however, was troubled by the proliferation of autonomous federal boards and commissions uncontrolled by the executive branch. He desired legislation that would unify federal transportation policy and simultaneously regulate rail, ground, and air transportation.[56]

Because of Roosevelt's refusal to support them, the McCarran-Lea bills, subsequently revised to provide tighter government control of aviation safety, regulation, and airmail rate reform, languished for more than two years. Finally, in July 1937, Roosevelt, in a memo to Harllee Branch, second assistant postmaster general, asked that the Interdepartmental Committee on Civil International Aviation (comprised of representatives from the departments of State, Treasury, Post Office, War, Navy, and Commerce) take up the matter of drafting an aviation bill to be submitted for the next session of Congress in January 1938.

The administration selected Clarence Lea to sponsor the legislation, and, after some compromises with the original draft produced by the Interdepartmental Committee, Lea introduced his bill (H.R. 9738) in the House of Representatives on March 4, 1938. A difficult legislative battle then took place between the supporters of the administration-backed Lea proposal and those of various other measures sponsored by Patrick McCarran, Royal Copeland, and Harry S. Truman (D.-Mo.), but a compromise was reached. On June 23, Roosevelt signed the bill into law.[57]

The hallmarks of the new law were a five-member Civil Aeronautics Authority (CAA) charged with responsibility for regulation (tariffs, airmail rates, and airline business practices); an administrator who functioned to foster civil aeronautics and air commerce, establish civil airways, improve air navigation, and protect and regulate air traffic; and an independent three-member Air Safety Board to investigate crashes, determine who was at fault, and recommend safety measures to prevent accidents. In the July 1938 issue of the *Journal of Air Law*, Clinton M. Hester, the newly appointed administrator of the CAA and a key member of the Interdepartmental Committee, wrote that on the law's "effective administration are rested the hopes of those interested in the future of aviation for a new era in the development of aviation."[58]

Ironically, the Civil Aeronautics Act of 1938 neither satisfied Roosevelt's concerns about the unification of federal transportation policy nor lessened his dislike of adding still another independent federal body to the growing list. On the one hand, by creating the office of administrator, who would be answerable to the president, the law satisfied Roosevelt that the executive's interests would be represented. But by separating the quasi-legislative functions of the newly created aviation regulatory agency from its quasi-judicial functions, the law established two virtually independent bodies. Although Roosevelt did sign the bill, his reasons for doing so were mysterious. His erratic behavior in regard to the Civil Aeronautics Act did nothing to convince the administration's detractors that its aviation policies were inconsistent at best, and misguided at worst.

It is little wonder, then, that even after the passage of the Civil Aeronautics Act, the aviation community was still unsatisfied. An *Aviation* editorial in August 1938 declared that "adding up the scores as charitably as possible, the aviation talent in the C.A.A. sloshes around like a gallon of gas in an empty tank." Robert Hinckley, one of five newly appointed members of the authority and originator of the CPTP, was perceived as a lightweight. "Mr. Hinckley," the editorial continued, "claims a long standing interest in aviation, is known to be a persistent airline rider, and once had an interest in a now defunct flying service in Ogden, Utah. Latterly, he has been WPA administrator for five western states, and is said to be a pal of Harry Hopkins. At best, his total aviation record could be outweighed by a hundred more qualified men that we could name."[59]

The CPTP and Preparations for War

This, then, was the political atmosphere within the aviation community and among its congressional backers at the time Robert Hinckley put forth the idea for the CPTP. To the air transportation segment of the aviation industry and the Army Air Corps, the Black Committee's hearings and the resulting airmail cancellations revealed a callousness, even recklessness, by the Roosevelt administration toward civil aviation. The remedial Black-McKellar Act of June 1934, described by Nick Komons as "a hodgepodge of conflicting ideologies," was no panacea and did little to reform air transportation. Eugene Vidal's controversial $700 Airplane for Everyman program was perceived by the lightplane manufacturers as impractical (had the idea worked, the increase in air traffic without an attempt to provide for adequate control of it would have caused panic in the skies) and an unwelcome government intrusion into the industry. Many members of the Senate held F.D.R. responsible for the death of Bronson Cutting, and Congress was certain that the New Deal was not doing enough to ensure the safety of the nation's air lanes. Finally, the confused state of the Roosevelt administration's aviation policies forced attempts at reform and had resulted in the ambiguous Civil Aeronautics Act of 1938.

All Hinckley's potential support for the CPTP—the aviation industry, the Army Air Corps, and Congress—had been embittered because of a lack of a coherent New Deal policy toward aviation and, perhaps more important, because of repeated bad judgment by the administration on important matters of aviation policy. Hinckley would have to salve many unhealed wounds if the CPTP was to be accepted.[60] The world situation in 1939 was troubling enough to overshadow other issues, however. Events in Europe and Asia were beginning to make it clear that the uneasy peace that existed might easily be threatened. The United States had pursued a course of isolation and neutrality in the interwar years, and Roosevelt's first two administrations had adhered to this policy, even going so far as to put a legal stamp of approval on it.

On August 31, 1935, Roosevelt signed the first of a series of neutrality acts. The initial act banned the shipment of arms and munitions to belligerent countries and authorized the president to prohibit Americans from traveling on ships of warring nations. The second Neutrality Act, signed on February 29, 1936, not only extended the previous act, but also prohibited the United States from making loans or providing credit to belligerents. The third Neutrality Act, signed on May 1, 1937, extended the first and second acts and added provisions that prohibited U.S. ships from carrying arms into the war zones of belligerent nations and required any country that purchased nonmilitary goods from the United States to carry these goods in their own ships.[61]

Even flagrant acts of aggression against American citizens and the U.S. Navy by the Japanese in China could not deter the country from its isolationist position in the late 1930s. Despite the bombing of American churches, hospitals, and schools; the killing of American missionaries and their families; and, finally, the "accidental" air attack by Japanese warplanes on an American gunboat, the U.S.S. *Panay* in the Yangtze River on December 12, 1937, the United States took no action until F.D.R. revoked the treaty of commerce with Japan in July 1939.[62]

Adolf Hitler's threatened takeover of Czechoslovakia in September 1938, however, made the United States painfully aware of the danger in Europe. For the first time, America felt its insularity threatened by the prospect of a foreign war. A *Fortune* magazine survey showed that 76.2 percent of the American people believed that the United States would become involved in a war in Europe. As William Manchester has observed, "the Czech crisis had awakened America from its long slumber, and the country was anxious, biting its nails, drumming its fingers. Bombs, invasion, war—all that had been unthinkable as recently as last summer—were suddenly very real."[63]

Despite strong pockets of American isolationist and pacifist sentiment, Roosevelt gave the green light to a military expansion. He was convinced that air power would win the next war, and that the United States had to build up its air forces and those of its European allies. On October 13, 1938, William Bullitt, the American ambassador to France, briefed Roosevelt on the situation in Europe. Bullitt stressed that the Luftwaffe was being used as diplomatic blackmail in the European crisis and suggested that the United States needed to strengthen its defense by increasing aircraft production.[64]

The following day, Assistant Secretary of War Louis Johnson asked the Army Chief of Staff Malin Craig to submit information about the current state of military aircraft and the requirements for bolstering America's air power. Chief of the Air Corps Henry H. "Hap" Arnold reported that 1,499 aircraft would be needed if the United States were to mobilize for war. On November 14, F.D.R. met at the White House with Generals Craig, Arnold, and George Marshall and Assistant Secretary of War Johnson, Secretary of the Treasury Henry Morgenthau, and WPA Administrator Hopkins. The president shocked the men by announcing that if an attack on the Western Hemisphere were to be prevented, twenty thousand aircraft were necessary. That number eventually was scaled down to ten thousand because the president believed that Congress would balk at the higher figure.[65]

In a press conference on November 15, Roosevelt mentioned the previous day's meeting and announced that the administration was "studying national defense and continental solidarity against possible attacks from other hemispheres . . . including the problem of aircraft. Yesterday's meeting was confined almost entirely to the problem of aircraft."[66] Military leaders wondered who would fly the war planes scheduled to roll off the assembly lines in greater numbers than at any time in the nation's history because both the Army Air Corps and the navy were ill-equipped to produce pilots in mass quantity. To gear up in the event of a national emergency would have been more than the military services could handle with only their peacetime resources to rely upon.

Despite the Army Air Corps' resentment of the Roosevelt administration because of the airmail fiasco of 1934 and other problems, the military benefits of the proposed CPTP legislation to U.S. preparedness were readily apparent. Unlike many countries in Europe, the United States had only a small reserve of pilots and no formal program of training. Only 3,800 commercial and 3,600 private pilots between the ages of eighteen and thirty were estimated to be in the United States in 1939. Many would not be able to pass the stringent physical requirements necessary to be military aviators. If a national emergency did arise, many more pilots would have to be trained, and the CPTP was a logical means of accomplishing this goal.[67]

Nonetheless, Hinckley's first barrier in clearing the way for the CPTP legislation was the military establishment. Harry Woodring, the secretary of war, was convinced that preparedness was a touchy issue and that, as Hinckley put it, "while preparedness was a good idea at any time, there was no use overdoing it." Moreover, training pilots for the military, one aspect of the proposed program, was a sensitive jurisdictional issue that the Army Air Forces (AAF) and the navy felt should be done under military sponsorship. One unnamed navy official went so far as to say, "We want no part of civilian aviation. We have a program which will train seven thousand pilots a year. That's more than we need. We don't want to be helped and we don't want to be interrupted."[68]

Despite these problems, Hinckley persisted. He found an ally in Assistant Secretary of War Johnson, who was enthusiastic about the program and began to remove the obstacles in its path. As Hinckley later put it, "He [Johnson] went to bat for us in the military and at the White House. He cut red tape every time it blocked us, and fought off protests from the training command of the air arm. Far more dynamo than diplomat, he bulldozed his way through all opposition and did more than any other man to make the military cooperate in getting us started." For the time being, at least, the military was satisfied that the program would not threaten its autonomy.[69]

On December 27, 1938, at a White House presidential press conference, F.D.R. paved the way for the larger CPTP by announcing the establishment of a small-scale experimental program. Roosevelt told reporters that he had given approval for the Civil Aeronautics Authority to promote the private aviation industry by giving flight instruction to a small number of college students. One hundred thousand dollars of National Youth Administration money would be used to set up the pilot project to train 330 pilots in thirteen colleges and universities throughout the United States.[70]

In a January 12, 1939, message to Congress on the national defense, Roosevelt made an urgent plea for a $525 million expenditure, most of which would be used for new military aircraft. In this message, and while plans were being laid for the experimental CPTP project, Roosevelt for the first time tied the CPTP legislation to American preparedness, asking for a $10 million appropriation for the CPTP. "National defense," he said, "calls for the training of additional air pilots. This training should be primarily directed to the essential qualifications for civilian flying. In cooperation with educational institutions, it is believed that the expenditure of $10,000,000 a year will give primary training to approximately 20,000 citizens."[71]

Hinckley Garners Support for the CPTP

Meanwhile, Hinckley attempted to overcome other obstacles in the CPTP's path. To quell potential opposition, Hinckley summoned to Washington a group of those involved in the small-scale demonstration of the CPTP in June 1939. Representatives attended from educational institutions, from which potential CPTP students would be obtained, and fixed-base operators, the flight schools that would train CPTP students. The conference would provide an arena in which to discuss problems that had arisen in the demonstration and that might arise in the full-scale program.

Earlier in the year, an article titled "Educators Split on Training Youths in Aviation" had appeared in the *New York Times,* quoting college presidents who were critical of the proposed CPTP legislation. One vocal dissenter, Ernest K. Wilkins of Oberlin College, was incensed because the CAA had told "several hundred educational institutions" what to do without prior consultation, and he condemned the CAA's thoughtlessness severely. "This seems to me," Wilkins said, "to have shown a serious disregard for the simplest principle of cooperation and to assume on the part of the government, a degree of control over the private educational institutions of the country which the government does not possess, and which, if it existed, would be repugnant to the nature of democracy."[72]

Wilkins's objections, however, were apparently not shared by the college and university administrators from such schools as the University of Alabama, University of Kansas, University of Michigan, New York University, Massachusetts Institute of Technology, and Purdue University, who had been invited to the conference. The New Deal had set a precedent by providing financial help to hardpressed institutions of higher learning through Federal Emergency Relief Administration work-study funds in 1934, so the schools were favorably disposed toward receiving government money for the CPTP. Moreover, since the 1920s, college curriculums, influenced by John Dewey's pragmatic philosophy of education, had been introducing practical subjects that would prepare students for employment. Finally, proponents of New Deal thinking about education, especially Rexford Tugwell and Leon Keyserling, stressed practical education that would benefit both the student and provide a workforce for corporations, government, and industry.[73]

In a statement to the press on the outcome of the meeting Hinckley said, "It was the unanimous expression of the representatives of the colleges that the training of these pilots represented a substantial contribution to citizenship, a contribution of the kind that a worthy institution of learning should give. Without exception they expressed themselves as delighted with the results of the course on the students who participated, upon the student body as a whole and upon the communities in which they are located."[74]

While he was conferring about the demonstration program, Hinckley met also with the fixed-base operators. Earlier in the year, *American Aviation Daily,* an industry trade paper, reported that "rather violent protests have been made to Washington by various aviation interests that the civilian training program for pilots will destroy the private schools which have struggled for existence." The *Daily,* however, supported the program, noting that "so far there is nothing in the civilian training programs that is harmful to private aviation except misleading publicity."

At the Washington conference, the operators proposed an extravagant $75 million appropriation, an amount, Hinckley commented, that "in the pre-war economy days of 1938, was enough to make the most extravagant Congressman's hair stand on end." The operators also wanted $41 million for publicity, and instructors were to be paid $25 an hour (the standard hourly rate at the time was $6). Despite these unrealistic demands, Hinckley reported to the press that "the operators of the flight instruction courses . . . were unanimous in the belief that these [demonstration] courses had proven a healthy stimulant to private flying as whole in each neighborhood in which the operation is carried on. All reported that there had been since February a distinct increase in private flying at their own and nearby fields."[75]

Another faction that the CPTP would affect, the lightplane manufacturing industry, was cautious in its attitude toward the program. The manufacturers were heartened by the CAA's announcement in the spring of 1938 that it would establish a Private Flying Division within the agency. The division would attempt to cut through the restrictive civil aviation regulations and make it easier for private flyers to take to the air. In an endorsement of the Private Flying Division, William Enyart, secretary of the National Aeronautic Association, commented in May 1938, that "the fact that private flying in recent years has lagged far behind air transport in rate of growth had undoubtedly helped to make it appear that scheduled air transport threatens to crowd out the private pilot."[76]

Moreover, in November 1938, *American Aviation* informally polled the heads of lightplane manufacturing companies. The poll showed that the industry was more concerned with the government easing private flying regulations and stimulating airport construction than it was with New Deal pump-priming subsidies. E. E. Porterfield, Jr., head of the Porterfield Aircraft Corporation, was one of the few lightplane industry executives who favored government funds. Porterfield argued that along with federal subsidy of "the majority of the cost of light planes selling under certain prices"—a variation of Eugene Vidal's $700 airplane idea—government payment of "a majority of the price of a flying course for eligible young men and women . . . would put our country in a most enviable position from a standpoint of national air defense." William T. Piper, head of Piper Aircraft, the largest and most profitable American lightplane company, felt differently. "Any government aid," he said, "which would increase private flying today would have to be perpetual or the result would be an over-production of planes and pilots when the subsidy was discontinued."[77]

Despite the lukewarm reception from the lightplane manufacturing industry, Hinckley was encouraged by public response. A Gallup poll in late January 1939 showed that the general public was receptive to President Roosevelt's announcement of plans to establish the CPTP. The poll asked, "as part of the national defense program the Government is planning to train young men in schools and colleges to fly airplanes. Do you favor this plan?" Eighty-seven percent of respondents answered favorably. Of those respondents under the age of thirty, 91 percent answered yes. Eighty-five percent of those thirty and older answered yes. A second question asked males between the ages of nineteen and thirty whether they would "like to receive such training." Seventy-four percent answered yes.[78]

Although he had received tentative approval for the CPTP from the representatives of the educational institutions and the fixed-base operators, tacit acceptance from the lightplane manufacturing industry, and a favorable response from the public at large, Hinckley was still grappling with the Congress, a major hurdle. Early in 1939, he prepared to testify for the full-scale CPTP bill before the House Committee on Interstate and Foreign Commerce. Congress's reaction could not be predicted, yet Hinckley was confident that he could win over skeptics and make the Civilian Pilot Training Program a reality.

CHAPTER 2

"Baptism of Fire": The CPTP and the Legislative Process

Although a relative newcomer to Washington's political scene, Robert Hinckley undoubtedly understood that his ability to persuade Congress on the benefits of the proposed CPTP, along with his personal dealings with members of committees, could make or break the prospective legislation. The program required an articulate spokesperson. Hinckley later recalled that he had confidently turned to Congress for support, but "thereby ran head-on into another combination of personalities and events that, too often, drive good men from government service, not a few of them screaming maniacal profanity at the lawmakers of the land. We had our baptism of fire 'on the Hill.'"[1]

Hinckley possessed keen political instincts, if not a firsthand knowledge of aviation. He was the quintessential New Deal bureaucrat—activist, can-do, and willing to experiment. The usually dour *American Aviation Daily* displayed uncharacteristic confidence in him, reporting in May 1939 that "if present trends continue Hinckley will be the outstanding government spokesman for civil aviation and he is one of the few who seem to be able to translate aviation's enormous possibilities into words which stir the imagination of (and secure support from) those on the outside who can help the industry." John R. M. Wilson, a historian of the Civil Aeronautics Administration, moreover, has commented that Hinckley's "agreeable personality, bluff but genial, made him friends wherever he went, including the highest levels of the Government. . . . His belief in the Government's playing a major role in promoting the rapid expansion of aviation, combined with his unquestioned administrative skill, disarmed would-be critics. . . . He enjoyed the confidence of all in aviation who met him."[2]

Despite Hinckley's winning ways, he could not predict congressional attitudes toward the proposed Civilian Pilot Training Program legislation. Some legislators would undoubtedly be skeptical given the New Deal's repeatedly inept handling of aviation policy matters. Added to this were congressional perceptions—based upon rumors of conflicts among the leaders of the Civil Aeronautics Authority and incoherency in its organization—that the newly created Civil Aeronautics Act of 1938 was not working. This uncertainty only added to congressional skepticism about the Roosevelt administration's ability to keep its aviation house in order. Responding to the notion that the CAA was in disarray, the House of Representatives cut its budget request for fiscal year 1940, and Senators James F. Byrnes (D.-S.C.) and Bennett "Champ" Clark (D.-Mo.) openly criticized the agency.[3]

Moreover, the possibility existed that other lawmakers with isolationist sentiments might see the CPTP as a thinly veiled military program and oppose it as warmongering. As David L. Porter has observed, the Seventy-sixth Congress (1939–40), in session as the CPTP bill proceeded through the legislative machinery, "held the awesome responsibility of deciding the pace of American involvement in the European War." Porter has divided the attitude of this Congress into three distinct phases: maintaining isolationism, shifting toward internationalism, and becoming interventionist. In 1939, Congress spent a good deal of time bitterly deliberating revision of American neutrality laws. The Democrats, who dominated the House and Senate, favored increased American involvement in foreign affairs and a change in the laws. The Republicans, in the minority, tended to favor nonintervention and to oppose changing the neutrality laws. Others in Congress could be classified as moderate, or undecided about the question of neutrality. Although they agreed with F.D.R. on maintaining an internationalist posture, Democratic legislators were heterogeneous and not always disposed to back the president's domestic initiatives. By 1938, from twenty to thirty senators had become "disenchanted" with the programs of the New Deal.[4]

Thus, Congress was divided over America's role in a crucial period in foreign affairs and struggling over how to proceed. To further complicate matters, the CPTP had something to satisfy or alienate everyone; the program had characteristics of New Deal economics as well as a dimension of war preparedness thrown in for good measure. How the Congress would react to the CPTP was anyone's guess.

With many in Congress antagonistic toward the New Deal and ambivalent about the status of the United States if war broke out in

Europe, Robert Hinckley began to lay the groundwork for the arduous approval process. Initially, he assumed that the authority for conducting the Civilian Pilot Training Program had been established by the Civil Aeronautics Act of 1938 because of its legislative mandate to promote aeronautics. "Our contention," Hinckley wrote, "was that flight training was a logical and practical form of aviation promotion." Two members of the House Committee on Interstate and Foreign Commerce, John Taber (R.-N.Y.) and Richard B. Wigglesworth (R.-Mass.), opposed this idea and argued that the act did not authorize the CAA to establish a pilot training program. Although other members of the committee supported Hinckley's reasoning, he was advised that the CPTP would require enabling legislation.[5]

Hinckley then sought the help of Committee Chair Clarence F. Lea for sponsorship of the CPTP bill. Lea (D.-Calif.) was a strong advocate of aviation and had written a version of the Civil Aeronautics Act (H.R.9738) that the White House had supported. On March, 16, 1939, he introduced the CPTP legislation (H.R.5093), and it began to make its way through the House of Representatives. Lea's proposal had three salient features. First, it authorized the Civil Aeronautics Authority to "train civilian pilots or to conduct programs for such training," which would include research to investigate "the most desirable qualifications for aircraft pilots." Second, it required students to be insured and to pay fees for ground-school training in an amount not to exceed $40 a student. Finally, it authorized an appropriation of $7,300,000 during fiscal years 1939 and 1940 as well as other funds to carry out the provisions of the program beyond that time.[6]

Hearings before the House Committee: Round 1

On March 20, 1939, Hinckley went before the House Committee on Interstate and Foreign Commerce to testify for what the published hearings called "A Bill to Provide for the Training of Civil Aircraft Pilots, and for Other Purposes." In his opening remarks, he stated the purpose of the legislation forcefully: to encourage and develop civil aeronautics in accord with the powers bestowed on the CAA by the Civil Aeronautics Act of 1938, and to select and train in a preliminary way civilian pilots who would be quickly available for national defense in an emergency.[7]

In his characteristic style, Hinckley declared that the United States was the cradle of aviation, but that foreign aggressors had temporarily assumed world leadership in civil aeronautics "on a purely military basis." Private flying, a segment of the American aviation industry crucial in building up a reserve of trained pilots who could be called upon in time of national emergency, had been neglected. There was a deficit of trained aviators in the United States. Only 7,400 pilots were between the ages of eighteen and thirty: 3,800 commercial and 3,600 private. The shortage was because of the lack of government support for civil aviation. World events showed that the country's educational system was ill-prepared to train people vocationally in the aeronautical sciences. Although the United States spent $22 million annually for vocational training in other fields, the educational system had completely disregarded aviation.[8]

Hinckley emphasized that the CAA intended its flight training program to develop civil aviation and strengthen America's aerial defenses, and that it had been conceived as "strictly in keeping with the American way of doing things." This was in direct contrast to conditions in Europe, particularly among the "aggressor nations," where private flying had been under the control of the military. Furthermore, the CAA would use the country's schools and the training personnel and equipment of the fixed-base operators to accomplish its goals. This course was chosen to preserve and cultivate private industry and "stimulate individual initiative."[9]

The plan was to provide each state with a quota of students based on population, college enrollment, and the number of certified flight instructors. The CAA would solicit applications from educational institutions that wished to participate. The fact that a vast organization of colleges and universities existed throughout the United States would make participation in the program democratic and avoid a concentration of students in any single geographic location. Thus, the program would be available nationwide to qualified applicants from all walks of life and tend to enlarge local awareness of and interest in aviation. The CAA was convinced that the program would build a useful supply of young men (as well as some young women) trained as pilots and encourage the development of private aircraft manufacturing. Only by taking the CAA's approach could the United States "adequately safeguard itself against the vast aerial militarization programs now being pressed with fanatic zeal by foreign powers."[10]

After Hinckley had made his opening statement, the committee deliberated over five basic issues: how safe would such a program be; how trainees would be examined physically; how much would the program cost, and would the government be getting a good return on its money; how did it compare with similar programs in Europe; and how would the program fit into the already established military pilot training programs.

Carl Hinshaw (R.-Cal.), Alfred L. Bulwinkle (D.-N.C.), and Oscar Youngdahl (R.-Minn.) were concerned about the potential for air accidents in a flight training program that proposed to train as many as twenty thousand pilots a year. Bulwinkle suggested that a provision about stringent physical examinations be written into the law. Hinckley agreed completely and explained that each trainee would be subject to the same examination as that given to army pilots, but he thought Bulwinkle's suggested provision unwise because the CAA wanted to recruit some trainees who were "substandard" in a physical sense in order to determine how well they might do as pilots.[11]

Youngdahl questioned the CAA's provisions in situations of accident or death. Hinckley assured him that each student would be covered by life and disability insurance and informed him that the insurance rate for the experimental CPTP program had dropped from $12 to $5 per thousand. Hinckley also pointed out that the airport operators were "required to furnish public liability and property damage insurance."[12]

James W. Wadsworth, Jr. (R.-N.Y.) contested the trainees' potential lack of obligation to the government in exchange for federal expenditure of funds for their training. Although not opposed to the training program, Wadsworth believed that by agreeing to it, the government would for the first time in its history be educating people "free of charge." Hinckley responded that it was "not altogether free," and that the CAA would ask for a laboratory fee, as it had already done in the CPTP demonstration program, which varied from $12 for a physical examination to $79, including insurance. Indeed, the issue of an adequate return for government funds expended would later become a concern of F.D.R. and others (chapter 3).[13]

Bulwinkle queried Hinckley about the benefits the military services would derive from the CPTP, whether the CPTP would take the place of the military's own pilot training, and how many student pilots the military could accommodate in its own training centers. Because the committee was considering the bill from a commercial and national defense viewpoint, Bulwinkle contended that "we should know what is going to be necessary for the Army and Navy to go into this program." The CAA's position was that the CPTP would probably ease the burden on the Army Air Corps and the navy to conduct primary pilot training, but that it did not intend to relieve them of responsibility for training their own flying officers. The CAA did not wish to train military pilots, but hoped only to establish a pool from which young men "with the equivalent of primary training" could be drawn now or "in time of emergency." From there, the military could take them into advanced training programs.[14]

When questioning was concluded, Hinckley was asked to go over several prospective provisions of the bill. Section 2, for example, gave the CAA general authority to carry out the program, prescribe regulations, and conduct research into the most desirable qualifications for pilots. Another provision of section 2—to be a continual source of confusion and contention during the legislative process— sought to postpone decisions on laying down "specific requirements as to the qualifications that must be met by students or as to the methods that are to be followed in their training." Although this seemed the best course to follow in a program that would continually change and be redefined, some legislators (especially during the House debates) wanted specifics written into the law concerning what would be required of the pilot trainees and how they would be trained.[15]

Section 3 gave the CAA authority to acquire real and personal property with which to conduct the program. Carl E. Mapes (R.-Mich.) and William P. Cole, Jr. (D.-Md.) were concerned that if the existing Civil Aeronautics Authority legislation authorized the CAA to purchase such property, would not the proposed CPTP bill give it additional authority to purchase property or to establish a military aviation training program comparable to those at West Point or Annapolis. Hinckley assured the legislators that this was not at all what the CAA had in mind.[16]

Section 4 specified that in carrying out the training program, the CAA would be given all the powers extended to it by the existing Civil Aeronautics Act of 1938. This section was included to preclude having to repeat in the CPTP bill some of the provisions of the 1938 legislation such as the authority to "employ personnel, to inspect aircraft, and to test and certificate pilots."[17] Section 5 gave the CAA authority to enter into contracts with "other executive departments and independent establishments." Section 6 was the "customary authorization for an appropriation." Section 7 had no relevance to the CPTP bill but was added so the CAA could use space at the new District of Columbia airport at Gravelly Point to establish its principal offices in a centrally convenient location.[18]

When he had finished testifying, the committee asked Hinckley to verify that there were twenty-three thousand civilian pilots in the

United States and to provide statistics for pilot training in other countries. Hinckley explained that he did not have the figures at hand but would be happy to provide the information in an extension of his remarks before the committee. After approximately two hours of testimony, the committee adjourned.[19]

The Civilian Pilot Training Program had passed its first congressional test and emerged relatively unscathed. The first round of hearings indicated that congressional opposition was based less on philosophical grounds than on practical procedure. The important question of the CPTP's relationship to pilot training conducted by the military was a source of confusion and would be a lingering issue throughout the program's history. The related question of CPTP students' "potential lack of obligation to government in exchange for federal expenditure of funds" would also be a source of future concern.

The discussions made it apparent that despite the program's New Deal ramifications, questions about its military aspects mattered most to the committee. With war clouds hanging over Europe, national defense was a concern. Preparedness in the form of a program to train pilots in the event of war had become palatable even to a Congress still in an isolationist mood.

Hearings before the House Committee: Round 2

The second round of testimony before the House Committee on Interstate and Foreign Commerce convened at 10 A.M. on March 27, 1939 in the Hearing Room of the New House Office Building and provided an opportunity for the military to clear up some of the questions the committee had asked a week earlier. The army and navy had a vested interest in the CPTP because such a program promised to relieve them from having to conduct elementary pilot training. Although outwardly cooperative, especially in testimony before the appropriate congressional committees, the military was ambivalent about the program. It wanted to maintain independence and insisted on complete autonomy in carrying out flight training programs.

The navy's testimony indicated this ambivalence. Appearing were Rear Admiral Arthur B. Cook, chief of the Bureau of Aeronautics, and Captain Theodore S. Wilkinson, substituting for Admiral J. O. Richardson, chief of the Bureau of Navigation, who had been called away to testify on the navy's appropriation bill. The navy's position was that the CAA's training program would be of "definite value to the national defense in case of emergency." It took issue, however, with a provision of the proposed bill that would lend aviation personnel, aircraft, property, and equipment or grounds and buildings controlled by the military to the CAA to carry out the CPTP. The navy felt that it could hardly support the CAA because its resources were already strictly committed to its own needs. It objected especially to the idea that reserve and retired personnel ordered to active duty to help in the CPTP should be paid out of navy funds rather than from CAA money. The use of regular naval officers on active duty would be impossible given the navy's already limited manpower.[20]

Cook replied positively to James W. Wadsworth's question about whether the CPTP might reduce the navy's burden of training pilots and outlined the way the navy undertook its pilot training. The naval reserve bases that conducted elementary pilot training (ten hours of flight instruction) were used to limit the number of applicants to the navy's main pilot training base at Pensacola, Florida. The Naval Academy at Annapolis provided some eighty-five pilot candidates annually, a number the navy hoped to increase to 150. Pensacola could train six hundred pilots a year, up to nine hundred in an emergency. That number would double if Congress approved the navy appropriation bill.[21]

Cook—and, presumably, the navy—felt that although the CPTP would shorten the time necessary to train naval pilots, CAA instruction alone would not qualify them as military aviators without further training by the navy. He estimated that it would take approximately 310 flying hours to produce a competently trained naval pilot under normal circumstances, half that time in an emergency.[22]

Brigadier General Barton K. Yount, assistant chief of the Air Corps, testified next. Like Cook, Yount outwardly supported the CPTP bill. The War Department was "wholeheartedly in favor of the training program provided for in this bill." Unlike Cook, however, Yount appeared to have an appreciation for the CPTP beyond the strict parochial requirement that a student should be ready for military service in time of national need. Even if never required in time of war, a trainee would become "air minded" and be influential in developing civil aviation. Yount also concurred with the Navy Department that if reserve officers were called upon to help the CAA carry out pilot training, the CAA should reimburse the Air Corps for pay, travel, and allowances.[23]

The Air Corps' official position was that the CPTP would supplement rather than overlap army pilot training programs. The Air

Corps was itself seeking to increase its numbers by sending five traveling selection boards to colleges and universities throughout the country to search for potential candidates. As part of that program, the Air Corps would ask for the records of pilot students enrolled in the CPTP. From the records compiled by the selection boards, the board chair could preliminarily select many qualified men. He could also find those who had been unable to complete the course, barring them from consideration for enlistment.[24]

Yount explained that the Air Corps' flight training had three phases: a primary one-year course comprised of seventy-five hours of flight instruction plus ground instruction and military training conducted at Randolph Field, Texas; a four-month basic course, also at Randolph; and, finally, a four-month advanced course at Kelly Field, Texas. The advanced course qualified students to become second lieutenants in the Air Corps Reserve. Future plans of the Air Corps for primary pilot training would involve contracting with civilian flight schools for more or less the same type of primary training as that at Randolph Field, except that the contract course would be given in nine months rather than a year. The Air Corps would select the schools from a list of contractors approved and accredited by the Civil Aeronautics Authority and planned to begin the contract program in July 1939.[25]

Yount was asked whether those pilots who had successfully completed the CPTP course would be immediately available for commissioning in the Air Corps. His response reflected the Air Corps' feeling that the CPTP alone would not be sufficient to make a qualified military pilot. "There is a great difference in the training which can be given at these colleges and the training which we give at our training center." Military aircraft were faster—three and four hundred miles per hour—with higher landing speeds, more difficult to fly than elementary trainers, and had greater potential for accidents. Yount speculated that if insufficiently trained pilots were placed in the Air Corps, they would not last long and would probably kill themselves and others.[26]

There was some skepticism about whether men trained in the CPTP would come forth in sufficient numbers to enlist in the military. If they did not, the program would not fulfill one of its stated goals. Yount, however, believed that potential recruits would not lack enthusiasm. The committee also questioned whether it would be better and more economical for the War Department to undertake the training if the bill's purpose was to build up a reserve of military pilots. Yount replied that the Air Corps was ill-equipped to undertake a training program of such magnitude.[27]

The Air Corps' attitude toward the CPTP during the House hearings is enlightening. The training that pilots received as civilians was thought to be of lower quality than that given to military recruits, even if it were done by civilian instructors. Military parochialism on the issue was a constant problem in the Air Corps' acceptance of the program. As the CPTP shifted into wartime high gear, the Air Corps' insistence on retaining its autonomy in matters of pilot training would have serious consequences.

The committee then turned to the question of how air education in the United States compared with that abroad. Hinckley read from a prepared statement, providing a synopsis of air training in Europe. From the figures Hinckley's office had compiled, one could infer that the United States lagged behind the Axis powers and other countries with established air programs. In Germany, for example, it was estimated that sixty-five thousand flight trainees were between the ages of eighteen and thirty-five, and the Nazis were turning out twenty-five thousand pilots, mechanics, and aeronautical engineers annually. Preliminary aviation training was mandatory for boys between the ages of ten and twelve, who, the report said, "are being instilled with the ambition to wear the wings of the German air force." It was estimated that about a million youths had been trained in this way. A hundred thousand youths between the ages of thirteen and seventeen, members of the Hitler Youth, were slated for some sort of aviation service. Finally, members of the Hitler Youth studied aeronautics in school and glider training and flying at more than four hundred summer camps.[28]

In Italy, air education was conducted in a similar manner. It was mandatory, for example, that each male child between the ages of six and twenty be a member of the Italian Youth of the Littorio, which was similar to the Hitler Youth movement. Aviation training began at age eight and continued through elementary school, high school, and college. Glider instruction began in high school, and powered flight training in college. Students who selected aviation as a profession were given flight lessons and ground instruction as part of their regular education, and this training prepared them for advanced military flying after they had completed their college degrees. It was estimated fifty thousand students were specializing in aviation, a figure that did not include members of the RUNA, a government-sponsored aeronautical society organized to foster interest in aviation. The Italian government gave the RUNA flight schools 4,000 lira (about $210) for each member who obtained the equivalent of a private pilot's license.[29]

In France, an estimated 153 flight training centers with twenty thousand members ranging in age from seventeen to twenty-one were encouraged to take preliminary flight instruction. Those completing the training successfully qualified to apply for advanced training in the French air force. In 1939, an estimated 80 million francs were appropriated for civil flight training.[30]

In Great Britain, the Civil Air Guard had been formed in the summer of 1938 to make flight training available to both men and women between the ages of eighteen and fifty. The Civil Air Guard was an umbrella organization that subsidized flying clubs and flight training schools throughout the country. The government paid $240 to the club or school for every member or student who obtained a private pilot's license. To encourage the continuation of private flying after initial licensing, the government also paid the equivalent of $72 to each member or student who renewed their private pilot's license.[31]

To conclude the hearings for that day, Sumpter Smith, chair of the Air Safety Board of the CAA, asked the committee to consider the question of accident prevention. "If the Congress is going to approve such a program," Smith testified, "it seems to us the most vital thing to consider is the time; that is, to give the Authority as much time as possible to get ready to start the program."[32] Smith enumerated several items that the CAA deemed "absolutely necessary" to accident prevention and that would take some time to prepare. First, because most colleges and universities ended their school year in early June, Smith recommended that plans for training be in the CAA's hands before the summer recess. Second, sufficient time would be necessary to select students, receive and process applications, conduct physical examinations, and prepare courses of instruction. Third, considerable time would be necessary to obtain aircraft and prepare airports near the schools for the program. Fourth, and no doubt most important in terms of safety, was the training of instructors. The CAA "should have at least six months if possible, to make these preparations and get everything under way so that when the schools open next September, we will not be faced with a lot of confusion in starting the program and with having a lot of these youngsters involved in crashes." Smith was concerned that if the legislation were not passed until the end of the congressional session in June, there would only be two months in which to prepare for the program. Although a minimum of six months was necessary, only five were available to the CAA to ready the program.[33]

Having heard approximately two hours of testimony, the committee adjourned. As in the first round of hearings, the legislators were interested less in the CPTP's philosophical underpinnings than in procedural matters, especially how it would be integrated into Army Air Forces and navy pilot training programs. Assurances from Admiral Cook and General Yount, however, seemed to satisfy committee members that the CPTP would be welcomed as supplementary and beneficial to the military's own system of flight instruction. Repeated questioning focused on whether sufficient numbers of men trained by the CPTP would enlist in military aviation programs. Although this question would continue to be raised, the committee felt that, at least for the moment, it did not present much of a problem.

Debate before the Full House

From March 27, the day of the final House of Representatives committee hearings on the Civilian Pilot Training Program, to April 19, the day of the House debate on the legislation, the Committee on Interstate and Foreign Commerce worked on the CPTP bill behind the scenes. On the afternoon of April 5, the committee met in executive session to consider the original CPTP bill (H.R.5093). The minutes of the proceedings specified that the committee give its approval for the chairman to reintroduce the amended bill "and report it out formally." The committee also gave the chairman authority to take necessary steps to present the bill to the House of Representatives. Instead of the $7,300,000 allowed in the original measure, the revised bill (H.R.5619) authorized only $5,675,000.[34]

On April 10, the House of Representatives produced a favorable report on the bill that underscored the twofold purpose of the legislation—New Deal economic recovery and war preparedness. It said that Congress had directed that the provisions of the Civil Aeronautics Act of 1938 "be administered so as to encourage and develop civil aeronautics." It argued that the CPTP bill would give the CAA another way of carrying out Congress's directions because training large numbers of civilian pilots would cause more aircraft to be built and sold, increase airport patronage, and provide more potential passengers for commercial aviation. Finally, it emphasized that, taken together, these actions would bring about "a much needed stabilization of the American aircraft industry."[35]

Moreover, the report said that the legislation would benefit the civilian aviation industry and "provide a means by which this country could better defend itself in time of national emergency" by selecting and training "a large group of civilian pilots who would be promptly available and immensely valuable in case of any such emergency." It found the proposed CPTP bill to be in harmony with the "traditional American way of providing for its military needs, not by extensive militarization, but by enhancing the strength and efficiency of the men and machines of civil life."[36]

On April 19, nine days after the Committee on Interstate and Foreign Commerce had submitted its favorable report, the House of Representatives began debate on H.R.5619. Most of the members of the committee were present.[37] Clarence Lea (D.-Calif.), sponsor of the CPTP bill, summarized the legislation. The bill would give the CAA control over a program of pilot training, and the proposed legislation had the approval of the army and the navy. Its fundamental purpose was to provide for the training of men between the ages of eighteen and twenty-five who wanted to become private pilots. If passed, fifteen thousand pilots would be trained by July 1, 1940. The CAA would arrange with colleges, universities, junior colleges, and civilian pilot training schools throughout the country to participate in the training program. Training would consist of between thirty-five and fifty hours of flight training and three hundred hours of ground school instruction. Based on Army Air Corps and navy pilot training experience, nearly 50 percent of the trainees would not finish the program, and the same physical standards used by the military would be in effect for the potential civilian trainees. Each trainee would carry some $3,000 worth of life insurance and contribute a fee of $40 from which insurance and incidental charges would be paid. As for the cost to the government, out of the authorization of $5,675,000, $4,875,000 would be used to train the fifteen thousand prospective pilots, $300,000 would be used for ground school, $250,000 for supervision, and $250,000 for research that would obtain information on the physiological and psychological elements relevant in training young men to fly.[38]

Lea believed that the CPTP would provide "a method by which the fullest resources of the United States now available for primary training purposes can be utilized immediately." The program would use airports and aircraft throughout the United States, as well as "local men who have certificates as instructors in air training." Lea also pointed out the advantages in "health, mental poise, and alertness" to the young men who would be trained as pilots and praised the program as an aid in "the progress and stability of civil aviation." The CPTP plan provided not only a pool of pilots who would be ready to serve military needs, but also would serve to disperse knowledge about how to operate aircraft and "develop air-mindedness in the young people of America." Lea likened the coming air age to the burgeoning automobile revolution at the turn of the century: "We have developed a nation that is thoroughly familiar with the automobile, and knowledge of its operation has become the common knowledge of the American people. When our people become likewise familiar with the airplane they will be invincible in the air."[39]

Stephen Pace (D.-Ga.) questioned how the CPTP would fit into military pilot training programs. Pace pointed out that the program was "strictly preliminary" and would not qualify a man to become an expert flyer. After a CPTP student had taken a year of preliminary training and shown the "proper ability," Pace said, "he will be transferred either to Randolph Field or to Pensacola for training." Pace also said that he anticipated that at least a hundred thousand men could be qualified to become military pilots through the CPTP.[40]

Oscar Youngdahl commented strongly on the role of the CPTP and national defense. Although he took the classic isolationist position against American intervention in what he considered foreign wars, Youngdahl nevertheless favored the CPTP. He vehemently criticized what he considered the current war hysteria and the vacillating U.S. foreign policy. Foreign policy, Youngdahl believed, should be "minding our own business." He stressed the peacetime objectives of the CPTP bill and its dual purpose to provide aviation careers and a pool of potential military pilots.[41]

Luther Patrick (D.-Ala.) favored the measure for much the same reason as did Youngdahl. "Most everyone says that America should attend carefully to its own business," Patrick said, "and yet practically everyone concludes that we ought to do that which we do as well as we can while we are at it, and that while we must stay at home and look after our own affairs and attend to them strictly, we should do it as securely and safely as possible. This is the philosophy behind this program."[42]

Some members objected to the CPTP because the program provided no mechanism by which trainees could be made to enlist in the Army Air Corps or navy if war came. James W. Wadsworth, however, felt that trainees should not be drafted in exchange for their training, and that such attempts would lead unduly to a militarization of the program. "To say to these young men when they apply for this training at these schools and colleges that they may not take it unless they enlist in some form of military or semimilitary organization, enter into some kind of a contract, is to change the picture, as I see it, to something very different from that conceived from the authors of this act."[43]

The main focus of the debate, however, was on some members' misunderstanding about whether young men not enrolled in colleges and universities could qualify for CPTP training. Even after being assured by members of the Committee on Interstate and Foreign Commerce that the CAA would allow trainees to come from outside the academic setting, some congressmen were not convinced. They demanded an amendment that specified the provision in detail.

Charles Halleck (R.-Ind.) addressed the controversy over the college requirement by stating that although men who did not attend college would not be excluded, the experience of the last war had shown that a higher educational requirement was desirable for officer candidates. Halleck stressed the "strength in reserve" aspect of the CPTP and its role in the preparedness of the United States. He added that the bill would stimulate the sales of private aircraft, encourage aircraft production, and add to the defense of the country in peacetime. The civilian aspect of the CPTP was important because, as he said, the army and navy "were not in a position to carry on such a program" because "they [had] all they [could] do to carry on the expansion program for which we have heretofore provided." Carl Hinshaw pointed out that the CAA had not meant to exclude any qualified person from CPTP training and that the program would be open "not only to colleges but also to junior colleges." Clarence Lea added that "a man can take this course without having gone to college at all."[44]

The discussion led James E. Van Zandt (R.-Penn.) to propose an amendment, which passed and specified in part that "students shall be selected from all walks of life who have at least 2 years' college training or equivalent thereof so far as aviation is concerned, but at least 10 percent shall be selected from applicants who do not present 2 years' college education as a qualification." Van Zandt justified the amendment by saying that the CAA officials who testified in committee would probably keep their word about admitting students who did not attend college, but if other CAA officials were to replace them, "this assurance to the committee may be forgotten, and then the boy who does not have a college education will be denied the privilege of taking advantage of this splendid program."[45]

Clarence Lea, however, opposed the amendment, saying he thought it "unnecessary and undesirable." Again, Lea tried to explain to Congress that a college education was not a prerequisite for someone to take part in the CPTP and that anyone, even though they had never been to college, could be admitted through extension programs. Halleck argued that Van Zandt's amendment was ambiguous, and Lea concurred. Van Zandt, however, would not be denied. Halleck's statement convinced him "that the money that will be appropriated for this program will be used exclusively to train college students and will exclude the poor boy who cannot go to college."[46]

William Miller (R.-Conn.) then proposed another amendment that stipulated that 5 or 10 percent of the students be selected from the ranks of people who did not have college educations. Hinshaw and Halleck again tried to explain the issue, but to no avail. Halleck made it clear that "part of the confusion arises out of the fact that . . . the Army requires 2 years' college education as its equivalent, under their rules." Despite the debate and attempts to clear up what appeared to be a muddleheaded modification to the proposed bill, the Van Zandt amendment as modified by Miller passed by a vote of 79 to 28.[47]

Then came an especially auspicious moment for blacks who had been attempting to break into the predominantly white world of American aviation. Everett M. Dirksen (R.-Ill.) offered an amendment that stated that in administering the act "none of the benefits of training or programs shall be denied on account of race, creed or color." Dirksen characterized black Americans as being "moved by the same patriotic ardor" and "possessed of the same aptitude in any field of national defense as anyone else" and pointed to their accomplishments in the American Revolution, the War of 1812, the Civil War, the War with Spain, and World War I. Dirksen was motivated in part to sponsor such an amendment because he had befriended a group of black fliers from the Chicago area who had recently formed the National Airmen's Association of America (NAA) to promote the cause of racial equality in aviation. With the help of Dirksen, Illinois governor Dwight H. Green, Chicago mayor Edward J. Kelly, and Enoc Waters, the city editor of the *Chicago Defender,* a black newspaper, the NAA began to seek political help in their crusade for inclusion of blacks in the CPTP and the segregated Army Air Corps (chapter 3).[48]

Clarence Lea again strongly opposed the Dirksen amendment because he believed that if the law were administered faithfully, it would "disregard" racial discrimination. He also pointed out that "we have a few colored educational institutions in this country that may be able to qualify as training centers under this bill. It seems to me," he said, "there is no contribution made to race equality to drag a thing like this forth that has no legitimate or necessary place in the legislation." Despite Lea's opposition, there was no further debate, and the amendment passed by a vote of 71 to 53.[49]

The Dirksen antidiscrimination amendment was an epoch-making event in the history of blacks in aviation. It demonstrated that for the first time the government was willing to intervene on the part of blacks who wanted to be a part of aviation, and it signaled the end of the pre-World War II struggle for recognition. Despite widespread discrimination, the period from 1936 to 1939 was marked by slow progress in the form of increased black participation in aviation. By 1938, for example, there were several hundred black aviators in the United States, concentrated primarily in Los Angeles and Chicago. Yet, exclusion of blacks was prevalent. They were unable to make their livelihoods as airmail or airline pilots or as workers in aircraft factories, nor were blacks accepted as military pilots. The Dirksen amendment showed that blacks had organized sufficiently to begin the next onslaught on the white aviation establishment: the Army Air Corps.[50]

After the vote on the Dirksen amendment, John M. Vorys (R.-Ohio) offered an amendment stipulating that "no student shall be accepted until he consents in writing to serve in the armed forces of the United States in case of war." Alfred Bulwinkle disputed Vorys and argued that Congress was concentrating "too much on national defense in considering this bill." The program, said Bulwinkle, was to do more than provide pilots in the event of war. It was meant to help them to enter civilian life as commercial aviators. To bolster Bulwinkle's argument, Carl Hinshaw reminded the Congress that the bill was supposed to foster civil aeronautics and not merely be a way to train pilots directly for the military. The bill's wider significance, according to Hinshaw, was to offer "a certain amount of vocational training to the young men of this country, a vocational training to which many of them will not be able to aspire, not having the funds for taking such a course."[51]

Because of Bulwinkle's and Hinshaw's objections to the Vorys amendment, the House rejected it by a vote of 68 to 30. After the vote was taken, John C. Schafer (R.-Wis.) offered an amendment that denied training to aliens, which was agreed upon unanimously. John J. Cochran (D.-Mo.) then moved to limit the amount of future appropriations for the CPTP, but Clarence Lea objected strongly yet again, and Cochran made no effort to put the question to a vote. When this business was finished, the CPTP bill passed the House of Representatives.[52]

The version of the CPTP bill that passed, H.R.5619, differed little from the one reported out earlier by the Committee on Interstate and Foreign Commerce. Among the features that distinguished it from the committee version were the antidiscrimination amendment, the proviso that at least 5 percent of the students taking part in the training "be selected from applicants other than college students," and, finally, the stipulation that the CPT program would run for five years. The House had not changed its mind about the sum to be appropriated, which was set at $5,675,000.[53]

As in the hearings on the CPTP bill, Congress involved itself in a debate that was more procedural and programmatic than philosophical. Would the CPTP be open to individuals not enrolled in institutions of higher learning? How would the CPTP interrelate with military pilot training programs? Which colleges and universities throughout the United States would be authorized to train pilots? Who would select these schools? And how they would be selected? Again, the expected opposition from isolationists did not happen.

Finally, Congress was concerned about whether trainees would be willing to come forth in sufficient numbers to serve in the military after receiving their pilots' licenses. Clarence Lea, Charles Halleck, Oscar Youngdahl, James Wadsworth, and Alfred Bulwinkle, however, were interested less in potential pilots for the military than in the program's peacetime, New Deal dimensions. They argued that the CPTP would be a valuable way to provide employment in the aviation industry and stimulate the sale of private aircraft. Although an attempt was made to amend the bill by stipulating that students be made to pledge enlistment in the military, collective wisdom dictated that the program remain civilian in content.

Hearings before the Senate Subcommittee

The Senate had also been working on its own version of the bill. This measure, S.2119, was sponsored by Patrick McCarran (D.-Nev.), a prominent advocate of civil aviation. Unlike Representative Clarence Lea, McCarran was not in F.D.R.'s camp. He had opposed the Roosevelt administration's Black-McKellar Act in 1934 and proposed instead a bill to create an independent agency to regulate civil aviation. To McCarran's dismay, however, the Black-McKellar legislation prevailed. Discouraged and distrustful after four years of battling the administration, McCarran told a *New York Times* reporter in November 1937, "I am fed up with the obstructions Washington bureaucracy tries to put in the way of honest legislative endeavor for aviation." McCarran had also carried on a bitter struggle with Senators Harry Truman and Royal Copeland over the final shape of the Civil Aeronautics Act of 1938.[54]

McCarran temporarily put aside his differences with the administration, however, and energetically supported the Civilian Pilot Training Program. His version of the CPTP bill omitted the antidiscrimination language and the provision that 5 percent of all persons selected for training not be from college ranks and authorized a $7,300,000 appropriation instead of the $5,675,000 proposed by the House. In all other respects, however, McCarran's bill was the same as Lea's.[55]

On April 20, 1939, the day after the House debate on the CPTP, the Senate Committee on Commerce's Subcommittee on Civil Aviation met to consider S.2119. Testifying were Robert Hinckley, General Barton Yount, and Captain John H. Towers. Although not a member of the subcommittee, Senator McCarran had been invited to sit in on the proceedings.[56]

Bennett "Champ" Clark, chair of the subcommittee, began by questioning Hinckley about the ambiguous and controversial college requirement, which had been the subject of so much discussion in the House debate the previous day. Hinckley replied that as originally conceived, the CPTP would admit men not enrolled in colleges and universities through extension programs. The academic setting would allow more local airports to be used for training than if the CAA were to set up training schools at random. This would enable the CAA to decentralize the program and increase its safety. Initially, the thirteen colleges and universities in the demonstration program were selected because of their strong aeronautical curriculums.[57]

McCarran asked Hinckley about the education a successful pilot should have. Hinckley replied that although the experience of the military had been that pilots should have at least two years of college, research on the question had not been comprehensive enough for the CAA to draw conclusions. One of the important aims of the CPTP was to determine just what made a good pilot. The research that resulted from the program would help to answer questions about pilot qualifications. Ideally, instruction should be adapted to the requirements of the military in terms of uniform ground school, uniform instruction, and the eligibility requirements of age and physical fitness.[58]

McCarran then asked how the CPTP would compare with similar programs in other countries. Hinckley replied that the expense would be modest when compared with, for example, Germany's ambitious program, which supposedly was training a million youths in various aspects of aeronautics. Other European countries were also well ahead of the United States. Furthermore, the United States did not want to follow Germany's militaristic model; Hinckley stressed that "we are endeavoring to do it in such manner that we will develop a resource that can be drawn upon in time of national emergency."[59]

James Mead (D.-N.Y.), the subcommittee's sternest interrogator throughout the hearings, took issue with the CAA's authority to administer the program because of what he considered the narrow mandate of the Civil Aeronautics Act. Why, Mead asked, did not the army train the pilots if the primary object of the proposed law was national defense? Hinckley responded that the Civil Aeronautics Act urged the CAA "to develop civil aeronautics." Mead persisted, digressing from the main issue to question the appropriateness of the CAA's involvement in airport construction and other areas he thought should be the responsibility of local municipalities and the airline industry. He warned that if the CAA began to get involved where he believed it had no business, then Congress would balk at appropriating the necessary funds.[60]

Hinckley defended the CAA's airport program and returned the proceedings to the main question of the CPTP. He reiterated that U.S. pilots lagged behind when compared to the number of trained pilots in other countries. The CPTP represented a democratic approach to the pilot shortage and would not be entirely state-subsidized like the programs of most other countries. The program would help those young men who wanted to learn to fly but could not afford to do so. Finally, it would have strong subsidiary New Deal economic benefits.[61]

Mead, however, continued to press. He asked a series of questions about pilot training programs in the United States and concluded that these were sufficient. Another pilot training program, not strictly military in nature and conducted by the CAA, was unnecessary. Hinckley countered by saying that the colleges and universities that participated in the CPTP would be responsible for the training, not the CAA, which would merely oversee the program.[62]

The subcommittee then questioned General Yount. As in the House hearings on March 27, Yount supported the CPTP, saying that the War Department endorsed the bill "wholeheartedly." To McCarran's question about the suitability of the Army Air Corps carrying out the program, Yount responded that because of a shortage of "resources, personnel and equipment" the War Department "could not attempt a program of this sort." To Mead's question about the Air Corps' ability to take on the training program in an emergency, Yount responded that it could be done but not without a "vast increase" in appropriations and personnel.[63]

Yount made it clear that the Air Corps was reluctant to take on training of the scope of the CPTP. Mead, however, suggested that the Air Corps might set up a center or centers to train a reserve corps of airline pilots with transport licenses. In wartime, these pilots would be eligible for military service as convoy, observation, and bomber pilots. The Air Corps' view was that, although desirable, such a center would be expensive. Mead continued to beleaguer Yount and concluded by asking, "Shall we encourage another agency to train pilots for you, or will the War Department expand its own facilities and keep the family intact?" Yount replied that the CAA had "two or three other very distinct objects" aside from national defense, and that the planned CPTP would ultimately benefit the military.[64]

The navy's representative at the hearings was Captain John H. Towers, assistant chief of the Bureau of Aeronautics and earlier the commander of the fleet of Curtiss NC flying boats that had made the first aerial crossing of the Atlantic in 1919. Towers, who within a little more than a month would be promoted to chief of the Bureau of Aeronautics, read a prepared statement endorsing the CPTP. "The vocational aviation training program of the Civil Aeronautics Authority," he said, "will be of definite value to the national defense in case of emergency. The existence of a large reservoir of trained civilian pilots will provide an immediate source of partially trained personnel, and thus reduce materially the time required to develop them into competent naval pilots."[65]

Mead suggested that if the navy were to set up an additional pilot training center, it might possibly accommodate another eight hundred pilots a year. The navy felt, however, that its shortage of personnel would hamper carrying out such an ambitious program of training. Before such instruction could begin, the other training center would have to be built, and that would take time.[66]

Towers hinted at the military's proprietary attitude toward the CPTP by suggesting that, in a national emergency, the army and the navy would step in to administer the program and supervise the training units that would be widely scattered throughout the country. He also warned the subcommittee not to place much credence in the twenty-two-thousand-pilot statistic Hinckley had cited earlier in the hearings as being the number of licensed pilots in the United States and that not all civilian pilots were potentially military pilots.[67]

After two hours of testimony, the subcommittee adjourned, and the Civilian Pilot Training Program had passed another congressional milestone. The Senate, too, had in large part been concerned more with procedural and programmatic questions than with the theoretical goals of the CPTP. However, Senator Mead's serious and persistent questions about the need for the CPTP emphasized the ambiguities of a civilian program designed as a feeder to the military. Indirectly, Mead also echoed some of the concerns that various members of the House of Representatives had about how the CPTP would fit into the pattern of military flight training and foreshadowed the program's later difficulties during World War II.[68]

Into the Home Stretch

After the Senate hearings on April 20, the CPTP bill languished in the Subcommittee on Civil Aviation of the Committee on Commerce. Busy with other legislative matters, subcommittee chairman Clark delayed the Senate's report on the bill for more than a month. Finally, on May 26, the subcommittee voted to report favorably on the bill. On June 7, forty-eight days after the Senate committee hearings, S.2119 was reported out with authorization to provide training for fifteen thousand pilots for the first year of the program. Amendments to the bill provided, among other things, that none of the program's benefits would be refused "on account of race, creed, or color," that a minimum of 5 percent of the students selected for training would not be from colleges and universities, and that the appropriation for the fiscal years 1939 and 1940 would be decreased from $7,300,000 to $5,675,000 and limited to $7 million in ensuing fiscal years.[69]

On June 19, the House agreed to the Senate amendments, but it was not until June 27, nearly two and a half months after the Senate hearings, that President Roosevelt finally signed the CPTP act. The final legislation, Public Law No. 153 (Appendix A), was in all respects identical to the bill reported on by the Senate, except that it did not specify the number of students to be trained in the first year of the program. [70]

Yet, even after the bill had passed and signed lawmakers could not agree on the program's budget or on the number of pilots to be trained in the first year. The CPTP bill that F.D.R. signed was merely the first step in making the program an actuality. The next was for Congress to decide the exact amount of money the program would receive and to appropriate the funds. On July 10, with Robert Hinckley, General Yount, and Admiral Towers testifying on its behalf, the House Appropriation Committee opened hearings on the Third Deficiency Bill, which carried the CPTP's funding. The committee, in a penurious mood, recommended that the CPTP appropriation be cut to $3 million for the first year and that the number of pilots to be trained be reduced from the fifteen thousand proposed by the CAA to 7,500. On August 2, the House passed the bill to which the CPTP appropriation was attached and sent it on to the Senate, which approved it two days later. On August 5, the House and Senate began considering the conference report on the bill, which raised the appropriation to $4 million. Finally, on August 12, the House and Senate agreed to a budget of $4 million. Hinckley estimated the number of pilots to be trained, which had become a separate question not part of the legislation, to be ten thousand, a figure he later increased to eleven thousand.[71]

Although the Civilian Pilot Training Program bill did not have an easy time in Congress, the potential opposition to the measure had not occurred in expected ways. During the House and Senate hearings and the House debate, the legislators repeatedly avoided the larger questions that the CPTP posed, whether it was too militaristic or whether its agenda was decidedly too New Deal. Thus, neither isolationism nor New Deal economics had been major congressional issues where the CPTP was concerned. Congress favored the economic dimensions of the CPTP as a way of advancing and stabilizing civil aviation. It also appeared to accept the program's war-preparedness aspects without much questioning, suggesting at least tacit acceptance that World War II was at hand and that isolationism was on the wane. Congress evidently believed that the CPTP would accomplish its dual purpose and was satisfied that the program would not involve the United States in foreign entanglements. Legislators saw the program as a national defense measure acceptable to isolationists, internationalists, and moderates alike.

The congressional process also showed that, for the moment at least, the objectives of the CPTP were in tenuous accord with those of the military. At this early stage of the program's development, the Army Air Corps and the navy, neither of which was prepared adequately for the advent of war, could afford to be magnanimous toward the CPTP, which would help them in their efforts toward mobilization.

The congressionally mandated antidiscrimination provision of the CPTP law made flight training widely accessible to blacks at government expense and opened an important area of vocational training from which they had been excluded. The opportunities the provision afforded also proved that blacks could learn to fly and would later make the Army Air Corps' exclusion of blacks appear inappropriate and irrational.

Robert Hinckley had seen the CPTP through the difficult legislative process successfully, but the struggle with Congress was not yet over. As he later recalled sarcastically, "the budding experts on the Hill watched us like hawks during the succeeding twelve months. . . . Hardly a day passed that one of us wasn't called to the Hill for a conference or kept busy late into the night, documenting what we were doing. To say that we met the demands from the Hill with smiling acquiescence and silent praise of the democratic process would be to deny the truth. There were times that the Congress burned hell out of us and seemed blissfully unaware of the fact that we were trying to do a difficult job rather than spend all of our waking hours telling them what kind of a job we were doing."[72]

CHAPTER 3

The Uneasy Transition from Peace to War

In the nearly two and one-half years between the time the full-scale Civilian Pilot Training Program received its appropriation from Congress in August 1939 and the Japanese attack on Pearl Harbor on December 7, 1941, the CPTP had many accomplishments to its credit. Among them were the successful completion of the demonstration program, the launching and execution of the bigger, more ambitious CPTP in late 1939, research in flying various types of unconventional aircraft, and psychological research in instructional methods and testing pilots.

Moreover, the CPTP began to address some of its New Deal aspects, either stated or implicit: pump-priming for the light aircraft industry, an ambitious program of air age education, and equality of training for blacks and women. However, the program also underwent several conflicts—the heated-up crisis in Europe, its safety, criticism of the lack of mandatory requirements for military enlistments, budget battles with Congress, and the lukewarm endorsement of President Roosevelt—that threatened its New Deal goals. The winds of war were beginning to have a profound effect on the program's civilian nature, testing its war-preparedness dimensions. The bends and shifts that these winds brought about in the CPTP foreshadowed the more extreme difficulties the program would face when the United States became involved in World War II.

Despite congressional delays in funding the full-scale Civilian Pilot Training Program, the CPTP's demonstration program, begun in February 1939, proceeded apace. The thirteen participating colleges and universities had been selected either because of their "pioneer" work in aeronautical engineering or because they had flight training programs. Prospective contractors for flight training were asked to submit bids to the CAA and were to be paid for up to fifty hours of flight training per student. With the $100,000 it had received from the National Youth Administration, the CAA selected 330 students between the ages of eighteen and twenty-five to take part.[1] Physical standards for trainees had been developed using military criteria, and the Army Air Corps agreed to provide flight surgeons to help the schools examine potential candidates. Students were required to pay a $35 to $50 laboratory fee that also covered life insurance. Ground school consisted of ten hours of classroom work on the civil air regulations (rules of the air) and thirty-five hours each on navigation and meteorology. Flight training consisted of thirty-five to fifty hours of flight instruction—eight hours of dual instruction, nine hours of dual check time, and eighteen hours of solo flying (Appendix B). Schools without an established flight training program were expected to contract with qualified local airport operators for instruction.[2]

The CAA's letter to the participating schools was explicit about the program's innovative approach: "We are instituting a special controlled-instruction course differing materially from the general training now required for a private pilot's license, though generally similar to that required in flying schools whose curricula have been formally approved by the Civil Aeronautics Authority." The CAA also pointed out that the lengthy course of instruction "not only [would] result in a much higher degree of safety than now exists in private flight instruction . . . but that it [would] enable all candidates to pass with ease the required test for a private pilot's certificate at the end of 35 hours' instruction."[3]

Early in 1939, Grove Webster, chief of the Private Flying Development Division of the Civil Aeronautics Authority, Harry Kinnear of the Works Progress Administration, Samuel Gilstrap of the National Youth Administration, and William Robertson of the CAA made a a twenty-one-day, twelve-thousand-mile tour of the United States, visiting all thirteen participating schools. Robertson saw to it that flight instructors received a check flight and that all aircraft were inspected.[4]

Webster reported on the overwhelming enthusiasm for the program. Of the 1,200 students who applied for entry to the CPTP at one school, four hundred were deemed eligible, and thirty were finally selected for physical examination. Based on the success of the CPTP's demonstration program, Webster predicted that the United States would have fifty thousand private aircraft and a hundred thousand licensed pilots within five years.[5]

On June 23 and 24, 1939, the CAA held a conference, with representatives of the thirteen schools and the fixed-base operators taking part in the demonstration program. Reports showed that the results of the fledgling CPTP program had thus far been encouraging. On the negative side, flight school operators at the conference felt that, considering the excellent safety record compiled to date in the program, something had to be done about their responsibility for bearing costly flight insurance. They suggested that if commercial underwriters could not be convinced of the need to lower rates, "it might be possible for the government to handle the insurance."[6]

Then in August came an announcement of significant importance not only for the operators, but also for the whole CPTP. The National Council on Compensation Insurance, a group that represented various insurance companies and was empowered to set rates, decided to lower operator rates 50 percent, from $1.50 an hour to 75 cents an hour. The CAA was pleased. If instructors' insurance rates were reduced, the cost of student participation in the CPTP would also be reduced. The net effect would be to attract more trainees.[7]

When the demonstration phase of the CPTP came to a close, the results seemed to suggest that the more ambitious full-scale program could be carried out. Of the 330 students enrolled in the demonstration program, 313 completed the course (approximately 95 percent) and received pilots' licenses. Total flying time logged in was 3,089 hours and 21 minutes. Only one fatality had occurred.[8]

In October 1939, the full-scale Civilian Pilot Training Program got under way. Hinckley's timetable for launching the big program, however, had been set back months by congressional delays. By August 1939, when the CPTP finally received its appropriation, most colleges and universities were not in session, making it difficult for school administrators, who could not proceed without authorization from their boards of regents or trustees. Nevertheless, by mid-September, the CAA announced the final requirements for the participating schools. It would accept applications from universities, colleges, technical institutes, four-year teachers colleges, and junior colleges. Prospective students had to be U.S. citizens between the ages of eighteen and twenty-five and could not have had previous flying experience. The CAA also stipulated that it would draw up contracts with each school for ground instruction and with airport operators for flight instruction; that it would subsidize flight and ground instruction; that the airport operators who would provide flight instruction would be chosen because of recommendations from the colleges and universities; that each school would be near a local airport with runways of specified length; that students and flight operators would have medical examinations and insurance; that schools and airport operators were to maintain a schedule for ground and flight school operations; and that schools would arrange for transportation to and from the airport.[9]

A typical course of flight instruction was similar to that used in the CPTP demonstration phase. It consisted of seventy-two hours of ground school, with segments on the history of aviation, civil air regulations, navigation, meteorology, parachutes, aircraft and the theory of flight, engines, instruments, and the use of radio and forms. For preliminary flight instruction, students would become familiar with the aircraft, then learn to taxi, take off, and land. While in the air, students would learn how to enter and recover from a spin and how to simulate a forced landing. Then they would solo. After that, students would take a minimum of fifteen hours of advanced solo work.[10]

During its formative days, the Civilian Pilot Training Program even managed to become, albeit briefly, part of the popular culture. In October 1939, Twentieth Century-Fox's publicity department promoted *20,000 Men a Year* as the first screen presentation based on the program. Starring Randolph Scott, Preston Foster, Margaret Lindsay, and Maxie Rosenbloom, the film was written by the prolific aviation screenwriter Frank "Spig" Wead and directed by Alfred E. Green. Scott portrayed a former commercial airline pilot who joins the staff of "Western College" as a CPTP flight instructor. Typical of the aviation film genre of the 1930s, *20,000 Men a Year* featured a lightweight plot interspersed with dramatic scenes of Paul Mantz flying the plane and the climactic aerial rescue of a student forced down over the Grand Canyon.[11]

The film received a lukewarm critical reception. In its inimitably cryptic style, *Variety's* anonymous review reported that it was "timely in presenting first film treatment of aerial training in colleges," and that "direction by Alfred E. Green [was] commendable, keeping picture moving despite trite story situations that crop up along the way." The *New York Times* critic Frank S. Nugent, similarly unenthusiastic, commented that the "flying sequences are exciting to watch," and that the cast had "played it competently enough." Nugent concluded that film was entitled to "a rating of 'fair' and a pair of wings from the CAA."[12]

That Hollywood had not been too successful in portraying the Civilian Pilot Training Program did not seem to matter. By the end of 1939, the program was progressing satisfactorily. In the continental United States, Alaska, Hawaii, and Puerto Rico, 9,350 men and women were being trained at 435 colleges and universities. In addition, the CAA was arranging to begin training seven hundred students not affiliated with colleges on a competitive examination basis by January 1, 1940. This training was apportioned throughout the country by a quota system, with states with large populations receiving bigger quotas.[13]

Early in 1940, the CAA announced that ninety of the 330 students selected for the CPTP demonstration program would undergo training in a prototype advanced course. Instruction would consist of a 146-hour ground school and fifty hours of flight training in aircraft larger than those used for the primary course. Advanced students would also undergo training in engines, aircraft radio, and night and cross-country flying and would practice handling aircraft powered by engines in the 125 to 165 horsepower range.[14]

In June 1940, the CAA also announced that contracts had been let to train sixty students in so-called unconventional aircraft, which had built-in safety features that supposedly made them spin- and stall-proof. Typical of this type of aircraft were the Engineering and Research Corporation (ERCO) Ercoupe and the Stearman Hammond Y-1, which featured two controls (elevator and aileron) instead of the conventional three (elevator, aileron, and rudder). Fewer controls made the Ercoupe and Stearman Hammond easier to fly and also safer.[15]

The program, to be held at airports in Baltimore and College Park, Maryland, and Palo Alto, California, had two objectives. First, it was designed "to determine the average amount of training required in *unconventional* aircraft to attain the same degree in safety in operation as would be required in the operation of *conventional* aircraft to qualify for a private pilot's certificate." Second, the program sought "to determine how much additional training would then be needed by the pilot taught to fly *unconventional* craft to reach the same proficiency in the operation of *conventional* aircraft."[16]

The CPTP Research Program

The CPTP also began to make inroads on the problem of testing potential pilots and developing improved instructional training methods. The research aspect of the CPTP was developed through the efforts of Dean R. Brimhall, Robert Hinckley's associate during the latter's WPA days and the CAA's director of research. Brimhall, who had been a professor of psychology at Brigham Young University, decided that it would be useful for colleges and universities to test CPTP students. The results of the investigations would be made known to the educational community through research reports published by the CAA.[17]

In conjunction with the CPTP research program, the National Research Council of the National Academy of Sciences established an
advisory group called the Committee on Selection and Training of
Civilian Aircraft Pilots. The committee, chaired by J. G. Jenkins of
the University of Maryland, was comprised of twenty-five scientists,
engineers, pilots, psychologists, doctors, military officials, vocational experts, and administrators. Through an executive subcommittee headed by Morris S. Viteles of the University of Pennsylvania,
the committee directed research at nearly forty universities throughout the country. The research program produced more than sixty
studies and reports (Appendix C) at a cost of $1 million.[18]

Two of the areas the research program explored were pilot selection and instructional methods. For pilot selection, the CPTP developed a battery of tests that the navy used later to evaluate potential
air cadets in the earliest phase of their training. These tests, which
"previewed" a student's flying ability, enabled the navy to eliminate
10 percent of those scoring lowest before they began flight instruction. By so doing, the navy eliminated 50 percent of those who
would eventually wash out of pilot training.[19]

Before the CPTP addressed the issue, flight instruction practices
lacked uniformity. In 1941, with the help of a grant from the National Research Council and funds from the CAA, CPTP researchers
at Purdue University under the direction of E. Lowell Kelly developed a way to help standardize teaching methods. Shortwave trans-
mitters placed in the cockpits of trainers enabled researchers to record and analyze conversations between instructors and students.
The transcriptions showed that teaching vocabulary and methods
varied widely from instructor to instructor.[20] The results of Kelly's
research produced two instructional guides. The first, a manual of
flight training vocabulary called *Patter for Elementary Flight Maneuvers,* was used widely by the CPTP and the navy. The second, *Fundamentals of Basic Flight Maneuvers,* was a standardized manual
that allowed students to go through various aerial maneuvers on the
ground before they did so in the cockpit.[21]

Techniques of recording what went on in the cockpit between instructors and students were refined in 1943 with the help of a device
perfected by the Armour Institute of Technology in Chicago and then
adapted by the CAA. The Airborne Magnetic Wire Recorder
(AMWR), which resembled a primitive tape recorder, recorded
sound on wire. It consisted of a small box that weighed fewer than
eight pounds, which suited it to the cramped quarters of an aircraft
cockpit. The AMWR recorded sound magnetically on a fine steel
wire, which passed back and forth from one spool to another

through a grip that converted electrical impulses into sound when the machine was in the playback mode.[22]

Later, the magnetic wire recorder and a motion picture camera were combined so that visual and aural observations could be made. The use of airborne photography to analyze pilot performance was pioneered in 1940 by Morris Viteles at the University of Pennsylvania. An on-board camera recorded not only pilot movements, but also those of the aircraft's ailerons and elevator. Researchers subsequently analyzed the footage and made observations about pilot posture, the ways in which the controls were grasped and manipulated, and how the ailerons and elevator responded as the controls were touched. The data were then plotted on graphs, inspected, and analyzed by computing quantitative indices that described the control movements.[23]

In his summary of the results of the investigations, Viteles noted that "analysis of the graphs and the quantitative indices resulting from treatment of the frame-by-frame readings of control positions revealed characteristic differences between the 'superior' and 'inferior' pilots when the graphs and mean scores on the indices were compared. With the exception of the 900 medium turns," he observed, "significant differences between the two groups were found in each of the flight maneuvers (Take-Off, Straight and Level Flight, 3600 Left Power Turn, and Landing)." Viteles cautioned, however, that "the investigation must be considered merely as preliminary to further research and the specific findings subject to the limitations set by the small number of cases. Its chief value lies in its exploratory nature and in the development of research tools and techniques such as the use of motion photography of flight performance."[24]

Such research contributed to establishing objective standards for predicting pilot success and measuring improvement and progress in instruction. As the CAA historian John R. M. Wilson has pointed out, "Evaluation of flight technique also benefited from the research. Subjective evaluations gave way to a standardized set of maneuvers, accompanied by filmed and computed records of a pilot's reactions, eye movements, perspiration, and other physiological responses. The seminal training program thus yielded a rich crop of side benefits."[25]

Another area in which CPTP research helped standardize flight training was in the methods flight instructors used to train pilots. This aspect of the program had also originated from research done by Viteles and others as part of the work of the Committee on Selection and Training of Civilian Aircraft Pilots. In the early days, flight training emphasized an instructor's flying ability rather than his teaching expertise. Despite changes in teaching made as a result of Kelly's research, the myth persisted that seat-of-the-pants flyers made the best instructors. As Viteles explained it, "the actual administration of flight instruction nevertheless remained, for the most part, in the hands of persons *with interest and experience in flying but little or no experience with methods of training.*" The belief persisted "that teaching others is a matter of a 'sixth' sense; and 'intuitive faculty' which defies explanation; a 'hunch,' appearing spontaneously in the teaching situation, that tells what is the right thing to do at the right time in training others."[26]

In 1943, the CAA asked the Committee on Selection and Training of Civilian Aircraft Pilots to develop a course on the theory and techniques of flight instruction. In April of that year, after the curriculum had been developed, a group of seven, selected as "Methods Instructors," was assigned to take the course at the University of Minnesota. The group then was asked to teach the methods course at several of the CAA's Instructor Training Centers. Later in the year, another instructors' course was set up at Ohio State University. Course materials also were given to the army, the navy, and the Royal Air Force, among other military flight organizations. From the practical lessons derived from the research on methods, a standard manual of instruction was prepared: *Lesson Plans for Training Methods Unit, CAA-WTS Controlled Secondary Instructor Course.*[27]

In his final report on the CAA research program, Viteles commented that although he viewed the effort as being largely successful, "not all of the research activities and investments were productive of useful outcomes." He cited "the unavailability of criterion data, or sudden changes in training plans made by governmental or other agencies," which "produced insuperable handicaps to the attainment of research objectives." Moreover, "there were instances where the original experimental design, apparatus, administrative procedures, or methods of analysis were inadequate for solving the problem under investigation."[28]

Yet the research arm of the CPTP did investigate many problems and answered questions about flight instruction, aviation psychology, pilot aptitude, and similar topics that had never before been addressed. Although the volume and diversity of report material cannot be ignored, the real benefits of the research can be found in the attempt to subject flying to rigorous scrutiny. Through the efforts of the CAA and the academic community in the United States, teaching people to fly, which had been largely uninvestigated, was given a firmer intellectual and scientific footing.

The CPTP had passed its first tests with flying colors, successfully completing the demonstration phase, launching the full-scale national program, and inaugurating an impressive series of research efforts aimed at improving training aircraft and instructional methods. Despite its delayed start, the results of the program's first fiscal year of operation were encouraging. By July 1, 1940, 10,281 students (10,197 in the elementary course and eighty-four in the secondary course) in colleges and universities throughout the United States, Hawaii, Alaska, and Puerto Rico had successfully completed training. A grand total of 371,000 hours had been flown.[29]

The Lightplane Industry,
Fixed-Base Operators, and Academe

A critical appraisal of the CPTP must take into account how well it fulfilled its subsidiary functions. How successful was it in meeting one of its primary goals, that of producing economic prosperity for the lightplane industry in the United States? Robert Hinckley and others intended this aspect to be part of the program's economic recovery aspect, and as such it can rightly be considered an integral part of the CPTP's New Deal dimensions.

Even before the passage of the Civilian Pilot Training Program legislation, the production of single-engine monoplanes with one or two seats—the typical lightplane—had increased 63 percent, from 947 aircraft in 1936 to 1,510 in 1937, and then leveled off at 1,400 in 1938. The production of domestic civil aircraft (produced solely for the civilian market) increased from 1,823 in 1938 to 3,715 in 1939, a gain of 49 percent. From January to mid-August 1940, domestic civil aircraft production reached 3,121, an average of 480 a month. Although production statistics for the remainder of the year are unavailable, projections show that at the average rate of production, 5,760 aircraft would have been produced by the end of 1940, an increase of 64 percent.[30]

These figures indicate that by the time the CPTP began in earnest, the lightplane industry was already growing. The need for the program as an economic booster was not as crucial as Congress had been led to believe. Moreover, production statistics may be misleading when one considers that major increases were limited to a small number of manufacturers. Piper Aircraft, for example, by far led the way, increasing its production 258 percent, from 658 aircraft in 1938, to 1,698 in 1939, to 1,501 in the first seven and one-half months of 1940—a projected increase of 71 percent.

One reason that Piper easily outdistanced its competition was because it produced the ubiquitous Cub, a relatively affordable, lightweight, high-winged cabin monoplane that became the standard training aircraft of the CPTP before the war. Piper even proclaimed in its late 1939 advertisements that a thousand had been turned out that year, and that the aircraft made up "more than 70% of all the planes used" in the Civilian Pilot Training Program.[31]

Taylorcraft, the next major company in terms of production, increased output from 281 aircraft in 1938, to 456 in 1939 (62 percent), to 464 for the first half of 1940. Next in line was Aeronca, with 260 aircraft in 1938, 501 in 1939 (an increase of 52 percent), and 264 for the first half of 1940. Other manufacturers like Howard—which produced eight aircraft in 1938, ten in 1939, and twelve in the first half of 1940—and Rearwin—which produced thirty-two aircraft in 1938, thirty-two in 1939, and thirty-eight in the first half of 1940— were much less fortunate.[32]

Thus, it appears that Hinckley and other CAA officials often overstated the extravagant claims they made about how the CPTP would aid the lightplane industry. Although, the CPTP appears to have had a significant effect on aircraft manufactured for domestic civil use in 1940, its first full year of operation, the effects were decidedly short term. By 1941, lightplane manufacturing for the civilian sector was less important as companies began to turn their attention to producing aircraft for the military.

Subsidiary to the issue of the economic effects of the CPTP on the lightplane industry is the question of its influence on fixed-base operators and college and university communities. This question is difficult to answer because the effects were hard to measure. One indication of an overwhelming response is that before the program began full-scale operations, CAA officials limited participation to three hundred colleges and universities, and applications far exceeded that number by October 1939. The *Washington Star* reported that "the final rolls will show between 390 and 400 schools in at least 47 states and the District of Columbia." Nevada, according to the article, was the only state that "had not yet been represented."[33]

Moreover, judging from the volume of enthusiastic correspondence that the CAA received, one can reasonably assume that from the beginning of the program until America's entry into World War II, the CPTP was eagerly sought after by fixed-base operators and college and university officials. For example, Wright Vermilya, Jr., of the Palm Beach Aero Corp. commented, "Frankly, I've never seen anything like it in all my 22 years in the flying business. Our private courses have jumped about 75 percent and it is almost impossible to estimate the potential business created. . . . There is probably more interest on the part of officials and business men than at any time since 1927." J. C. Sedgwick of Oak Air Service in Mobile, Alabama, remarked, "as to business benefits I think a few figures tell the story—our gross receipts April 1939—$687.10—Gross receipts April 1940 to date—*exclusive* of C.P.T.P.—$1,817.03—and while some of this increase is due to increased fuel, oil, and shop revenue from transients at least a goodly portion of it must be credited to increased interest in flying locally through C.P.T.P." And Robert F. Turner of the Palmetto Air School of Spartanburg, South Carolina, wrote, "My outside flying [exclusive of CPTP contracts] has been doubled since the beginning of this program and I am glad to say that it has put aviation on a highly respected basis. . . . I have sold eight new planes this year. So you see the CPTP has made a new life for me as well as hundreds of others that I know of."[34]

College and university officials were equally enthusiastic. Samuel K. Wilson, S.J., of the Office of the President, Loyola University in Chicago, expressed appreciation to "the Civil Aeronautics Authority for the very excellent training the course provided. . . . There is a great deal of interest here at Loyola in the proposed advanced training course for next year." H. C. Byrd, president of the University of Maryland, also wrote, "It will be a pleasure again to cooperate with you with regard to the Civilian Pilot Training Program for the next scholastic year." Finally, Harmon Caldwell of the University of Georgia, observed, "The students in the University of Georgia are very interested in the work offered under the supervision of the Civil Aeronautics Authority and the number of applications far exceeds even the amount of the quota for which we are asking."[35]

The CPTP and Air Age Education

The questions of how well the CPTP lived up to its stated New Deal goal of providing so-called air age education for American youth and, more important, the quality of that education must also be addressed. An adjunct to the pilot training conducted by the CPTP, this effort was the visible embodiment of Robert Hinckley's idea of "air conditioning," the notion that young people not only should but also must be introduced to the air age in such courses as science, geography, social studies, and industrial arts, as well as through participation in activities that would familiarize them with aeronautics.

Air age education also fit into the New Deal's broad pragmatic education philosophy. In 1933, the Federal Emergency Relief Administration (FERA) and, later, the National Youth Administration provided federal assistance for a nationwide system of work-study programs for high school and college students. The theory behind the work-study plan was that providing incentives to stay in school would reduce the number of young people who were untrained and unemployed. They would be kept off relief rolls, and the level of educational attainment in the United States would rise.[36]

Although different in method from the FERA-NYA work-study program, the air age education movement was on one level similar to it philosophically because it provided training incentives for practical employment in what was perceived as the glamorous and burgeoning airline and aircraft industry. On another more significant level, however, air age education, as the sociologist William Fielding Ogburn characterized it, was "an attempt to inculcate air-mindedness in American youth—a recognition of and interest in making the airplane a living tool in their lives."[37]

Perhaps the clearest statement of the latter purpose was provided in January 1940 by John W. Studebaker, commissioner of education, in an article titled "Air Youth's Place in the Schools." Studebaker warned that "if the use of aviation in the schools merely meant the advancement of an industry or the promotion of a method of transportation, the Office of Education would be loath to enter into a discussion of the subject; but, at the present time, aviation takes a foremost place in national and international affairs and, therefore, deserves a place in our thinking." Despite his altruistic disclaimer, it was obvious that the widespread incorporation of aviation into the curricula of the nation's schools would be a boon to textbook publishers and producers of educational materials. It would also perpetuate what the aviation industry had labored long and hard to establish: the acceptance of aviation on a large scale and, with it, a steady flow of employees.[38]

Air age education had several antecedents. The first was the Daniel Guggenheim Fund for the Promotion of Aeronautics, which for several years, beginning in 1927, provided grants for aviation education through New York University. Other efforts were by the Air Cadets of America, established in 1933 by the American Legion; the Junior Birdmen of America, founded in 1934 and sponsored by the Hearst newspaper chain; and Air Youth of America, founded in 1940 by Laurence S. and Winthrop Rockefeller. Although each organization's methods varied and some were more commercial than educational, their common goal was to indoctrinate youth into the air age and thus ensure that flying and the aviation industry would grow and prosper.[39]

After the Japanese attacked Pearl Harbor in December 1941, the idea of air age education was officially sanctioned by the government and promoted by the Civil Aeronautics Administration and the Department of Education. On December 18, 1941, Robert Hinckley convened the first meeting of the Advisory Committee on Aviation Education. Among its members were N. L. Engelhardt, an educator and prominent proponent of air age education, Ben D. Wood, director of Collegiate Educational Research at Columbia University, and the CAA's Dean R. Brimhall. The committee recommended that the program be designed "to maintain our competitive position in aviation as such," and that the "focus of effort would be on creating a vast reservoir of air-minded personnel, so that all personnel needs, all along the line could be met, so far as human resources permit." The appeal of the program "would be popular and elementary, would not eschew decent propaganda or 'childish glamour,' and would be directed at making aviation as much a part of conscious thinking and 'attitude' of our people as schools, churches, railroads, penny newspapers and radio are now."[40]

In February 1942, Hinckley, who had assumed the post of assistant secretary of commerce for air, and Wood set out to act on the Advisory Committee's recommendations and make aeronautics part of the everyday secondary school curriculum. With the help of John Studebaker and educators throughout the country, Hinckley and Wood identified two important problem areas: a shortage of qualified teachers and a lack of curriculum materials.[41]

To tackle the teacher shortage, the CAA and Department of Education solicited the help of various colleges and universities in the summer of 1942 to establish teacher training institutes, where teachers could become familiar with the methodology for air age education. By July 1, 170 educational establishments had responded, and the teacher workshop segment of the program was well underway. The most ambitious initiative, however, took place in curriculum materials. In six months, the Air Age Education Series, published by the Macmillan Company, turned out twenty textbooks produced by Columbia University Teacher's College and the University of Nebraska under the sponsorship of the Institute of the Aeronautical Sciences (Appendix D). As Ben Wood observed, the series provided "text and teaching materials for older students in high schools in the field of pre-flight aeronautics" and "pertinent aviation materials which may be woven into existing courses in the curricula of the secondary schools and, wherever feasible, of the elementary schools."[42]

Textbooks in the Air Age Education Series focused on biology, English, geography, industrial arts, mathematics, science, social studies, and preflight aeronautics. *Flying High,* an anthology of aviation literature edited by Rose N. Cohen, was aimed at junior high school students. They were asked to read essays and poems about flying or the mythology of flight and then answer questions based on the readings. After reading John Townsend Trowbridge's poem "Darius Green and His Flying Machine," for example, students were asked, "What kind of a boy was Darius? Why did he believe he could build a flying machine? List his arguments. Do you agree with them?" George T. Renner's *Human Geography in the Air Age,* a textbook for high school students, outlined in nine chapters the effect of the airplane on geography and asserted that by changing ideas about living in a three-dimensional world the airplane had "created a new geography of the United States, of North America, of the world." Hall Bartlett's *Social Studies for the Air Age,* also for high school students, examined the effect of the airplane on commerce, governmental and military affairs, world peace, and the local community.[43]

Although critics have argued that educators employed air age education to make schools little more than "vocational adjuncts of the military," the movement seems not to have had sinister motives. Rather, it was faddish and experimental, fitting in nicely with Joseph Corn's description of the "gospel of aviation," the belief that the airplane would eventually transform the world into a better place. Judging from the overwhelming number of favorable articles written in educational journals, air age education was widely accepted by educators. Although enthusiasm for it declined after World War II, the movement endured well into the 1950s, and persisted into the 1980s.[44]

Not all contemporary reactions to air age education were favorable, however. Cyril C. Trubey, who taught physics and electricity at Classical High School in Salem, Massachusetts, was one of the few who took issue with the movement. Writing in the September 1942 issue of *The Nation's Schools,* Trubey cited the methodological superficiality of teaching aeronautics in American schools. "I think that it is a mistake to assume that each and every pupil, girl or boy, who elects aviation will find either the romance or the value that are automatically assumed." Trubey concluded by conceding that "the teaching of so-called aviation in the schools may be beneficial," but,

on the other hand, he cautioned, "it may turn out to be a passing fad."[45]

The CPTP, Blacks, and Women

Yet another question that must be addressed is how strongly the
CPTP endorsed its explicit legislative provision that prohibited exclusion from the program for reasons of "race, creed or color." Until
the CPTP legislation was passed, blacks in the United States, subject
to Jim Crow exclusionary laws, had been as routinely prohibited
from receiving flight instruction and pursuing careers in aviation as
they had from other areas. Moreover, the belief that blacks were inferior in intelligence to whites and, therefore, incapable of becoming
pilots was widely held.

An example from the literature of the period illustrates not only
how desperate blacks were to become pilots, but also how those who
aspired to aviation careers were treated. In *Native Son* (1940), Richard Wright's nightmarish novel of black youth, the protagonist, Bigger Thomas, and his friend, Gus, look up as a sky writing plane over-
head spells out an advertisement for Speed Gasoline. "Them white
boys sure can fly," says Gus. "Yeah. . . . They get a chance to do everything. I *could* fly a plane if I had a chance," Bigger responds. "If
you wasn't black and if you had some money and if they'd let you
go to that aviation school, you could fly a plane," Gus replies
sarcastically.[46]

In the 1920s and 1930s, flying had become the bold expression of
a new era of speed, change, and modernity. The perception existed
that those who took part in it would be treated with the respect and
admiration reserved for heroes. William J. Powell, for example, believed firmly that aviation offered limitless opportunities for black
enterprise. Having graduated from the University of Illinois in 1922
with a degree in electrical engineering, Powell's interest in aviation
led him to apply to the U.S. Air Service at Chanute Field in Rantoul,
Illinois, but he was turned down because of his color. After investi-
gating the matter further, Powell discovered, much to his dismay,
that none of the military air schools would admit blacks.[47]

Powell's rejection by the armed forces, however, steeled his deter-
mination to break into aviation. He applied to commercial aviation
schools in Chicago, St. Louis, Kansas City, Cleveland, and other
cities but was again refused admittance. In 1927, Powell went to
France in search of flying lessons, but his financial resources began
to dwindle before he could complete the course of instruction, and

he returned to the United States. Through his French contacts, he was admitted to the Warren College of Aeronautics in Los Angeles, where he completed instruction in aeronautical engineering. Despite his proven abilities, Powell was refused admission to the Curtiss-Wright School of Aeronautics in Los Angeles.[48]

Powell persisted, however, and later received a commercial pilot's license and accreditation from the California State Board of Education to teach aeronautics. With these credentials in hand, Powell decided that because the white aviation world would not readily admit blacks into its tight circle, he would found a school of aeronautics for blacks. Under the provisions of the Roosevelt administration's Emergency Education Program, Powell obtained permission to teach a course in aeronautics at the Jefferson Evening High School in Los Angeles.[49]

The program was a complete success. In its earliest days, enrollment grew from fifty students to more than 250. In due course, thirty-two persons became qualified for pilots' licenses, with Powell providing free instruction for as long as he could sustain the arrangement financially. He then decided to establish an aircraft construction and repair shop, which was furnished with the help of some of his associates. The shop was incorporated late in the 1920s under the laws of California, and soon the enterprise became known as the Craftsmen of Black Wings, a nonprofit educational organization.[50]

In 1934, Powell had published *Black Wings,* a book-length treatise that outlined his belief that aviation was the key to black success and appealed to black men and women to fill the sky "with skilled black wings." Powell urged black youth to carve out their own destiny—to become pilots, aircraft designers, and business leaders in aviation. In the midst of the Great Depression, he offered the prospect of new jobs and a transportation system free of discrimination.[51]

For C. Alfred Anderson and Albert Forsythe, flying was not only a possible means of obtaining professional advancement and of compelling the government and commercial aviation to employ blacks in the aviation industry, but also a way of instilling racial pride. Anderson and Forsythe's long-distance flights in 1933 (Atlantic City to Los Angeles and back; the United States to Canada) and the Pan-American Goodwill Flight of 1934 (Miami to Nassau and points in the Carribean) were carefully planned and well-thought-out attempts to prove that blacks deserved a place in the predominantly white world of aviation. During the course of their flights, the team worked with the National Urban League to promote black involvement in aviation.[52]

Anderson and Forsythe's Pan American Goodwill Flight of 1934 in a Lambert Monocoupe called "The Spirit of Booker T. Washington" was intended to promote interracial harmony and demonstrate the growing skills of black pilots. The flight was a much more ambitious undertaking than it first appeared. Besides making the flight, the two had to obtain the proper clearances from the Department of Commerce's Bureau of Air Commerce. Once permission was granted, the Office of the Secretary of Commerce had to be persuaded to coordinate with the Department of State to obtain permissions from the countries over which the flight was to be made.[53]

The bold-flying Anderson-Forsythe team attracted widespread attention. In the Caribbean, the Department of State and Pan American Airways provided active and cordial support. At home, the flight provided the black community with a source of pride. Anderson and Forsythe hoped that the long-distance flight would inspire black youth to see in aviation a new avenue for advancement.[54]

In 1939, at about the same time that Congress was debating the race issue in regard to the CPTP, a group of black aviation enthusiasts in Chicago banded together to form the National Airmen's Association of America (NAAA). With the help of Congressman Everett Dirksen and others, the NAAA, one of the first organizations of its kind, not only attempted to broaden the base of black participation in aviation, but also—and more important—led the crusade to include blacks in the CPTP and the Army Air Corps. In May 1939, under the auspices of the NAAA and a black newspaper, the *Chicago Defender*, Chauncey E. Spencer and Dale L. White made a three-thousand-mile flight from Chicago, to Washington, D.C., to New York to dramatize the goal of black inclusion in the Army Air Corps and interest black college students in flying.[55]

To be sure, it was aviators such as Powell, Anderson, Forsythe, Spencer, White, and others who led the struggle for black acceptance in aviation. Their efforts, rather than those of the CAA, eased the way for blacks to be admitted to the Civilian Pilot Training Program. The antidiscrimination provision of the CPTP bill had not been one of the hallmarks of Robert Hinckley's original grand plan for the program, but for obvious political reasons he and the Roosevelt administration did not see fit to challenge it. Nor did CAA officials ever promote the idea of including blacks in the CPTP as beneficial to the society as a whole. They remained silent and acquiesced to what they considered political pressure to include blacks.

Hinckley's—and, by extension, F.D.R.'s—ambivalence was characteristic of the New Deal's general attitudes about race. The historian B. Joyce Ross has written that, on the one hand, the "New Deal marked for the first time since the Reconstruction era the revival of federal auspices of racial equality." On the other hand, "federal auspices of racial equality during the Roosevelt administrations often enhanced the trend toward separate but equal accommodations for Negroes." The National Youth Administration was an example of how "the administration's policy was tacit acceptance of separate, albeit ostensibly equal, consideration of blacks in the programs of the southern and border states. Thus," Ross concludes, "the greatest shortcoming of the New Deal was its failure to link inextricably the principle of federal auspices of racial equality with the concept of a desegregated society."[56]

This failure was undoubtedly true of the Civilian Pilot Training Program. Pilot training for blacks was small in scale, largely segregated, and conducted at black colleges and universities. Moreover, the attitude of CAA officials about including blacks in the CPTP can be characterized succinctly by a statement in a memo from Brimhall to Hinckley in late September 1939. "It looks," he pointed out, "as if we will have *pressure* to have seven schools at which Negroes will be trained."[57]

Initially, six schools were allowed to participate: the West Virginia State College for Negroes in Institute; Howard University in Washington, D.C.; Tuskegee Institute in Tuskegee Alabama; Hampton Institute in Hampton, Virginia; the Delaware State College for Colored Students in Dover; and the North Carolina Agricultural and Technical College in Greensboro. Later, other black schools were added, among them Lincoln University in Chester County, Pennsylvania and the State College for Negroes in Etrick, Virginia. Yet, limiting acceptance of blacks who wanted to fly only increased their frustration. Until March 22, 1941, when the all-black 99th Fighter Squadron was formed, there was no way that blacks could enlist in the Army Air Corps.[58]

Moreover, even after the creation of the 99th Fighter Squadron, many blacks smarted at what they perceived as their underrepresentation in the program. In an October 1942 letter to John P. Morris, director of the CPTP, John W. Davis, president of West Virginia State College, complained bitterly, "I do not accept your conclusion which indicates that at a later date the scope of the CAA program may permit the inclusion of additional schools for Negroes . . . I do not accept your conclusion because America is in war and we need to train now all eligible persons without regard to race for war tasks in which they can best serve."[59]

Hinckley and the CAA, however, defended their position. As Roscoe Wright, director of information and statistics service for the CAA, wrote to Congressman Thomas C. Hennings, Jr. (D.-Mo.) in October 1940, "It seems to us here that the most important and significant thing about the Civilian Pilot Training Program so far as the Negro is concerned is that for the first time in the history of aviation it is affording him the opportunity of demonstrating his ability in aeronautics on a broad scale." In a letter to Eleanor Roosevelt, Hinckley pointed out that by June 1941, "500 Negroes will have been trained as pilots under our program during the two years it has been in existence. As nearly as we can determine, this is more than twice as many Negro pilots as were on record from the entire country at the time this program began."[60]

Despite the program's obvious shortcomings, the CPTP was not only instrumental in opening the door to blacks who wanted to fly, but it also showed that large numbers of blacks could learn to fly. By the middle of 1942, blacks were enrolled in eighty elementary CPTP courses in five black colleges and thirty elementary courses scattered throughout several white schools, and in sixty advanced courses at Tuskegee Institute and the Coffey School of Aeronautics in Oak Lawn, Illinois. By the time the CPTP ended, the number of black pilots in the United States had increased from a handful in the 1920s and 1930s to approximately two thousand. Most went on to serve in the four segregated combat squadrons that the Army Air Forces (AAF) established in World War II.[61]

Intimately connected to the CPTP's relationship with blacks was its attitude toward admitting women. Although women had originally been allowed to enroll in the CPTP, they did not fare in the program as well as blacks. Initially, enrollment had been limited to four women's colleges: Lake Erie College in Painesville, Ohio; Adelphi College in Garden City, New York; Mills College in Oakland, California; and Florida State College at Tallahassee. In the other colleges and universities that took part in the program, women were accepted only at a ratio of one woman to ten men. To make matters worse, when war threatened and CPTP graduates were required to enlist as part of their agreement with the CAA, women were automatically excluded. Despite protests—Eleanor Roosevelt asked for an explanation—the order stood.[62] In January 1942, Robert Hinckley attempted to resolve the predicament by promising that the training of women would "resume . . . at the earliest possible date." In an attempt to keep this promise, the CAA in 1942 proposed a program to train women as flight instructors for the army and navy. The Bureau of the Budget, however, turned down the request for funding the program in May 1943, and the idea was not revived. Notwithstanding these obstacles and the early demise of training opportunities for women, the CPTP increased the number of women pilots in the United States from 675 in 1939 to almost three thousand by July 1, 1941.[63]

Trouble on the Horizon

In spite of the Civilian Pilot Training Program's obvious successes and obvious shortcomings, European events in 1940 and the inevitability that the United States would have to speed efforts toward mobilization were to test the program's civilian, New Deal dimensions severely. On May 16, 1940, President Roosevelt addressed a joint session of Congress and requested a billion-dollar defense appropriation with provisions for a fifty-thousand-plane air force. The figure was approximately equal to the number of aircraft that had been produced in the United States since 1903, when the airplane was invented. If military aircraft production was increased to meet Roosevelt's request, additional pilots would also be needed.[64]

Responding to this need, Hinckley announced in June that the CAA would expand the CPTP to train forty-five thousand elementary and nine thousand secondary students, an increase of 500 percent over the goals of the previous year. The ambitious forecast was more than pride in the program's good first-year results; it was an indication of Hinckley's increased concern about national defense. Congress responded by increasing the CPTP's allocation more than ninefold—$37 million for fiscal 1941, compared with $4 million for the previous year.[65]

Because of the increasingly dark international scene and the possibility of entering the war, it became imperative that the CAA produce the forty-five thousand pilots it had promised. In June 1940, Hinckley announced that the goal would be met in three stages. The 1940 summer school term would turn out fifteen thousand pilots; the fall term, another fifteen thousand; and the spring term, still another fifteen thousand. This ambitious undertaking meant that pilot production would have to be increased nearly sixfold over the previous year. Not only was the promised goal met, but the program also surpassed its expectations for fiscal year 1941 by training 57,972 pilots.[66]

Yet not even the early operational success of the CPTP nor its increased budget satisfied everyone. An editorial by Wayne W. Parrish in the September 15, 1940, issue of *American Aviation* charged that the enlarged CPTP was "hastily prepared," that "instructors were insufficient in number," and that the limit on the number of flying hours permitted in a twenty-four-hour period were "cheerfully ignored." Parrish also accused the CAA of hiding accident and fatality data, criticized the program for producing few if any military aviation candidates, and declared that it was of little or no value to the armed forces. "Stark realism," he wrote, "forces the conclusion that the $37,000,000 civilian training program is of such negligible value to the military services as to be a waste of government funds and a hoodwinking of the Congress that appropriated the money."[67]

Then in February 1941 came another bombshell. In the "Washingtonia" section of *Aero Digest,* correspondent Arnold Kruckman told of how F.D.R. had criticized the CPTP in a recent press conference as "a failure from the standpoint of the Army and Navy." Kruckman reported that the president "declared . . . that the CPTP was not particularly successful in making military flyers, and that only a small percentage of the students were sufficiently enthusiastic to join the Air Corps or the Navy. The plan for the future is designed to teach a smaller number, but to give them stiffer courses and to frankly make them aware that they are regarded as potential material for military aviation. In all likelihood from now on the CPTP will be focused wholly on national defense."

What Kruckman had written was basically true. In his January 7, 1941 press conference, F.D.R. did comment unfavorably on the CPTP program's "30-some million"-dollar price tag. "The Army and the Navy," he continued, "don't think we are getting enough out of these schools in the way of military and naval pilots. That doesn't mean the abandonment of those schools; it may mean that the training in those schools will be greatly improved to meet the needs of the Army and Navy; and secondly, that all these people who go into these schools, largely at the expense of the Government, with thereby some obligations on their part to serve in the Army or Navy—which there never has been up to the present time."[68]

In response to a question about CPTP students who declined to serve in the armed forces, the president stated that the number was "quite large," and he left no doubt about the military implications of the program. "It was a grand idea that we were going to teach everybody to fly," F.D.R. said, "and now, from practical experience, we think we ought to do some pretty careful combing of the people so as to make them useful for military and naval needs."[69]

In view of such criticism, the House Appropriations Committee voted to slash the CPTP's budget for fiscal year 1942 by more than

half, to $18 million rather than the $37 million of the previous fiscal
year. Later, however, the committee restored $7 million of the cut,
saying that the initial reduction was "much too drastic." By the time
the program's budget had reached the Senate Appropriations Committee, Donald H. Connolly, the CAA's administrator, was informing
members that the CPTP was being revised to bring it more into line
with Army Air Corps requirements, particularly the need for pilot
instructors.[70]

How fair was the criticism of the CPTP? Parrish's objections that
the program was unsafe and that the CAA had deliberately con-
cealed accident data could be characterized as hyperbolic journalism. Jerome Lederer, the director of the Bureau of Safety Regulation
of the Civil Aeronautics Board, admitted that between June 15 and
September 15, 1940, nine fatal accidents and eight accidents involv-
ing serious injuries had occurred. Lederer, however, went on to say
that "it would be unlikely that the occurrence of any accident of
any gravity in the Civilian Pilot Training Program could escape the
knowledge of the Safety Bureau, and it seems quite impossible that
any appreciable number of accidents could so escape."[71]

The validity of the charge that the CPTP failed to produce sufficient candidates for military aviation and that its instruction did not
prepare men well enough for military aviation is difficult to judge.
On the one hand, it was true that the percent of CPTP students who
entered the nine primary flight training courses offered by the Army
Air Corps in 1941—and the one offered in 1942—was low when
compared with the percent of students not from the CPTP who entered the same courses (Table 1). Only 19.5 percent of entrants were
CPTP students; 80.5 percent were not. The percentage of CPTP-
trained entrants, however, rose steadily, from 12.3 in the early
classes (A–D) in 1941 to 29.7 in the last class (I) in 1942. Furthermore, although CPTP-trained students made up only 30 percent of
the entrants for Air Corps Class A in 1942, they comprised 45 percent of those who completed military pilot training (Table 1). Finally, 88.2 percent of CPTP-trained students finished the course,
compared with only 56.6 percent of those not trained by the CPTP
(Tables 2 and 3).[72]

The conclusion, then, is that the CPTP was a qualitative rather
than quantitative success. Although the CPTP produced considerably fewer entrants, a higher percentage of those with CPTP training
tended to complete the courses than those without CPTP training.
This indicates that the CPTP was good preparation for military aviation. Proponents of CPTP training, for example, Dean Brimhall, using Bureau of the Budget figures, estimated that "53,000 cadets must

Table 1. Percent of CPTP and Non-CPTP Students Entering and Completing Primary Air Corps Classes, 1941–42

Class	CPTP		Non-CPTP	
	Entered	Completed	Entered	Completed
A–D (Incl.)	12.3	16.2	87.7	83.8
E	18.4	26.1	81.6	73.9
F	19.3	27.9	80.7	72.1
G	26.8	31.4	73.2	69.6
H	20.9	29.4	79.1	70.6
I	29.7	40.8	70.3	59.6
A (1942)	30.0	45.0	70.0	55.0
	19.5	27.0	80.5	73.0

Table 2. CPTP Entrants to Air Corps Classes, 1941–42

Air Corps Primary Classes	Cadets Entering Course	Cadets Completing Course	Percent Completing	Percent Failing
A–D (Incl.)	843	707	83.9	16.1
E	262	227	86.5	13.5
F	330	283	87.3	12.7
G	373	323	88.5	11.5
H	433	392	90.5	9.5
I	602	558	93.2	6.8
A (1942)	565	517	92.5	6.5
Total	3,408	3,007	88.2	11.8

Table 3. Non-CPTP Entrants to Air Corps Classes, 1941–42

Air Corps Primary Classes	Cadets Entering Course	Cadets Completing Course	Percent Completing	Percent Failing
A–D (Incl.)	6,043	3,644	60.3	39.7
E	1,163	643	55.2	44.8
F	1,399	729	53.9	46.1
G	1,362	708	53.5	46.5
H	1,646	941	57.2	42.7
I	1,494	812	55.2	44.8
A (1942)	1,192	631	55.0	45.0
Total	14,300	8,108	55.6	43.4

start flight training in Air Corps schools in order to provide 30,000 who complete its primary course." Brimhall argued convincingly that the high rate of Air Corps eliminations (washouts) in the primary course (43.4 percent) could be lowered if entrants were required to have completed the CPTP flight training course before being admitted to Air Corps training (Table 3).[73]

Donald S. Lopez, former deputy director of the Smithsonian Institution's National Air and Space Museum, a CPTP graduate, and a fighter pilot in the 14th Air Force in China, corroborates the view that the program was good preparation for military flying. Lopez was a freshman at the University of Tampa in 1941 when he enrolled in the primary CPTP course. He found physical examinations to be rigorous, flight training "first-class" and subject to rigid standards, and washouts frequent. The CPTP was valuable for military pilot trainees because after passing the course they were not only used to being in the air, but also were aware of objects on the ground.[74]

Nonetheless, the CPTP continued to receive negative publicity and be threatened by military takeover. As could be expected, Robert Hinckley defended and praised the program profusely. On December 1, 1941, the eve of Pearl Harbor, in a speech before the National Aviation Training Association annual convention in Kansas City, Hinckley pointed to the qualitative aspects of the program and stated, "our records show that more than 20,000 of our trainees have gone to the armed forces of our own country; half of them as pilots and half of them to other activities. Some have gone as skilled meteorologists, others as map makers, others as mechanics. Some have gone to industry as aeronautical engineers, others are teaching ground school, still others have become mechanics. But every one of them is a better man in his field because he has had actual piloting experience."[75]

On the one hand, Hinckley was correct in pointing to the CPTP's accomplishments as a civilian program. On the other, he was being evasive about how many CPTP graduates had enlisted in the Army Air Forces and the Navy. Available statistics for the Army Air Forces (Table 2) show that in 1941 and early 1942, 3,408 CPTP students entered AAF flight training courses, and that 3,007 successfully completed training. It is difficult to prove Hinckley's assertions that approximately ten thousand CPTP graduates had gone into the military in previous years. The CAA did not make available—either in published or unpublished sources—statistics on students' rates of enlistment. In view of criticism on this score, and the fact that the CPTP was intended to provide personnel to the armed forces, the

CAA committed an unconscionable error (although an understandable one from a bureaucratic point of view) in not attempting to track how many CPTP personnel went to the military. However, it is likely that the results of such information might have been embarrassing.

Despite the uproar over how many military pilot candidates the CPTP produced, it was, in fact, a civilian program created by Congress and mandated to fulfill New Deal economic goals and provide a measure of war preparedness in a civilian context. Although Congress had debated the question of whether to make enlistment in the military mandatory for enrollment in the CPTP, enlistment had hitherto been voluntary by the terms of the legislation. The program could never completely free itself from this dilemma, which would create further difficulties once America entered World War II. By late 1941, however, conditions in Europe and Asia had begun to contribute to the fever for mobilization, overtaking political considerations. The CPTP was swept into the vortex of wartime preparation. Ultimately, it would be transformed by military needs.

CHAPTER 4

The CPTP Goes to War

The period from mid-September 1940 through 1941 had been a difficult one for the Civilian Pilot Training Program and Robert Hinckley. Caught in what appeared to be an unresolvable situation between civilian and military demands, Hinckley attempted a limited accommodation with the Army Air Forces (AAF) and the navy by discussing various plans that would stimulate voluntary enlistment and make the program more responsive to national defense. At the same time, he strongly resisted changing the nature of the CPTP from a civilian program to a military one.

During this time of crisis, Hinckley had responded in expected bureaucratic fashion with a flurry of speeches and press releases extolling the CPTP, pointing to the number of men the program had sent to the armed forces, and emphasizing that—in contrast to enlistees not trained by the CPTP—CPTP-trained men tended to complete flight training successfully. He continually justified the CPTP as a civilian program, saying in early 1941, that until July 1940, it "was built upon a civilian philosophy, as part of the development of civil aviation. Although the viewpoint has been shifted materially since last July, we have had to work on a civilian basis, which means as a sideline to each student's normal college life. I wish neither to condemn nor praise this," Hinckley concluded, "it is simply a fact if a direct relationship [between the student and the armed forces] is the need, then our trainees should be placed in some definite status related to the armed forces before we begin their training."[1]

That students had been required since September 1940 to sign a pledge to enter military aviation if they were qualified and necessary for national defense did not seem to matter. Like other civilian-based programs, the CPTP had by 1941 been co-opted by the military in its attempt to lead the preparedness bandwagon. Rife with confusion of purpose, conflicts with the military, and criticism from all sides, the CPTP was caught in the contradictory welter of competing plans and agencies aimed at mobilizing for what was now the inevitability of war. In the broader context of preparedness, Eliot Janeway has pointed out that F.D.R.'s ambivalent "scheme for balancing civilian against military power ended by producing a concentration of military power." As a result, "the civilian agencies lost control of the home front to the military; and Roosevelt himself, in spite of all his manipulations, ended by losing the balance of power between the two forces."[2]

The change from civilian to military control of government programs was equally true in the CPTP. Although it had come increasingly under military influence from mid-1940 onward, the nature of the CPTP changed entirely when the United States entered World War II. On December 12, 1941, five days after the Japanese attack on Pearl Harbor, President Roosevelt, in Executive Order 8974, officially transformed the CPTP into a wartime program. Henceforth, all Civil Aeronautics Administration civilian pilot training efforts would be "exclusively devoted to the procurement and training of men for ultimate service as military pilots, or for correlated non-military activities."[3]

By early 1942, the program, almost of necessity, had lost much of its early flavor and character. The New Deal elements of "air conditioning" American youth and stimulating the lightplane industry inherent in Hinckley's original plan had given way to the exigencies of wartime. In addition, the AAF and the navy began to force changes to bring the program into line with their needs. To formalize the military aspects of the CPTP in wartime, the name of the program was changed on December 7, 1942, to the War Training Service (WTS), but its scope and direction had already begun to be altered drastically by the demands placed on it in the year following Pearl Harbor.[4]

In addition to changing the nature of the CPTP, Executive Order 8974 decreed that the secretary of commerce's "control and jurisdiction over civil aviation" be "in accordance with requirements for the successful prosecution of the war, as may be required by the Secretary of War." The secretary of war, in turn, was "authorized and directed to take possession and assure control of any civil aviation system, or systems, or any part there of, to the extent necessary for the successful prosecution of the war." Such language threatened the independence of the CAA, and agency officials feared that the AAF might attempt to take over all civil aviation, not just the CPTP, as a wartime emergency measure.[5]

In the wake of Executive Order 8974 came the news in January 1942 that Donald H. Connolly, an army officer who had been the

CAA's administrator, was resigning to go on active duty as head of the War Department's newly created Office of Civil Aviation. Connolly had been tapped for the post by the chief of the AAF, Lieutenant General Henry H. "Hap" Arnold. Commenting on the appointment, *American Aviation Daily* observed that Connolly's new office would carry out Executive Order 8974, "granting powers to the Secretary of War over all civil aviation." It also would have "broad powers, through directives to existing agencies, over movements of transport airplanes, traffic & other regulations, airline equipment, airports, CPT training, & all other air activities." It was not surprising that the CAA interpreted Connolly's appointment as an ominous warning.[6]

At about the same time that he appointed Connolly, Arnold queried the Judge Advocate General's Office about the legality of transferring the duties and responsibilities of the CAA to the War Department. The judge advocate, Lieutenant Colonel E. H. Snodgrass, advised Arnold not to take such action until the War Department considered the transfer absolutely necessary. Snodgrass also said many favorable things about the CPTP and recommended that the program not be changed but rather expanded "to full capacity." He concluded that, on the whole and "in specific detail," the CPTP "has proved so valuable an asset to the science of Aviation, and directly and indirectly, to Military and Naval Aviation, that it is regarded as undesirable and possibly inimical to the latter services to basically disturb the existing organization through which this program has been so efficiently conducted."[7]

Despite Snodgrass's explicit legal opinion, the AAF made continual attempts in 1942 to call up CAA personnel who were reservists and to obtain direct control of CAA facilities. In response to Assistant Secretary of War for Air Robert Lovett's recommendations in July 1942 to compromise by maintaining a "nucleus of a CAA organization both for certain types of operation and for training" Arnold wrote, "The only sound solution, to my mind, is to transfer the CAA to the War Department for the duration."[8]

The dispute between the CAA and the AAF finally was resolved in August 1942, when the secretaries of war and the navy wrote to the secretary of commerce that the CAA would retain its independence. This meant that it could not be subsumed into the War Department. Thus, the CPTP, one of the key elements of the CAA's function as overseer of civil aviation and with a legal mandate in force until 1944, could not be taken over by the air force. The AAF would have to make some accommodation with the CAA about how the CPTP would be used in a wartime setting.[9]

General Arnold's Uncompromising Attitude
toward the CPTP

A compromise between the CAA and the AAF concerning the CPTP, however, would not be easy. The air force, particularly in the person of its chief, Henry H. "Hap" Arnold, placed many stumbling blocks in the way of the program from 1942 to 1944. Although no direct proof linked Arnold and the air force to an attempt to sabotage the CPTP, circumstantial evidence indicates that the AAF deliberately refused to cooperate with the CAA and Congress in making full use of the program, imposed unrealistic training goals and quotas on it, and then did nothing to assist in getting required training aircraft and spare parts. The AAF preferred instead to train its own pilots without what it considered civilian interference.

The source of the conflict between the CAA and the AAF on civilian versus military prerogatives and the use of the CPTP in wartime was jurisdictional. The CAA felt that it had a legitimate right to continue its normal functions, including the CPTP, as long as they contributed to the war effort. The AAF, on the other hand, believed that the CAA was a civilian interloper in what it saw as primarily a military task. With the onset of the conflict, General Arnold, speaking for the AAF, became more convinced that the quality of the pilots the CPTP produced was inferior to those trained in air force schools. This was a far cry from the AAF's conciliatory attitude toward the program during the congressional hearings in March and April 1939, when Barton Yount, the AAF's training expert, declared wholehearted endorsement of the CPTP and welcomed it as a way of easing the air force's training burden in time of war.

While Yount was praising the virtues of the CPTP, his superior General Arnold was telling a different story before the Senate early in 1939 about the Air Corps' use of civilian contractors to train its own pilots. Arnold's testimony was a harbinger of the impending disharmony between the AAF and the CPTP. "It is essential," he said, "to build up a reserve capacity for training personnel and we can't do it in time of peace unless we resort to civilian institutions. So we propose to utilize private schools accredited by the Department of Commerce and authorized to give commercial licenses to pilots. It will be necessary, however, for us to train their instructors to Army standards at our training center. . . . We will have to examine all the cadets who go there, the same as we do now, so as to be sure they measure up to our educational and physical standards . . . our instructors will check each one of them to be sure they measure up to our flying standards."[10]

Arnold firmly believed that the AAF provided superior pilot training. Early in 1941 he wrote to his assistant, Major General Davenport Johnson, to observe that although the CAA's training program doubtlessly provided some benefits, it was essential that only the AAF be able to mandate the suitability of personnel to be trained, the type of training given, or the number of people who received training each month. None of these things, Arnold concluded, could be accomplished "if the Army does not have complete and unqualified jurisdiction over its primary training."[11]

Arnold was concerned also that the CAA's efforts to legitimize itself as a civilian agency necessary to the war effort might draw attention away from the AAF. In April 1942, he ordered Yount, now head of the Flying Training Command, to conduct a study of a publication titled *CAA for Defense,* which, Arnold termed "the 'bible' of the CAA for tying on National Defense with its activities." The study was to consider the AAF's use of CAA pilot training facilities; it should under no circumstances "build them up" with added personnel, equipment, or materials at the expense of the AAF's own training program or "war effort."[12]

In many respects, one might well applaud Arnold for his intransigence. After all, primary and secondary CPTP courses were only an introduction to flying. Combat pilots, besides to having to learn to fly more complex and powerful aircraft, were subject to an entirely different set of physiological and psychological demands. Besides, Arnold believed that military pilot candidates trained in a civilian setting were not instilled with a proper sense of military discipline. Yet, it is curious that the navy had made full use of its CPTP graduates.[13]

Captain Arthur W. Radford, director of training in the Bureau of Aeronautics and later chair of the Joint Chiefs of Staff under Dwight D. Eisenhower, characterized the navy's attitude toward the CPTP. He admitted that the navy had been skeptical about using the CPTP to train its pilots. "Like the old farmer who refused to trust anyone else with the job of greasing his wagon," he said, "the Navy held to the belief for years that only the Navy could train Naval aviators." This attitude had changed, however, when the navy realized that it could not turn out pilots in sufficient numbers to fight a two-ocean war without the CPTP's aid.

The CPTP, in turn, agreed to "raise its training standards and standardize its methods" to accommodate the navy. One way of accomplishing this was *Patter for Elementary Flight Maneuvers* (chapter 3), designed to make instructional vocabulary uniform. Another was the use of a test that the CPTP developed to evaluate naval air cadets before they began flight training. By releasing the 10 percent of each class that scored lowest, the navy was able to eliminate 50 percent of its cadets who would eventually fail its flight training program. In addition, the navy credited trainees for passing the advanced CPTP course, and unlike the AAF, had no qualms about admitting CPTP students into its combat training program. "Without question," Radford concluded, "the Navy is profiting greatly from the CPT program; it saves time in planes, saves time for instructors and prevents loss of wastage by reducing the number of students eliminated." The navy's successful use of the CPTP as a screening device was obviously working. Its pilot elimination rate was 17 percent, compared to the AAF's rate of 43 to 50 percent.[14]

But there may have been more deeply seated reasons for the ways in which the navy and the AAF viewed the CPTP. In accommodating to the CPTP, the navy apparently had less to lose than did the AAF. The navy was an established service with a long tradition. The AAF, on the other hand, had little or no tradition and had struggled to be accepted by the regular army establishment and then to become quasi-independent. Arnold was adamant about AAF prerogatives because he worried that the total independence of the air force after the war depended heavily upon its image as an integral part of the war effort. He was determined that nothing get in the way of his organization's quest for autonomy.[15]

Despite Arnold's firmly held convictions, the AAF was roundly criticized for what appeared to be a deliberate attempt to avoid making use of the CAA's pilot training program. American Aviation, in July 1942, and the Congress shortly thereafter, took the air force to task for failing to use existing CPTP facilities in favor of constructing new AAF training centers, for which $312 million had been appropriated. Estimates placed the use of CPTP facilities at one-fourth of their capacities.[16]

The AAF's most vocal critic was Richard L. Stokes, a Washington correspondent for the St. Louis Post-Dispatch. In a July 5, 1942, column, Stokes commented that in the past, the CPTP had made good use of facilities provided by colleges, universities, and flight schools. "Under the current program," he said, "it is alleged a considerable volume of these resources will go begging, while the Army yields to the intoxication of building a throng of 'Hollywood' air schools, vast and ornate, which are said to consume inordinate quantities of critical materials, especially steel and cement." Moreover, Stokes charged that the AAF was spending huge amounts of money on these new facilities, "complete with flying fields, housing quarters, classrooms, cafeterias, recreational facilities. . . . few . . . will be turning out pilots before the end of 1942 or beginning of 1943."[17]

Stokes recounted privately that he had received a telephone call summoning him to Arnold's office to discuss his *Post-Dispatch* story. Arnold informed Stokes that he would get his fingers "burned plenty" if he continued to write "this Fifth Column tripe." He then told Stokes, "This whole story is wrong. It is a mistake and you have been misled by Hinckley and that political gang over there who are trying their best to horn in on the military program." Arnold also stated flatly, "I won't have any sissies in my Air Force," to which Stokes replied, "Well, they've been doing pretty well up to now, these CAA boys, haven't they?" Arnold responded, "It's because they come in the Army and we have to start all over to train them the way we want them." Stokes stood his ground, earning Arnold's respect in the bargain. Despite the acrimonious exchange, the meeting ended amicably, and Stokes was told that he could see Arnold any time he wanted.[18]

The March 31, 1942, issue of *American Aviation Daily,* which reported that seven new AAF flight schools were being opened in Texas, Wisconsin, Arkansas, Florida, and New Mexico, corroborated Stokes's story. On April 3, 1942, the *Daily* reported that six new AAF schools were being opened in Marianna, Florida; Carlsbad, New Mexico; and Greenville, Lubbock, Hondo, and Big Spring, Texas. Each cost more than $5 million. Some members of Congress, indignant that CPTP facilities were operating at 15 percent capacity while the AAF spent a multimillion-dollar appropriation for new training facilities, began to clamor for an investigation. As an unnamed senator commented bluntly, "Ordinarily, we have no desire to meddle in the Army's conduct of this war. However, this is becoming so obviously a case of gross neglect by the Army of its responsibility to the American people . . . that I for one am willing to make such an issue of it that the Army will either have to make 100% use of the Civil Aeronautics Administration's civilian pilot training facilities, or explain in very clear terms why use of those facilities would not help speed up the war."[19]

Robert Hinckley recalled that when Stokes's story appeared, a spokesman for the AAF reportedly said, "If the Civil Aeronautics Administration doesn't stop squawking, the Army will take 'em over, lock, stock and barrel." Hinckley replied that "we should be in favor of the army taking us over if we thought that would win the war a minute sooner. We don't believe it would. And we are not squawking. We are merely pointing out, in a temperate manner, that this is a total war; that this country's utmost resources will not be too much; and that a substantial proportion of CAA facilities is not being used."[20]

Difficulties in Reaching an Agreement

There was a good deal of truth in what Hinckley said. For six months, from January to July 1942, the CAA and the AAF tried to come to an agreement on how to make full use of the CPTP in wartime. (At the same time, the navy was making arrangements with the CAA to provide CPTP flight instruction to prospective student pilots in the Naval Reserve.) Although the AAF had promised early in the year to increase its use of CPTP facilities, it reneged on that promise. During the first six months of 1942, it continually vacillated about what use should be made of the program and was slow in implementing stated policy regarding the CPTP. Unable to deal with a pilot training program that it had neither created nor was interested in perpetuating, the AAF seemed determined to announce one thing and then do another in regard to the CPTP.[21]

Negotiations between the CAA and the AAF appeared to be proceeding favorably, when on January 2, 1942, the agencies signed a memorandum that outlined preliminary plans for coordinating the CAA's pilot training with that of the AAF. From mid-January to the end of the month, officials conferred daily to work out a completely coordinated program. In February 1942, Donald Connolly was conciliatory when he appeared before the House Appropriations Subcommittee, announcing that at General Arnold's request the air force and the CAA had agreed provisionally to "a joint plan under which this program would be used to its maximum capacity as a feeder to the Army air program."[22]

On February 21, 1942, after almost two months of conferences between representatives of the CAA and the War Department, Secretary of War Henry Stimson advised Secretary of Commerce Jesse Jones that, in using the facilities of the CAA, preference should be given to training students who could meet the criteria for appointment as aviation cadets and were members of the Air Corps Enlisted Reserve, a way of obtaining qualified pilot candidates for the AAF by enlisting them and placing them on inactive status until they could be called upon to fill training quotas. In this way the AAF believed it could weed out those who were unfit to be pilots. Stimson also recommended that additional trainees who did not meet the qualifications for aviation cadet be accepted for flight training in other pilot specialties—as flight instructors, for example—that could be "adapted to serve the national interest, directly or indirectly." Stimson stated that he was providing the opinion of the War Department on the subject "in very broad outline." He suggested that the chief of the AAF and the administrator of the CAA work out particulars.[23]

About three weeks later, on March 12, 1942, the War Department issued a press release after receiving a preliminary copy of the agreement. All pilot training facilities of the CAA would "soon be devoted to the War program, under a plan worked out in cooperation with the Army Air Forces." The announcement emphasized that CAA training facilities would be "greatly expanded" and that the current volume of twenty-five thousand students in elementary pilot training would increase to forty-five thousand a year. The number of students in secondary training would increase from ten thousand to thirty thousand. The announcement also stated that "first priority in CAA training" would go "to students who can meet the requirements of the Army Air Corps for appointment as Aviation Cadets, and who are members of the Air Corps Section of the Enlisted Reserve."[24]

At this point the AAF began to go back on its stated intention. Although the announcement had been approved by his office, General Arnold was apparently so displeased by the story, which had appeared nationally, that he ordered it changed. (It is difficult to determine the exact source of Arnold's irritation. One suspects, however, that he may have objected to the statement that preference would be given those who could qualify as aviation cadets and thus enter AAF combat flight training.) On March 26, representatives of the CAA met with Arnold's representative, Major J. G. Ayling, to rewrite the news release, which was then resubmitted for air force approval.[25]

On March 27, Ayling met in Washington with a group of coordinators from colleges and universities that were sponsoring the CPTP. When asked if the CAA would train air force reservists on furlough, Ayling said that it would not because the AAF had "determined other uses for them." To the question of whether CAA field representatives and college officials could be helpful in the air force recruitment program, Ayling replied, "You are going to be very helpful to us telling a story by direct contact. You can be helpful in overcoming parental attitudes against the Air Forces and aviation. We hope that by correlating our work and your work you will be able to help us."[26]

The next day, however, Major Ayling denied a CAA attempt to get approval for a press release publicizing the CAA's efforts to use the CPTP to train AAF enlisted reservists. He said that the AAF did not

want the CAA to mention plans to recruit men for the enlisted reserves. When CAA staff members pointed out that the War Department's announcement of March 12, approved by Arnold's office, had
already alluded to such plans, Ayling informed them that a mistake
had been made.[27]

A few days later, Arnold admonished his staff concerning recent
press releases contrary to AAF policy. "You must bear in mind," he
wrote, "that every civilian activity is endeavoring to ride on the tail
of national defense in order to justify their existence. While we have
no brief against these activities carrying out their normal functions,
we cannot have them take advantage of national defense and by so
doing, endeavor to insure our backing in their activities unless they
are in accordance with our policies."[28]

The AAF evidently bowed to pressure from Arnold because in
late April 1942, without consulting with or informing CAA officials,
it embarked on a month-long advertising campaign in major newspapers and college publications to promote enrollment in the AAF enlisted reserves. Prepared by the firm of Geyer, Cornell, and Newell,
the half-million-dollar campaign was directed toward 150 colleges
and universities throughout the country. Meanwhile, a telegram and
letter signed by Arnold explaining the program went out to college
and university leaders all over the country. At about the same time,
officials of twenty-five key universities and colleges met in Washington at the War Department's request to plan AAF recruitment of approximately eighty-one thousand collegians in 1942, with well over
two hundred thousand more scheduled to be recruited during the
next two years.[29]

CAA officials viewed this maneuver as a deliberate attempt to
steal the CPTP's thunder. CAA administrator Charles I. Stanton
fumed that the "CAA which pioneered air training in the colleges
and which has a pilot training program in more than 700 today, was
neither invited nor represented at the meetings or officially informed
of what went on." Meanwhile, AAF cadet selection boards began
recruiting through colleges from coast to coast without mention of
the CPTP.[30]

In late May 1942, at a Bureau of the Budget hearing, Arnold's representative, Colonel Luther Smith, announced that the AAF had
scaled down its original plan to train forty-five thousand reservists
in elementary courses; now only 13,350 would participate. These
people were to be trained as instructors, service pilots (ferrying aircraft and towing targets), field artillery liaison pilots (flying light aircraft for observation and artillery spotting), glider pilots, and airline

copilots but not as combat pilots. The decision confirmed that the AAF believed the CPTP was second-rate and should take a back seat to its own combat pilot training program.[31]

Despite the continual changes of air force policy in regard to the CPTP, on July 1, 1942, the CAA finally agreed to employ its training facilities exclusively for AAF enlisted reservists in noncombat pilot specialties. The CAA would also give preliminary flight instruction to some twenty thousand naval reservists, who would then go on to be trained as combat pilots. The agency also would recruit for the AAF and the navy by examining and selecting candidates who would then be sent to army and navy centers for voluntary enrollment in the enlisted reserve.[32]

The agreement had been won at the price of an emerging enmity that would plague the relationship between the two organizations for the duration of the CPTP. The AAF's eccentricity in regard to the program in the first six months of 1942 was no accident; it was determined to delay agreement as long as possible and make it as difficult as possible to achieve. The next eighteen months would be even more bitter and difficult.

The Changing of the Guard

At about the time that the AAF and CAA had reached an accord on the use of the CPTP, other changes were about to take place that would profoundly affect the program for the remainder of its history. Its New Deal foundations had begun to give way to wartime emergency planning, and a new cast of characters was about to take control.

The CPTP's originator, Robert Hinckley, had played little or no part in the deliberations between the CAA and the AAF. He preferred instead to let Charles Stanton assume the responsibility while he publicly defended the CPTP and promoted his idea of air age education. Hinckley's deferral to Stanton was out of character. He had always viewed himself as a public servant and a team player, although he sometimes walked a fine line between invoking the wrath of the aviation community for an unpopular, politically motivated decision or incurring F.D.R.'s displeasure at his unwillingness to go along with White House aviation policy.

But Hinckley had become demoralized by the controversy over the CPTP and the capriciousness of the AAF. Criticism of the CPTP and the failure of the AAF to make better use of the program were evidently the final blows. On June 20, 1942, the *New York Times* quoted Hinckley, in a speech before the National Aeronautic Association, as saying, "It sometimes happens that a government agency becomes so strong that it loses touch with the people who really own it, and it begins to fight not for the people but for itself." According to the *Times*'s account, Hinckley "denied that he had the War Department in mind," but there was no question that he referred to the air force's obstinacy about the CAA and the CPTP.[33]

This was to be Hinckley's parting shot. A few days later, he resigned as assistant secretary of commerce, effective July 1, to become assistant to the president of the Sperry Corporation. In his letter of resignation, he stressed how difficult his decision had been because "the progress of civil aviation has become almost an obsession with me. . . . It is only because I am to undertake work of great importance in the war production program which is so closely related to aviation that I do so."[34]

Reaction to Hinckley's departure was predictable; the usual valedictory accolades cited his invaluable contributions to aviation. F.D.R. accepted the resignation "with extreme reluctance" and praised him for his accomplishments and contributing "a decided emphasis on the creative and developmental as contrasted with the purely regulatory aspects of aviation." The *New York Times* applauded Hinckley's "broad vision and devoted interest in the 'air conditioning'. . . of America."[35]

The tone of the *Aero Digest*'s editorial, however, was bitter. "Much can be read between the lines in the resignation of Robert H. Hinckley," it said. "The net result, however, is that aviation loses a Washington representative who has been instrumental in the training of 80,000 civilian pilots, of which number 34,000 are now in the Air Force. . . .But the brass hat boys don't like to admit that Hinckley's activities have contributed immeasurably to the personnel of our Air Forces. They prefer to minimize the CPT, asserting that its trainees have to unlearn what they have been taught before they are any good to Naval aviation or to the Air Forces." The editorial concluded that it was "shocking to contemplate the pigheadedness of some of those entrusted with the awful responsibility of bringing us through the war successfully. Unwilling to see any viewpoint but their own, these stuffed shirts are hamstringing aviation either because they are grossly ill-informed regarding the modern ways of war or so headstrong as to demand that things be done their way or not at all."[36]

In the wake of Hinckley's departure, a new set of participants came on the scene. William A. M. Burden, R. McLean Stewart, and

Robert Lovett would play a significant role in shaping CPTP policy. Their appointment was typical of the Roosevelt war administration's change in direction from New Deal administrators like Robert Hinckley and toward Wall Street bankers, financiers, and businessmen such as James V. Forrestal, Edward Stettinius, and Donald Nelson who had been in the ascendancy during the push for mobilization. As Richard Polenberg points out, "In the early 1940s the federal service underwent a major overhaul. Some New Dealers remained but usually their influence was greatly reduced. Many left government employment altogether . . . still others resigned when their objectives were frustrated or they became physically exhausted."[37]

Taking Hinckley's place but not his position as assistant secretary of commerce was William Burden, whom Secretary of Commerce Jesse Jones named as his special assistant in matters relating to the CAA. Burden, a wealthy, well-connected New Yorker, had transferred from the Defense Supplies Corporation and, as in his previous post, agreed to serve without compensation. He was widely known in the aviation community, having been an aviation securities analyst with the prestigious Wall Street firm of Brown Brothers, Harriman & Co. from 1928 to 1932; head of aviation research at Scudder, Stevens & Clark, from 1932 to 1939; and vice president of the Institute of the Aeronautical Sciences. He was respected as a hard-driving advocate of aviation.[38]

In January 1943, Burden named another Wall Streeter, R. McLean Stewart, to be executive director of training for what was by then the War Training Service. Stewart had been born and educated in Canada but became an American citizen in 1937. He had most recently been vice president and director of Harriman-Ripley & Co., a New York investment banking firm. His selection had another purpose. Stewart would report to Charles Stanton and thus be Burden's man in the front office of the CAA. Secretary of Commerce Jones had assigned Burden to supervise and direct Stanton, who believed in running the CAA in a manner free from the interference of the Department of Commerce. Moreover, Stanton had been perceived as an ally of Robert Hinckley and one of the last vestiges of the Hinckley era.[39]

Like Burden, Robert Lovett's background was in Wall Street finance, having joined Brown Brothers in 1921 and eventually becoming head of the firm's international activities. Lovett had also been a pilot in World War I and had served in the renowned Yale Unit, a squadron comprised of undergraduates from Yale University. In 1940, he had been tapped by Secretary of War Henry Stimson as a special assistant for aviation matters. A comprehensive report that

Lovett made on the shortcomings of the aviation industry had so impressed Stimson that he hired him on the spot.[40]

As special assistant to Stimson, and later as assistant secretary of war for air, Lovett was responsible for broad AAF policymaking on aircraft production and procurement, training, and other important issues. He was a perceptive and influential civilian in a world of military men and a trusted and valued advisor to General Arnold. Eric Larabee comments that although Arnold "had the dream and the inner drive to undertake a great mission," he had "neither the brains nor the organizing capacity to carry through on it. Fortunately, he also had the good sense to recognize his limitations and to form an alliance that compensated for them." As Larabee observes, "a combination of luck and business-world enterprise sent him an ally in the person of Robert A. Lovett, who, wrote Arnold, 'possessed the qualities in which I was weakest, a partner and teammate of tremendous sympathy, and of calm and hidden force.'"[41]

Lovett's banking experience stood him in good stead in overseeing his broad responsibilities for the wartime aircraft industry. Lovett's "mode of operation," his biographer Jonathan Foster Fanton has pointed out, was characterized by "careful attention to factual analysis of production capability, a belief in realistic production goals coordinated with strategic considerations, widespread consultation through formal and informal channels, and finally, a capacity to resist pressure from above for a wrong decision."[42]

Lovett's approach to the CPTP-WTS was much the same as his attitude toward production goals—impartial and factual but no doubt influenced by General Arnold's belief in the superiority of air force training methods. Burden and Stewart agreed that the CPTP should be redefined to make it more productive. Unlike Hinckley, who had created the CPTP virtually out of nothing, defended it in Congress, and nurtured it through difficult times, Burden and Stewart could more easily divorce themselves personally and ideologically from the program. Because they lacked Hinckley's personal investment, they were more objective about the CPTP's shortcomings and more willing to cooperate with the military than he had been.

The Uneasy Marriage between the AAF and the CPTP

Despite the changes in leadership, the CPTP continued to experience difficulties with the AAF for the rest of 1942. The agreement made in July of that year had broken the ice, but the program was still running at only 15 percent capacity, only 25 percent by Septem-

ber. The AAF was sensitive to criticism that it was not making sufficient use of CPTP facilities; nevertheless, it was dissatisfied with the
CAA's management of the program on many fronts, not the least of
which was its perception that the CAA was unable to meet agreed-
upon quotas. As for the CAA, extenuating circumstances sur-
rounded its compliance problems, for example, shortages of training
aircraft and spare parts.[43]

Despite the disagreements between the air force and the CAA, the
CPTP was, as a result of the July 1, 1942, agreement, sending trainees
directly to the AAF and the navy in a variety of pilot specialties.
Naval aviation cadet candidates, for example, usually took the eight-
week elementary course (240 hours of ground instruction and thirty-
five to forty-five hours of flight training) and the eight-week secondary course (240 hours of ground instruction and forty to fifty hours
of flight training). Trainees who were sufficiently proficient after the
elementary course could bypass secondary and go right to active
duty. After successfully completing these courses, they were called
to active duty for combat training and commissioned as ensigns.[44]

Although the AAF had determined earlier that no CPTP trainee
would enter its combat pilot training programs, it offered enlisted
reservists a variety of alternatives. Trainees could go from the elementary and secondary courses to the eight-week cross-country
course (108 hours of ground instruction and forty-five to fifty hours
of flight instruction). From there, they would proceed to the flight
instrument course, also eight weeks long (108 hours of ground instruction and twenty to twenty-five hours on the Link trainer, a rudi-
mentary aircraft simulator), then to an eight-week instructor training
course (seventy-two hours of ground instruction and fifty to sixty
hours of flight training). The AAF would then train the candidates
and assign them as civilian flight instructors or service pilots, the
physical and mental requirements for which were less stringent than
for combat duty. In contrast, navy enlisted reservists who went
through the flight instructor program were commissioned as military
flight instructors.[45]

Other alternatives after completing the first three CPTP courses
were flight officer training or airlines school (325 hours of ground
instruction, fifty hours of flight training, and twenty to thirty hours
on the Link trainer). Flight officers were given positions as airline
copilots and used to ferry aircraft for the AAF or the navy. Flight
officer trainees could also go to airline school to be taught to fly mul-
tiengined aircraft and be subsequently qualified for jobs as copilots
with the Air Transport Command, the militarized airlines. Other op-

tions were liaison pilot training (flying small observation and artillery spotting aircraft) or glider pilot training, both of which took ten
weeks (240 hours of ground instruction and fifty-five to sixty-five
hours of flight training) and led to assignment in an army field artillery school or an AAF glider unit.[46]

By the end of fiscal year 1943 (July 1, 1942, to June 30, 1943) the
CPTP was delivering 3,695 enlisted reservists a month to the AAF
and the Air Transport Command. At the same time, it was training
4,124 AAF aviation cadet candidates a month. In fiscal year 1944,
the figures for AAF enlisted reservists trained decreased significantly to 919 a month, but the number of aviation cadet candidates
increased to 14,053. In fiscal year 1943, CPTP-WTS was also training
4,031 officers, aviation cadets, and enlisted men for the navy, a figure that jumped to 4,887 a month in 1944.[47]

Yet these statistics failed to impress the AAF because it claimed
that the CPTP was not meeting the quotas it had requested, and that
the men trained were not up to AAF standards. On September 9,
1942, Lovett pointed out to Burden that the CAA had encountered
difficulties in delivering graduates on time after the July 1 agreement, but offered no statistics to substantiate his claim. He was dis-
appointed that most trainees "were civilians and not members of the
reserve"; the air force had presumed that the CAA would not train
anyone other than members of the enlisted reserve after July 1, 1942.
The CPTP, he felt, was wasting time by training these men instead
of enlisted reservists who could be sent directly to the AAF. Lovett
concluded, "I want to call all of the above facts to your attention,
not so much in the spirit of complaint as in an endeavor to help
coordinate the efforts of the C.A.A. and the A.A.F. so that Civilian
Pilot Training may be a factor to be counted on by the Army, as a
reliable source of flying material."[48]

A few days later, Lovett told Acting Secretary of Commerce
Wayne C. Taylor that because the CAA had problems "in meeting
commitments to the Army Air Forces," he would honor the director
of the CPTP's request and hold back on additional increases in training quotas until the CAA could guarantee satisfaction in meeting the
AAF's demands. Again, he offered no figures to back up his assertions. In his reply for Taylor, William Burden remarked, "I am sure
you must realize, [the] CAA can no more guarantee production of
specific numbers of men, trained to specific degrees of competence,
on specific dates than can [the] Army's and Navy's own aviation
schools." Burden assumed that Lovett referred to the charge that the
CAA, from the beginning of the current fiscal year to date, had not

produced the numbers of pilots scheduled in the agreed-upon training quotas that the air force requested in May 1942.[49]

In a later memorandum, Burden stressed that deficiencies were critical in aircraft and Link trainers—especially those required to carry out elementary, secondary, and cross-country training—as well as unused training facilities. He warned Lovett that his data showed that trainees could not readily go into advanced training "under existing arrangements," and that "unless employment can be found for the facilities which have been used throughout the past six months to give elementary and secondary training for the Army Program, it seems unlikely that the existing organization for the provision of training will disintegrate to an extent which will defeat the possibility of carrying these men forward on an acceptable basis."[50]

By the end of 1942, the CPTP had encountered another difficulty, however. On December 5, President Roosevelt signed Executive Order 9279, which prohibited enlistments in the army and navy. This action was designed to expand the readily available supply of military personnel and guarantee that each branch of the armed forces would get an equitable share. Its effect, however, was detrimental to the CAA because it terminated the agency's recruitment role for the air force, thus ending one of its main efforts. The CAA would have to devise a new method of obtaining recruits to be trained for the armed forces.[51]

As a result of the presidential order and the manpower problems the AAF had experienced during 1942, Robert Lovett queried Major General George E. Stratemeyer, chief of the Air Staff, in mid-December about what use "from this time on" should be made of CPTP schools and training facilities. Lovett had already asked Burden and Stewart to explain "as promptly as possible" how the CAA could perform the services it had been providing under the changed conditions. Although he did not elaborate on its shortcomings, Lovett thought that the CPTP had been unsatisfactory in many respects. Schedules had not been met, and the "quality of the product" did not match the wishes of the AAF. Nevertheless, he believed that improvements had occurred recently because of Stewart's organizational efforts. Despite these perceived deficiencies, the AAF would require the CPTP in 1943 to train seven hundred instructors every two months, five hundred pilots for Air Transport Command every two months, and 240 liaison pilots every month. Air Transport Command, Lovett also noted, could use five hundred pilots every month rather than every other month as had been specified if the supply were continuous and the training complete.[52]

Lovett had recently called a staff meeting to discuss the work that the CPTP was doing for the AAF. The group agreed that the nearly four hundred schools now operated by the CPTP should be cut to about a hundred, even to fifty. Such a reduction would then enable the AAF to contract directly with each individual school, as it arranged for flight training in its elementary schools. As an alternative, the AAF would contract with the CPTP to operate all air force schools. (Some of the group preferred the former option to the latter, but Lovett asked them to consider the question further before a final decision was made.) He was convinced that consolidating CPTP schools would avoid such situations as those existing at the airfields where only one or two training aircraft were available for use by five or six instructors and a large number of students. Lovett also suggested using CPTP facilities to screen potential pilot trainees, thus reducing the number of eliminations that normally happened in the AAF's own training schools. This would increase correspondingly the production of AAF schools and perhaps fill the requirement for instructors, Air Transport Command pilots, and liaison pilots. Lovett was unconvinced that the suggestion was workable under all circumstances but recommended that it be investigated.[53]

Burden and Stewart, Lovett emphasized, recognized completely "the past defects of the CPT organization" but believed that these could be remedied. He felt that the program's shortcomings could be traced to the fact that many CPTP students did not measure up to the AAF's physical requirements and that many who had completed elementary training either would not continue with their instruction or, having done so, "would not report for duty." Such problems, however, would take care of themselves when all CPTP students were selected from the ranks of those inducted into the AAF. Better organization and supervision by CPTP administrators would eventually eliminate other faults.[54]

About a week later, on December 22, Stratemeyer told Lovett that, "based on past performance," the CPTP would not be able to instruct those students now in training "in the numbers specified by the expiration date of the contract and that the quality of these students will not be wholly satisfactory." Stratemeyer produced figures that pointed out the "past deficiencies of the CPT" that illustrated what he termed "an unsatisfactory situation."[55] The CPTP, for example, was required to provide 680 liason pilots from September to December 1942; it delivered 264 plus an additional 190 promised by December 30, only ninety-three of whom were qualified. It delivered 1,538 of the 1,900 instructor course graduates required in August

1942, but only seventy-three were members of the enlisted reserve. This meant that they could not go on active duty, and most of the seventy-three were subsequently eliminated. The others were questionably qualified, according to the AAF.[56]

Stratemeyer also noted that Air Transport Command had "stated very emphatically that CPT pilots are highly unsatisfactory. These pilots are professionally unqualified as well as being a poor type of personnel. It must be remembered that this personnel has been rejected from our aviation cadet program and recruited from the highways and byways." The truth of this statement cannot be determined readily, but Stratemeyer echoed General Arnold's belief that CPTP accepted inferior personnel.[57] Stratemeyer chided the CPTP for failing to set up the kind of organization over which it could exercise sufficient control and criticized the inefficiency of the operators because of haphazard organization. In addition, he criticized the AAF for failing to "furnish CPT with a comprehensive program showing specific requirements" and for not making more of an attempt to supervise the operators.[58]

Stratemeyer, responding to Lovett's earlier suggestion, recommended that the AAF consolidate CPTP activities into a smaller number of schools, put them on a contractual basis similar to the AAF's arrangement with civilian contractors to train its own pilots, and place the schools under military supervision. Moreover, he proposed that, beginning February 1, 1943, the CPTP be used to conduct suitability screening of the monthly backlog of fourteen thousand AAF aviation cadets. Stratemeyer noted that the navy's successful use of the CPTP to screen unfit pilot candidates had resulted in a 17 percent preflight elimination rate compared to the AAF's rate of 43 to 50 percent. "In the event that AAF requirements cannot be met," Stratemeyer counseled Lovett, "dissolve CPT and place the facilities thereof at the disposal of the Army Air Force Flying Training Command."[59]

Ironically, on December 21, the day before General Stratemeyer's memo, Burden, speaking in Kansas City to the National Aviation Training Association (NATA), an organization of airport operators who supplied services for the CPTP, had confidently proclaimed an expansion of CPTP programs. "While I can make no definite predictions in this field as yet, it is my firm conviction that before long, as part of our war job, we will be called upon to do other types of training of persons in a civilian capacity."[60]

Burden's optimism would be short-lived. During the next year and for the remainder of its history, the CPTP would find its energies dissipated by several interrelated, critical problems: its relationship to the air force, the pay and status of its trainees, who would have administrative and budgetary control of the program, and shortages of aircraft and spare parts. The extent to which these problems could be resolved would shape the program's destiny.

Yet Another Agreement and Still More Problems

The first problem the program faced, the role of the CPTP-WTS in the air force's pilot training scheme, had been pointed to in the exchange of memos from Lovett to Stratemeyer in late 1942. Unquestionably, the AAF believed it would have to exert more control over the program to make it useful. By early January 1943, *American Aviation Daily* reported that there were rumors that additional changes in the WTS program were under way, with "a strong possibility" of "more Army control and administration." In the latter part of the month, however, the AAF issued a statement, in apparent contradiction to the Stratemeyer memo, which suggested it would expand the use of CAA training facilities in connection with its own production of combat and service pilots. "The new plans," the AAF said, "which have been under discussion for several weeks, have the complete approval of the Department of Commerce."[61]

Thus, the crises of 1942 and the change in the CAA's recruitment role for the air force had necessitated another agreement between the two organizations, signed on January 19, 1943 (Appendix E), on the continued use of the War Training Service. The CAA-AAF memorandum of agreement, however, seemed at worst to bear out the rumors of an air force takeover and at best to suggest tighter military control. The WTS would continue to train enlisted reservists for noncombat pilot specialties. In addition, it would provide ten hours of elementary flight instruction for men selected for the AAF's college training program.

The agreement first specified that 13,500 enlisted reservists would be in training. The number included the 9,500 enrolled in WTS courses and 4,000 who awaited assignment to training. Second, WTS would continue to train elementary, secondary, cross-country, Link instrument, instructor, and flight officer candidates. Third, the number of trainees produced each month would be in line with strictly prescribed AAF schedules. Fourth, trainees who were members of the enlisted reserve would be supervised by WTS personnel and be on inactive status; all expenses for enlisted reservists would be paid out of CAA appropriations. Fifth, parts and materials necessary for the safe and efficient operation of WTS facilities would be made available insofar as their production did not interfere with the production of combat aircraft. Sixth, the AAF would call 20 percent of the seventy thousand enlisted reservists to active duty and place them in selected colleges for instruction; the WTS would give them a minimum of ten hours of elementary flight instruction. Before committing itself to allow more than ten hours of instruction, the AAF wanted to be sure that the WTS could successfully produce the required number of trainees.[62]

Opinions on the agreement varied widely. Dean Brimhall, the CAA's director of research who had helped to pioneer the CPTP, was skeptical. In January 1943, he expressed his misgivings to Robert Hinckley: "We are now vulnerable to almost every kind of sabotage if the Army people really want to perform that way." "On the other hand, it may be that the Army will work itself into such a dilemma that it will be forced to have us give more that the 10 hours now specified. . . . I have been told by reliable authority that Luke [General Luther] Smith fought to the last ditch against any kind of an [Army-CAA] arrangement and that Lovett forced the arrangement. Just why Arnold would agree to Lovett pressure, if all this is true, I do not know."[63]

R. McLean Stewart was more sanguine. Responding to queries from C. R. Mooney secretary of the NATA, on the future of the WTS program during more stringent military controls, Stewart wrote glowingly, "the new program is one of substantial magnitude. The highest standards of performance will be required of those engaged in it. It cannot be carried through successfully without the close cooperation and earnest effort of the flight contractors, instructors, and CAA personnel who have been responsible for the success which has attended the training program during its first and second phases."[64]

Stewart's reassurances notwithstanding, uneasiness continued among the training contractors, and the rumor persisted that the army would take over the WTS. In mid-February, Stewart felt compelled to squelch that rumor publicly. "The CAA War Training Service will continue," he said, "the rumor that it will be taken over by the military has no factual foundation. The Service is and will continue to be the contracting agency through which flight instruction contractors will deal in respect to all matters having to do with the conduct of pilot training programs for the Army and Navy at centers where such training is now being provided under the supervision of the CAA."[65]

The NATA flight contractors were also concerned that a consider-able number of training contracts would be eliminated as a result of the January 1943 reorganization. The number of flight contractors participating in the CPTP-WTS had shrunk by nearly 60 percent, from 441 nationwide in June 1942 to 262 in April 1943. The reduc-tion was a result of the AAF's belief that the program should be con-centrated in as few hands as possible for greater efficiency in train-ing, use of aircraft, maintenance, administration, and discipline. After the January 1943 reorganization, the AAF awarded contracts to the larger, well-established flight schools, a policy that caused hardship for the smaller schools squeezed out of the program.[66]

The trend toward consolidation, as John R. M. Wilson points out, "reflected a general Government predilection during the war to con-centrate contracts with large manufacturers; but while the practice may have been defensible to insure productivity in early war con-tracts, the CPTP schools were operating smoothly enough before the military began to play a large role in the program. Thus, the Army seemed almost deliberately to increase concentration and reward bigness, even when the benefits to be derived from such a shift were negligible. Hinckley's original conception of the CPTP as a boon to the fixed-base operators was fundamentally altered by this produc-tivity-oriented military approach."[67]

The second problem facing the program—the pay and status of men in the enlisted reserve who were awaiting training—arose while the revised 1943 program was waiting to be implemented. The predicament was a result of the agreement that the CAA and the AAF had reached in July 1942. The trainees whom the CAA was to recruit for the AAF would then be placed in enlisted reserve status until arrangements could be made for their training. In 1942, how-ever, the CAA recruited more men than could possibly be trained in a reasonable period. The resulting backlog delayed instruction for many.[68] In addition, many had quit their civilian jobs and were not being compensated while in or awaiting training. As a result, they suffered financial hardships.

A letter from a constitutent of Senator W. Lee O'Daniel of Texas was typical. The writer explained that he was among a group of sixty-five young men undergoing flight training and enrolled in the War Training Service. "All of us," he wrote, "are members of the Army Air Forces Enlisted Reserve Corps and do not receive any pay whatsoever. At the time of our enlistment, we understood we would complete the program in eight months; most of us are not financially able to go without pay for a longer period. Yet, at the completion of each phase of the program, we are being released to shift for ourselves for periods of more than two months. At that rate we would not complete the program for nearly two years."[69] The trainee asserted that, because of rigorous schedules, "the program is more exacting than that required of regular army cadets in aviation. Such treatment has caused morale to ebb to a low degree and discouragement is evident at every hand. We have been promised uniforms, have never received them. We were told we would be taken in the Army and given our wings, but rarely does this occur. Naval cadets taking exactly the same training are on active duty and are being paid." (The navy placed its enlisted reservists awaiting training on active duty and paid them $75 a month.)[70]

To remedy the inequity, Senator Patrick McCarran (D.-Nev.) sponsored an amendment to House Joint Resolution 115, a deficiency appropriation, which would have compensated the enlisted reservists. Hearings were held before a subcommittee of the Senate Committee on Appropriations on April 19 and 20, 1943. The amendment was added despite protests from the chair of the committee Senator Kenneth D. McKellar (D.-Tenn.) and from Senator Henry Cabot Lodge (R.-Mass.). President Roosevelt signed the legislation in June. A few days later, AAF enlisted reservists were issued compensatory checks for $50 a month, retroactive to December 15 of the previous year.[71]

Related to the problem of compensation for the enlisted reservists was the question of how to thin the ranks of the surplus recruited in 1942 before Executive Order 9279 put an end to the recruitment. The CAA and the AAF worked out a plan to release a large number of enlisted reservists because there were too many to be trained in the allotted twelve-month training period, not enough aircraft in which to train them, and the need for them had lessened. Early in June 1943, these men, approximately 13,500 in number, were given various options. Those between the ages of eighteen and twenty-six who were physically qualified could apply for aviation cadet training. They could also apply for active duty in the AAF as enlisted men, but with no promise of being assigned to flight duty. Finally, they could request a discharge from the AAF, but by doing so be subject to the draft. Although many lost the opportunity to become service pilots, most were absorbed into the AAF in various capacities.[72]

The third problem confronting the WTS had to do with whether the CAA would maintain administrative and budgetary control of the program. Passage of Senator McCarran's amendment to House Joint Resolution 115 had raised the legal problem of the CAA, a civilian agency, paying enlisted reservists on active duty. On January 6, 1943, Comptroller General Lindsay C. Warren informed Secretary of Commerce Jesse Jones that in placing these men on active duty and paying them $75 a month the navy changed their status from civilian to military. The appropriations set aside for the WTS program, however, were obtainable only for the training of "civilian" pilots. Warren argued that "while enlisted members of the Army and Naval Reserves when on inactive duty may be classed and considered as civilians, and, as such, may be furnished training under the appropriations for civilian pilot training, when they are ordered into active service they cease to be civilians and become members of the military or naval forces and the expense of any training furnished members of the Naval Reserve on active duty would be chargeable to available naval appropriations and not to the appropriation for civilian pilot training." The navy resolved the problem by transferring to the WTS some $25 million from its appropriations to continue the training to the end of the fiscal year. The Bureau of the Budget sought to resolve the problem of the AAF enlisted reservists by transferring control of the CAA's budget for the War Training Service to the air force.[73]

This time, Senator McCarran and Representative Clarence Lea came to the rescue. The two men sponsored amendments (S.1037 and H.R.1670) to the Civilian Pilot Training Program legislation that sought to keep WTS funds under the control of the CAA. The bills proposed to make funds authorized for the defunct CPTP available to the War Training Service and authorize the CAA to train men on active military duty.

On May 28, 1943, McCarran went before the Senate to explain the legislation. He contended that his bill would rectify the problem "so that the appropriation may come through the Commerce Department, thus to be handled by the CAA, so as to enable it to train enlisted enrollees." He asked "to have the word 'civilian' stricken so that the act may cover not only civilian, but military enrollees as well."[74] Eventually, Clarence Lea's version of the legislation, which specified that the CAA could expend its own funds to train military pilots, was adopted, passed, and signed by President Roosevelt.

The fourth problem facing the program, potentially more serious than all the rest, had to do with the difficulty of obtaining single-engine aircraft and spare parts. The shortage of aircraft and parts was beginning to be felt as early as the fall of 1942, as Burden had pointed out to Lovett in December 1942, and had helped to delay the training of large numbers of enlisted reservists. In early January

1943, the NATA had complained in its newsletter that the WTS was "breaking down on airports all over the country because flight contractors are unable to obtain repair parts and supplies." A survey conducted among the seven CAA training regions showed that sixty-five aircraft were inoperative, some from as long ago as September 1942, and estimated that ten thousand flight hours had been lost as a result.[75]

The roots of the parts problem can be traced to the actions of the Joint Aircraft Committee in late 1942 and early 1943. In December 1942, the committee, comprised of representatives of the principal customers of the American aircraft industry including the navy and AAF, whose purpose it was to see that aircraft and engines were allocated equitably, met to discuss priorities for the WTS program. The committee asked the CAA to summarize WTS requirements. Although the committee approved the maintenance requirements for the navy and CAA-owned airplanes, it tabled requirements for the army "pending further decisions in regard to the continuance of the Program by the Commanding General [Arnold], Army Air Forces."[76]

On January 10, 1943, Deputy Chief of Air Staff Brigadier General T. J. Hanley, Jr., told the director of military requirements that "the question of whether or not the Army Air Forces will continue to support request[s] from [the] CAA for additional airplanes and maintenance of those now being used by CPT, must be decided with reference to our need for the CPT Program." Hanley argued that if the program was "performing no useful purpose," the AAF should say so explicitly and not agree to "a further diversion of the materials." If the air force concluded that the program was useful to its training, the AAF "should maintain it in accordance with [its] needs."[77]

About two weeks later, Hanley proposed to the Joint Aircraft Committee's Office of the Recorder a policy to maintain aircraft used in the WTS program that would correspond to the priority "accorded the Army Air Forces for the maintenance of Liaison Type airplanes." Because this priority was very low, the action was tantamount to cutting off the parts necessary to maintain WTS training aircraft.[78]

In addition to the scarcity of parts, there was difficulty in obtaining additional aircraft for training. The shortage was a serious problem; without adequate training planes, the WTS could not meet the AAF's quotas. The January 19, 1943 agreement between the CAA and the AAF specified that the CAA could not carry out the training program unless it could purchase "71 instrument equipped aircraft of not less than 120 horsepower" and "33 link trainers equipped with the required instruments." If the WTS could not obtain these aircraft and Link trainers could not be obtained from private owners, the agreement would be renegotiated and the program revised in accord with whatever equipment was available. Although the AAF had promised the WTS additional aircraft in February 1943, three months later they had not yet been delivered and were found sitting idle in Houston, Texas.[79]

The AAF also failed to keep its agreement that training quotas be adjusted to reflect the number of available aircraft. Early in 1943, the AAF's director of individual training, Luther S. Smith, now a brigadier general, asked Stewart if trainees could receive more training than had been specified in the January 19, 1943 agreement. Stewart replied that he would be happy to cooperate but cautioned that the WTS's ability to satisfy Smith's requests—made in a letter dated February 19 and a discussion held on March 4—would be "determined by the availability of planes and other equipment." He then suggested that the AAF could help the WTS substantially in accomplishing training goals by making elementary training planes available, as well as some commercial planes that could be used for cross-country training. "If those light planes could be released to us," Stewart wrote, "the personnel now engaged in buying other light planes from the public could be put to work exclusively on the job of finding planes and other equipment for the advanced courses."[80]

To ease the situation, the War Production Board, in late January 1943, issued General Limitation Order L-262, which froze aircraft of five hundred horsepower or less and Link trainers in the hands of their owners by prohibiting their sale or rental. The board also made it possible for the CAA to purchase these aircraft through the Defense Plant Corporation, a quasi-independent federal wartime financing agency. The action had been taken to prevent the price gouging and speculation that the shortages created and to channel light aircraft directly into the hands of WTS flight contractors.[81]

In February 1943, the CAA signed an agreement with the DPC, providing funds to purchase the necessary aircraft and then leasing them to the WTS, which turned them over to flight contractors. The aircraft were to be issued under a revocable license, with contractors responsible for maintenance. In July 1943, however, the comptroller general challenged the agreement on the grounds that it was intended as a "subterfuge designed to relieve the CAA of the duty and responsibility of submitting to the Congress an estimate for additional funds." Procurement proceeded unhindered when procedural changes that satisfied the comptroller general were agreed upon.[82]

Although a good many of the major policy problems experienced
by the WTS in 1943 had been solved by late in the year, it was becoming apparent that the air force was again questioning the program's usefulness. Wartime mobilization had gained momentum, the
need for pilots lessened, and the WTS required a level of maintenance that the AAF thought was exceedingly burdensome and not
cost-effective.

In November 1943, Robert Lovett asked his executive officer, Colonel George A. Brownell, to investigate how long the AAF would
make use of the War Training Service "in the two fields in which
they are now working for us; vis. the training of the flight instructors,
and the dual control training in the colleges." Lovett wanted the program evaluated because of an extensive request William Burden had
made on November 3, 1943. Burden wondered whether the War Department could work out arrangements to use WTS facilities further
after the current round of training was completed. He pleaded on
behalf of the contractors engaged in training AAF personnel for the
CAA, a group that stood to lose a great deal after the CAA and the
AAF ended their agreement. "These centers," Burden told Lovett,
"are in a position to provide valuable service in the training of pilots,
and it is our view that their continued employment in this work will
not only contribute to the war effort but will aid as well in maintaining throughout the country a civilian training organization
which may prove of high importance to our national economy after
the war."[83]

Brownell cautioned General Robert W. Harper, assistant chief of
air staff for training, that "if the decision of the Training Command
and of yourself is to be that we will terminate our use of the War
Training Service some time in the course of 1944, we should start
now to lay our plans accordingly, and we should also endeavor to
give the CAA appropriate advance notice so that they will not claim
that they have not been given time in which to effectively and economically make the necessary changes in their organization."[84]

Harper made it clear to Lovett that his office wanted to retain the
WTS program because of its "value as air indoctrination," but he
also saw "no reason why the Army Air Forces should not make contracts with the individual contractors rather than support a CAA su-
pervisory organization" because there was "duplicate inspection
and supervision by the Army Air Forces Training Command in each
of the colleges in the program. Other than the college program,"
Harper concluded, "this office can find no use for CAA War Training
Service facilities after the present program is concluded the middle
of 1944."[85]

Earlier in the year, at a hearing of the subcommittee of the Committee on Appropriations, Harper, speaking for General Arnold, had informed Burden and Stewart that the AAF did not object to the CAA paying Air Corps enlisted reservists who were on inactive duty and undergoing training with the WTS. Harper emphasized that the AAF was now working with the CAA to "clear up the hump existing in the present Civilian Pilot Training Program" (nearly fourteen thousand enlisted reservists awaiting training) and that Arnold wanted the work done "as rapidly as possible." However, Arnold did not wish "to further use the C.A.A. in an extension of the Civilian Pilot Training Program."[86]

Despite Burden's urgent appeal the handwriting was on the wall. Shortly after the beginning of 1944, the AAF announced that it was planning to end all WTS secondary, cross-country, Link instrument, and flight instructor training within a matter of days. The official AAF statement explained that the production rate of pilots within the AAF's own system in addition to pilots returning from combat were adequate to handle current needs. "Discontinuance of the Flight Instructor Program is in no sense attributable to dissatisfaction with the training performed by CAA-WTS. It is desired to express appreciation of the excellent work accomplished by the Flight Contractors, ground schools and CAA personnel who have been engaged in the training of pilots for the Air Forces." Yet, it was obvious to insiders that the AAF was dissatisfied with the WTS, and that its dissatisfaction had a great deal to do with its decision to end the program.[87]

A few months later, the AAF announced that as of June 30, 1944, it was concluding the only remaining WTS course, the college training program for air crew indoctrination. Again, the AAF's rationale was ostensibly that its own resources were more than adequate to fulfill training requirements after midyear. Gradually, the program was geared down until it had been completely eliminated by the latter part of 1944.[88]

Franklin D. Roosevelt, Eleanor Roosevelt, and members of the Roosevelt family prepare to fly to Chicago aboard a chartered American Airways Ford trimotor to accept the Democratic party's nomination for president in July 1932. Although F.D.R. was perceived as an advocate of aviation, his administration's record in regard to aviation policy was inconsistent. (National Air and Space Museum, Smithsonian Institution)

Robert H. Hinckley (left) poses with Brigadier General Barton K. Yount (center) and Colonel F. M. Kennedy of the U.S. Army Air Corps at Wright Field in 1939. Hinckley was one of the original members of the Civil Aeronautics Authority and "father" of the Civilian Pilot Training Program. (National Air and Space Museum, Smithsonian Institution)

Eugene L. Vidal was director of the Bureau of Air Commerce from 1933 until 1937. Vidal's proposal for a $700 aircraft was perceived by many in the aviation industry as an outlandish and impractical idea. (National Air and Space Museum, Smithsonian Institution)

Clarence F. Lea (D.-Calif.), chair of the House Committee on Interstate and Foreign Commerce and a strong advocate of aviation, introduced the CPTP legislation in the House of Representatives on March 16, 1939. (Harris & Ewing, Washington, D. C., courtesy of the National Air and Space Museum, Smithsonian Institution)

The venerable Piper J-3 "Cub" was the workhorse of the CPTP training fleet. Its manufacturer, the Piper Aircraft Corp., claimed that more than 70 percent of the light aircraft used in the early days of the CPTP were Cubs. (National Air and Space Museum, Smithsonian Institution)

A CPTP instructor discusses a flight maneuver with a student at the Coffey School of Aeronautics in Chicago. Both blacks and women participated in the program. (National Air and Space Museum, Smithsonian Institution)

Chief of the Army Air Forces Lieutenant General Henry H. "Hap" Arnold receives the Distinguished Service Medal from Assistant Secretary of War for Air Robert A. Lovett in October 1942. Both men played a significant role in shaping CPTP policy after America entered World War II. (National Air and Space Museum, Smithsonian Institution)

William A. M. Burden, a one-time aviation securities analyst on Wall Street, was responsible for administering the Civilian Pilot Training Program after Robert Hinckley resigned as assistant secretary of commerce. Burden attempted to usher the CPTP into the postwar era. (National Air and Space Museum, Smithsonian Institution)

The Fulton Airphibian, a combination automobile-airplane, symbolized the anticipated postwar boom in private aviation, a time in which Eugene Vidal's prewar dream of an Airplane for Everyman would be fulfilled. The CPTP was seen as an essential element of the boom. (National Air and Space Museum, Smithsonian Institution)

CHAPTER 5

The CPTP
and Postwar Aviation

The end of the Civilian Pilot Training Program-War Training Service promised to take its toll financially and in more personal terms on three groups of participants: military personnel consisting of some five thousand trainees in varying stages of training, enlisted reserve flight instructors, and the fixed-based operators who conducted flight training. The end of the program meant frustration and, in some cases, a loss of livelihood for these people.

The qualified trainees were given the option of volunteering for duty in the aviation cadet corps, training as glider pilots, or receiving technical training. The instructors were given the opportunity of qualifying as AAF pilots if they could pass a flight examination and a physical. Because the AAF was resolute in its belief that the men had to measure up to its stringent standards of physical fitness and the equally stringent requirements for pilot training, absorption into the AAF was not automatic, a policy that caused considerable resentment on the part of trainees and instructors.[1]

As a result of the program's abrupt end, neither the CAA nor the AAF had planned for assimilating trainees and instructors into the force. The haphazard manner in which the transition had been handled and the perceived arbitrariness of the AAF's decisions made the men feel that they had been badly used. In testimony before the House Military Affairs Committee, one former CPTP-WTS trainee summed up the group's feelings. He accused the AAF of "repudiating" its agreement by not routinely offering the men commissions, giving them additional training without stipulation, employing them as instructors in AAF flight training programs, and retaining them in the enlisted reserve. The AAF, however, maintained steadfastly that no agreement had ever been made that guaranteed the rights of former trainees and instructors. It denied any responsibility other than to make opportunities available to qualified men.[2]

Another group affected greatly by the termination of the CPTP-WTS was the fixed-base (flight school) operators, whose contracts had been discontinued and who felt that they had been left holding the bag. They were still smarting from the wholesale cancellation of contracts in early 1943. Their reaction to the end of the program was made clear at the annual National Aviation Training Association (NATA) conference in December 1943 at St. Louis. In-coming president Roscoe Turner, the flamboyant racing pilot turned fixed-base operator, railed excitedly at the government and said that he was tired of being "kicked around." Turner warned the government that the NATA would fight to protect its interests. Moreover, the NATA conferees passed a resolution to continue the WTS program for the duration of the war and extend the Civilian Pilot Training Program after it expired on June 30, 1944.[3]

The fixed-base operators, organized under such umbrella organizations as the NATA and the like-minded Aeronautical Training Society, had heretofore not known much prosperity and had barely been able to make ends meet during the depression. They were plainly loath to relinquish a federally subsidized program that put money into their coffers and that had caused flight training and small airport operations in the United States to prosper as never before. Through the NATA newsletter, the *N.A.T.A Dispatch,* members were informed that it was "imperative that all influence possible be brought on Congress to . . . decide this issue [the CPTP extension bill]."[4]

The reasons for continuing the CPTP after the war by extending the life of the CPTP legislation were compelling economically not only to the fixed-base operators, but also to the colleges and universities that had also benefited directly from the program. Before the war, the CPTP had significantly carried on the New Deal policy linking government and academe that had begun in 1933 with the Federal Emergency Relief Administration's (and later, the National Youth Administration's) work-study programs. During its predominantly New Deal, civilian phase from fiscal year 1940 to fiscal year 1942, the CPTP was one of the largest government-sponsored educational programs, training 125,762 persons and consuming a budget of $68 million. (By comparison, the FERA-NYA spent more than $93 million on college training, but over a period of eight years.) Although the CPTP-WTS had been superseded in size and scope by many military training programs that took place on college campuses, by the end of World War II the program had spent nearly $500 million to train 378,479 persons.[5]

Because the CPTP-WTS was so heavily tied to the campus, it made use of college and university facilities all over the United States. Before the war, this was a boon to institutions still suffering the effects of the depression. As with the FERA-NYA work-study programs, federal assistance for the CPTP, and later the WTS, stimulated expansion of college facilities, the growth of enrollment, and the increase of aeronautical engineering curricula. Moreover, because aviation was regarded as an important source of professional employment after the war, colleges and universities viewed their role as preparing American youth for roles in the aviation industry. The continuation of the CPTP would help achieve that goal.

In a broader, social-cultural context, the CPTP was perceived as the linchpin in the postwar movement to promote private aviation. Even before the war ended, a powerful sentiment existed that the hold that private aviation would take on society after the war would be so strong that the way people lived would change. The rhetoric of postwar private flight promoters was apocalyptic, and the feeling was that aviation's effects would be felt at the innermost core of society. As Joseph Corn has pointed out, "The question as to when Mr. and Mrs. John Q. Public would be flying, and the implied question of how many new aircraft would be in the air once peace returned, generated the most extensive discussions, particularly during the last years of the war. . . . not only simple predictions but also market research and public-opinion polls addressed the question. Businessmen trying to forecast postwar buying trends, aircraft manufacturers planning peacetime production, and government planners thinking about future airfield requirements and the reconversion of the economy, were just some of the groups wanting information regarding the public's aerial expectations and intentions."[6]

Many such forecasts discussed aviation education and saw the CPTP as a pivotal element of the postwar boom in private aviation. In their comprehensive study for William Burden, *Postwar Outlook for Private Flying* (1943), John H. Geisse and Samuel C. Williams underscored the importance of private aviation education for American youth. If neglected, "it is not impossible that in future years we may find that this advantage has passed to other countries."[7] Moreover, Geisse and Williams linked the Civilian Pilot Training Program to private aircraft production and the volume of flying. Although, as they pointed out, persons trained in the CPTP were "for the most part, college students and most of them obviously could not afford to buy their own planes . . . it can be assumed that when they do become financially able to participate in private flying, they will be more likely to become prospects by reason of their early training." Geisse and Williams also observed that "if the student permits issued in those two years [1940–41] to C.P.T. students are eliminated from the totals, the number of non-C.P.T. permits were above the trend line, indicating that the program tended to stimulate an interest in non-C.P.T. training rather than to detract from it."[8]

Other surveys, for example, *Civil Aviation and the National Economy,* published by the Department of Commerce, pointed to the CPTP's obvious benefits to civil aviation. The report noted that at the end of 1939, there were approximately thirty-one thousand licensed civilian pilots; by the end of 1944, "the total was 132,000. . . . Considering only the period when the program was purely civilian," the report stated, "we find that the total number of pilots in the United States increased to 100,000 by the end of 1941—gains of 101.9 percent from 1939 to 1940, and 59.7 percent from 1940 to 1941, compared with gains of 36.0 percent from 1938 to 1939, and 30.0 percent from 1937 to 1938."[9]

Finally, adding fuel to the argument for continuing the CPTP after the war was a widespread belief that the surplus of trained military pilots who returned from the war would not be enough to sustain the expected boom in private flying. The general feeling was that a constant supply of postwar pilots trained by an extended CPTP was essential if private flying were to grow. In an address to the NATA's annual convention in St. Louis in December 1943, R. McLean Stewart, director of the War Training Service, stated that a future estimate of postwar flight requirements must include provisions to instruct at least a hundred thousand young people. "We need such an influx of young pilots," he said, "if we are to retain our command of the air. We need them for civil aviation. We need them as a reserve to which we can turn if we are called on again to exert our armed strength in the air. We cannot rely on those who will then be the veterans of this war. In a year or two after the peace they will have settled down to civilian pursuits."[10]

Such considerations caused the machinery for perpetuating the CPTP to go into high gear. On Wednesday February 2, 1944, not long after the announcement that the CPTP-WTS program would be canceled, the subcommittee of the Senate Committee on Commerce met in the District of Columbia Room of the Capitol Building to hear testimony on S.1432, a bill to prolong the life of the CPTP act beyond its legally mandated expiration date of June 30, 1944. Senator Patrick McCarran, who had seen the program through serious difficulties the previous year, presided. In his opening statement McCarran said that he had invited those interested in civilian pilot training "to come here and express themselves as to what their experience has been in the past . . . and what they visualize as to the future . . . as regards the adoption of the bill by the Congress. Unless this bill does go through, or some similar measure," McCarran pointed out, "there will be no appropriation made for civilian pilot training at the on-coming appropriation for the Commerce Department."[11]

When McCarran had concluded his remarks, he called on Robert H. Hinckley to open the hearings. Although Hinckley had not been associated with the CPTP since 1942, he maintained a keen interest in the program. He began by recapping the history of the CPTP and, as in his testimony five years earlier, spoke emphatically in its favor. This time, however, he stated that the CPTP's national defense value to postwar aviation was similar to its significance before the war. "Today," he said, "we face the certainty of peace in a far different kind of world than we have ever known before—a three-dimensional world. . . . In that kind of a world, a nation of fliers is the best protection in time of war and in time of peace. No aggressor nation would dare attack a nation of fliers, a nation really equipped to live in a three-dimensional world." Hinckley argued persuasively that the machinery in place for the CPTP was capable of "making a nation of fliers," that the program had "proved its worth," and that it was "an efficient, going concern that can step in almost at a minute's notice to begin again its work in the air-conditioning process. . . .We should not," he continued, "allow that mechanism to disintegrate. We should not allow the skills of its personnel or it facilities to go unused."[12]

Hinckley also argued that, instead of being dismantled, the program should be expanded to include high school students. "Over 14,000 of the Nation's 28,000 high schools are now conducting courses in pre-flight education," he said, "and just as students are required to take practical laboratory courses in chemistry, physics, and biology, so should they take laboratory courses in aviation. This means flight training. In this way the present organization could and should be continued until peace returns, when operations can go ahead on an all-out basis in high schools and colleges."[13]

Finally, Hinckley declared that the money spent on the aviation training should rightfully be called "venture money" and not a subsidy. "The use of Government money for such a program," he said, is not a subsidy any more than the use of a business concern's funds for expanding, developing, and conducting research is a subsidy." Hinckley compared the CPTP to "an investment—an investment in people for all the people. The air-conditioning process," Hinckley said, "is much too big a program for any one agency to handle alone. This program for a nation of fliers, an air-conditioned population, requires teamwork—teamwork among governmental, educational, and business agencies."[14]

After Hinckley had concluded, McCarran introduced an impressive array of witnesses, all of whom favored extending the Civilian Pilot Training Program. Among these were such college presidents as Raymond Walters of the University of Cincinnati, Edward C. Elliott of Purdue University, Everett Needham Case of Colgate University, and Harmon W. Caldwell of the University of Georgia. Others were members of the training establishment, for example, NATA president Roscoe Turner and C. R. Mooney of Parks Air College in East St. Louis, Illinois; members of aviation interest groups, including W. P. Redding of the National Aeronautic Association; regional coordinators of the WTS program; and various officials of the Department of Commerce, including R. McLean Stewart and William Burden.[15]

Case spoke convincingly on behalf of the program. He viewed the CPTP as "an example of American foresight and enterprise at its best," a "successful collaboration between private operators who invested their skills and their capital, educational institutions which provided living and instructional facilities—and in time of peace an admirable reservoir of young men ambitious to become pilots, and the Government which aided in defraying the costs of operation." Case admitted that the colleges had "a selfish interest in the continuation of the program." He also argued that if the continuation of the program "can be shown to stand in the way of the effective prosecution of the war" he would "be content to see it disregarded." He noted, however, that this was not the case. The program would be "liquidated not because its effectiveness is challenged, but primarily because adequate facilities are now available without it." Case argued that it would be "fair to ask whether the loss from a broadly national standpoint does not exceed any possible gains." Finally, he cited Colgate as "typical of the situation in hundreds of colleges." He feared, like other college and university presidents, that investments made by the fixed-base operators, communities, and academic institutions "would, at the moment of peak efficiency, be dispersed" and that "not all the operators could survive the loss. It seems to me," Case said, "we would enter the period after the war very much the poorer for the loss of facilities which have already proved they are useful to the country."[16] On March 30, 1944, about two months after Senator McCarran's hearings, the Senate passed S.1432, with provisions that the CPTP act would be extended for five years, until June 30, 1949, and that $30 million would be appropriated for it.[17]

The House also produced various CPTP extension bills (H.R.4079, H.R.4092, and H.R.4181) sponsored by Representatives Richard F. Harless (D.-Az.), Ezekiel C. Gathings (D.-Ark.), and Jennings Randolph (D.-W. Va.), respectively. These bills, however, languished because members of the House Committee on Interstate and Foreign Commerce thought Clarence Lea's proposal for an independent Civil Aeronautics Administration (H.R.3420), which would have created a permanent CPTP for pilots and mechanics, should take precedence. The omnibus Lea measure, however, contained several controversial elements—including CAA independence—that were unpalatable to President Roosevelt, who threatened veto. Moreover, some committee members objected to the notion of a permanent CPTP because it would flood the market with civilian pilots and thus deprive returning veterans of jobs. For these reasons, it had little chance of becoming a reality.[18]

Finally, in early June, the House Committee on Interstate and Foreign Commerce conducted hearings on McCarran's CPTP extension bill. In its report, the committee, evidently fearful that the Senate bill was too extravagant, drastically reduced the number of years the program would be extended from five to one and removed the $30 million appropriation, an action that would have grave consequences for the future of the CPTP.[19]

On June 19, S.1432 was debated in the House. Unlike the Senate hearings held in February, which had focused on the CPTP's importance to the economic future of private aviation, the House debate centered on the necessity of continuing the program in view of the military's desire to carry on its own pilot training programs after the war, a sensitive issue in wartime.[20]

Carl Hinshaw (R.-Calif.) pointed out that the bill would not conflict with the desire of the AAF and the navy to continue to train military pilots. Joseph P. O'Hara (R.-Minn.) agreed: "We would not be properly considering the needs for the future if we were to cut it off now simply because the Army and the Navy say they have their own program. It would be giving very little thought and very poor consideration to matters of future national defense." Charles A. Wolverton (R.-N.J.) commented that although he supported the extension, "now, that these service branches have taken over the training of pilots, and, on account of the great numbers of pilots that will be available when they war is over, it may be that there will be no real need to justify a civilian pilot training program."[21]

John Taber (R.-N.Y.) objected strongly to removing the appropriation from the bill: "Just how an extension of this proposition is going to work any good without any money being provided to carry it along is beyond me," he said. "It looks to me just like an extension of life without any life. I do not like that way of approaching the problem, nor do I like that way of handling the Government's business." In response, Congressman Wolverton pointed out that the "Appropriations Committee can, by its study of the subject, ascertain whether there is need for its operation this coming year and can act accordingly. This bill merely permits the program to continue if the Appropriations Committee finds it advisable to appropriate funds."[22]

The issue of the length of the extension was finally settled on June 23, when the Senate and the House compromised by extending the CPTP for two years. The bill subsequently passed both houses and was signed by the president on June 30. That the bill had become law, however, did not ensure the CPTP's continuation; there was as yet no appropriation.[23]

Meanwhile, William Burden appointed a special committee comprised of John E. P. Morgan, director of the Personal Aircraft Department of the Aeronautical Chamber of Commerce; Lowell H. Swenson, director of the National Aeronautic Association; John H. Wilson, executive director of the National Aviation Trades Association; Dexter Martin, president of the National Association of State Aviation Officials; William A. Lloyd, representative of the Association of Land Grant Colleges; Francis I. Brown of the American Educational Council; and Walter C. Eells, executive secretary of the American Association of Junior Colleges. The group met on July 8 to study the place of the CPTP in a peacetime setting. Of primary concern was a justification for the program's existence after the war that would satisfy Congress sufficiently to provide an appropriation.[24]

Although members of the committee had discussed extending the CPTP's influence into the high schools, the group recommended that the program be confined to the college level. The decision was largely because of the committee's awareness that an ambitious CPTP would not be underwritten by a postwar Congress that, in all probability, would be stingy with funds. Subsequent meetings failed to produce a consensus about what kind of report the committee should submit to the legislators. However, the group felt that the program would best be sold to Congress on the basis of its impact on national defense rather than on economic grounds as had been advocated earlier by Geisse and Williams.[25]

The Burden Committee's decision may have been a tactical error. When the CAA submitted its request for an appropriation of $11.7 million for the CPTP in fiscal year 1946, the Bureau of the Budget rejected it. The bureau's action was prompted by the executive branch's mood of fiscal austerity; nothing except essential defense-related expenditures could be funded. By fiscal year 1947, the CAA had reduced its appropriation request for the CPTP to $3 million, yet the Budget Bureau denied the request again. On May 22, 1946, shortly before the enabling legislation for the Civilian Pilot Training Program (Public Law 39) was scheduled to run out, Senator McCarran again proposed legislation (S.2227) to the Committee on Commerce to extend the program, but this time no action was taken and the idea was never revived.[26]

The failure to gain an appropriation that would enable the CPTP to continue after the war was because of several reasons. In the broader context of events, the two-year period (roughly from mid-1944 to mid-1946) in which Congress could have provided such an appropriation was marked by the last, critical fifteen months of the war and the troublesome first nine months of the postwar era.

During the fifteen-month period, the Roosevelt administration and Congress, in the midst of a presidential election year, were largely preoccupied with matters relating to ending the war. In the succeeding nine months, the Truman administration and Congress were kept exceedingly busy coping with the labor unrest that swept the country in the wake of cancellations of government contracts, a shrinking work week, and the end of payments for overtime.[27]

The plethora of national problems diverted attention from the issue of private aviation. Congress and the Roosevelt and Truman administrations had more important issues to deal with than the continuation of the Civilian Pilot Training Program. More important, however, the CAA and the CPTP lobby groups again found themselves at cross-purposes over how best to convince Congress that the program was in the best interests of the country. The perception, especially in Congress's view, of the CPTP as a wartime mobilization program that did not need to be carried on after the war was reinforced by the Burden Committee's insistence on promoting the CPTP's continuation as a national defense measure. Taking its cue from the Burden Committee, the NATA began to lobby for an integrated, civil-military pilot training program that would incorporate elements of ROTC and make use of CPTP-WTS facilities on college campuses and in nearby communities. The NATA also recommended that a joint training committee, comprised of army, navy, and CAA representatives, be formed to plan such an integrated program.[28]

The AAF and the navy had other ideas. Even before the end of the war, the two forces had been locked in debate over the structure of the postwar military force. The controversy focused on the questions of whether the armed forces should be unified into a single entity of combined land, sea, and air forces and whether the AAF should be made a separate and coequal branch of the armed forces. The navy objected to both proposals because it believed that if a unified armed forces were created, the navy would lose its identity. If the AAF were made separate and coequal, the navy might lose its own ship-based and land-based air arm to the AAF. The AAF, on the other hand, favored both proposals because it believed that either would ensure that its hard-won identity as separate and distinct from the army would continue after the war. Because each service was so intent on establishing and maintaining its postwar individuality, there was little chance that the NATA's joint training plan would ever be adopted.[29]

The AAF was especially single-minded about maintaining autonomy and pushed hard for status as a separate branch of the armed forces. In testimony before the Senate Military Affairs Committee, Lieutenant General James H. Doolittle summed up the AAF's view when he stressed the importance of keeping "the training, the doctrine, the thinking and the habits of the men who we will train to fight the next war" under the control of a single entity. Allied with this thinking was an Army Air Forces' postwar summary of wartime training: "it has been the AAF's policy to conduct as much of its own training as possible at schools located near its own air fields." The rationale for doing so, the report pointed out, was that "normally, it was easier to give military and physical instruction and to supervise the life of the students outside the classroom in schools at such locations." The report also justified the expansion of hundreds of airfields around the country and the expenditure of "hundreds of millions of dollars" for that purpose between 1939 and 1943. Civilian facilities for training, the report pointed out, were used to meet wartime emergency needs, when the emphasis was on quantity rather than quality. Given such considerations, the idea of civilian interference in such an integral part of AAF affairs as training was entirely out of the question. There was little evidence that the AAF's thinking on the matter would change after the war.[30]

Although no direct evidence exists that either service sabotaged the continuation of the CPTP, the War Department and the navy had been opposed to extending the program early in 1944 and had informed Congress of their decision. Secretary of War Henry L. Stimson based his objection on the Bureau of the Budget's advice that the bill "should not, at this time, be considered as being in accord with the program of the President." Secretary of the Navy Frank Knox rejected the idea on similar grounds.[31]

The CAA, however, believed that the AAF was putting obstacles in the path of a renewed postwar CPTP. At the House Interstate and Foreign Commerce Committee hearings, Charles Stanton and R. McLean Stewart testified that the AAF was opposed to continuing the CPTP because it favored its own program of pilot instruction based on compulsory military service. Stanton also testified that recent AAF attempts to recruit high school students were a "plain indication that the Army sees the necessity of looking ahead to a continuous flow" of pilots.[32]

In spite of its long-term plans for a strong and independent organization after World War II, demobilization, as Alfred Goldberg points out, "seriously disrupted the Air Force's training establishment. . . . During the first eight months of 1945, the Air Force graduated each month an average of more than 20,000 flyers—pilots, navigators, bombardiers, radar observers, and gunners—but this figure fell to 322 in December 1945."[33] This drop in pilot production steeled the AAF's resolve to lobby for perpetuation of its own training programs after the end of the war. By July 1946, Carl A. Spaatz, the new commanding general of the Army Air Forces, informed his predecessor General Arnold that for fiscal year 1947 the AAF planned to mobilize 120 air reserve bases and "to actively train 22,500 pilot officers, 27,500 non pilot officers, and 120,000 enlisted personnel." Such ambitious plans provided further proof that the AAF's policy of conducting its own training would be strictly followed after the war.[34]

The parochialism of the AAF and the navy in regard to a joint training committee that included Civil Aeronautics Administration representatives, coupled with the ideas that postwar pilot training programs conducted by the military services were sufficient and that the CPTP's efforts toward national defense would be largely superfluous, operated against continuation of the CPTP. Yet the Burden Committee would probably not have been any more successful in

getting an appropriation had it taken the obvious alternative of trying to obtain funding for the program as a strictly economic stimulus
to private aviation. By 1946, New Deal-type spending for economic
stimulation was virtually dead, having been displaced as early as
1941 by economic mobilization in preparation for war. Added to this
was the fact that the G.I. Bill of Rights provided financial aid to returning veterans who wanted to learn to fly, and, as *National Aeronautics* put it, "a latent attitude [on the part of Congress and the
Bureau of the Budget] that the wartime crop of something near a
half-million pilots should be enough to last for a while."[35]

Perhaps even more significant was the spirit of postwar financial
austerity in which the CPTP appears to have been caught and from
which it could not escape. In April 1946, after again excluding the
CPTP from the Commerce Department's budget for fiscal year 1947,
the House Committee on Appropriations, warned the departments of
State, Commerce, and Justice about the need to curtail expenditures.
"There seems to have developed during the war years," the committee observed, "what some have termed a 'spending psychology' and
the committee is fearful that this spending psychology has become
somewhat too deeply entrenched in the minds of the officials responsible for the operation of our Federal establishments. It must be
eliminated."[36]

The CPTP appears to have been one of many aviation programs
that were either starved of funds or denied enabling legislation by
the frugal 79th Congress. Concerned that aviation spokesmen were
ineffective in supporting legislation that would benefit the industry,
National Aeronautics pointed out in its January 1947 issue that out
of "113 bills or resolutions affecting aviation introduced in both
House and Senate . . . only nine were enacted." Although these figures were exaggerated because some of the legislation was duplica-
tive, it is clear that the 79th Congress was willing to pass only those
laws relating to aviation that it considered essential, i.e., federal aid
to airports, lowering the postage rate on domestic air mail, theft of
aircraft, and establishing meteorological observation stations in the
Arctic region.[37]

Thus, the CPTP again had again encountered the civilian-military
dichotomy. Having succeeding in surviving by adapting the CPTP to
the needs of the armed forces in wartime, proponents such as William Burden and the members of his committee erroneously believed that another accommodation with the military after the war
would prolong the program. However, the jurisdictional struggle between the AAF and the navy precluded any chance of the CAA's

becoming involved in postwar pilot training. Moreover, it is unlikely that in the atmosphere of postwar fiscal austerity the program would have succeeded in obtaining funds had it been promoted as an economic stimulus to the private aviation industry. The economic climate had changed markedly between 1939 and 1944, and the program's supporters, caught between two alternatives, simply could not mount an effective campaign to justify the CPTP's existence.

Conclusion

Spanning the years from 1939 to 1946, the Civilian Pilot Training Program evolved during a tumultuous time in American history, an era marked by economic crisis and recovery, war preparedness, war mobilization, and postwar adjustment. The pivotal event during this period was World War II, which put an end to Roosevelt's sweeping New Deal program of economic recovery, reform, and long-range planning. More important, the war shifted the administration away from purely domestic considerations toward those of foreign policy, war preparedness, and, eventually, all-out mobilization. The shift not only brought the CPTP into being, but also had an enormous impact on it for a considerable part of its existence.

One could argue that the Civilian Pilot Training Program went through three distinct stages, all influenced by the needs and requirements of the military. In the first, or New Deal, era from January 1939 to late 1940, policy and expectations were based largely on civilian goals, but the program began to be criticized severely for not contributing substantially to military preparedness. In the second, or war-preparedness and mobilization, era, policy and goals were increasingly directed toward military ends. This meant that the CPTP's initial decentralized approach, with administrative power and functions residing largely in the colleges and universities where the training was taking place, gradually gave way to centralized control by the military. In the third, or postwar, era, the program languished, not only because its goals were ill-defined and unreasonable expectations were placed on it, but also because these goals were perceived to be in conflict with military programs of a similar nature.

During its first period the CPTP reflected basic New Deal socioeconomic goals thought to be ostensibly in concert with those of the military. The first goal was based on the idea that government should subsidize vocational education. Subsidiary to this idea was the belief that aviation was, and would continue to be, so important to the social and cultural fabric of the United States that it should fall within the area of those subsidies. Through a college and university-based system of training in conjunction with local flight schools, the CPTP would provide such vocational education.

The second goal was based on the New Deal plan to provide economic help to industries affected by the depression. By increasing the number of pilots, the CPTP would speed recovery of the private flying industry, a long-ignored sector of aviation, and provide work for fixed-base aviation operators, the owners of flight schools and flying fields at which the CPTP would be conducted. The third goal was based on the New Deal idea of long-range economic planning. By accomplishing its other objectives, the CPTP would provide the basis for private aviation's long-term economic development after the war.

To a great extent, however, military considerations were as instrumental in the inception of the CPTP as New Deal socioeconomic thinking. At the same time that it was to fulfill its New Deal mandates, the CPTP, as part of its war-preparedness and mobilization mandate, was also to provide a ready supply of military pilots in time of emergency. This goal was based on the notions that airplanes would be important in a future war and a pool of trained pilots would play a significant part in America's war-preparedness efforts.

The dichotomous nature of the CPTP can be seen as a attempt by the Roosevelt administration to take preliminary steps toward war preparedness and provide for the country's peacetime economic needs. Because considerable isolationist sentiment existed during the earliest days of the CPTP, F.D.R. was reluctant to commit the country to all-out mobilization. By meeting peacetime and wartime needs, the CPTP was intended to bridge New Deal economic policy and the inevitable preparation for war.

Adding to its complexity was the fact that the CPTP was the last in a long line of controversial, incoherent, and often ill-conceived prewar aviation policies that the New Deal had promoted since 1933. By 1939, the CPTP's first year of operation, the New Deal had failed to win any segment of the aviation community. From its beginning the CPTP struggled to enlist support among important sectors of the aviation industry, the military, and Congress.

Although at its outset the CPTP faced a long, uphill battle in Congress, the opportunities it presented for reviving private aviation, as well as the need for American preparedness, convinced most doubters. After a highly successful demonstration program in late 1939, the full-scale CPTP got underway with good first-year results. An allied program of educational and psychological research into the best methods of selecting and training pilots, which began in 1941, was similarly productive. Although admirable, other initiatives that were in resonance with New Deal thought—such as the air age education program designed to prepare American youth for the coming age of aviation, the congressionally mandated inclusion of blacks into the program, and the short-lived attempt to make the program available to women—produced mixed results.

One of the most important New Deal aspects of the program—economic stimulation of the lightplane industry—produced less than favorable results. Light aircraft manufacturers did benefit, albeit briefly, from the CPTP in the years before America's entry into World War II. Lightplane (aircraft defined as costing less than $2,000 and/or weighing less than 1,300 pounds gross weight) production jumped more than 400 percent—from 2,851 between 1933 and 1937 to 13,797 between 1938 and 1941—largely as a result of the CPTP and the increasing number of private pilots and fixed-base operations necessary to train them.[1]

Yet, the industry was already on the upswing by 1939, and most of the gains that resulted from the CPTP were confined to three major lightplane manufacturers: Piper (which by far received the most benefits), Aeronca, and Taylorcraft. In the three years before Pearl Harbor, Piper sold 8,020 of the 17,727 aircraft listed in the private category by the industry, a prodigious 45 percent of the market.[2]

During its five-year span, the CPTP only partly lived up to Robert Hinckley's ideal to permanently air condition young Americans to "a three-dimensional world." Air conditioning was one of the cultural manifestations of the CPTP, an idea that had a New Deal impetus and was an integral part of what Joseph Corn has termed the "gospel of aviation." Aviation advocates had pursued this idea almost religiously since powered flight began. The gospel promulgated the notion that aviation, once it realized its full potential, would be of inestimable benefit to society, and that airplanes would bring about fundamental beneficial changes in American life.[3]

Air conditioning had two focuses. The first was the pilot training carried on by the CPTP, which was intended to provide government-sponsored vocational education in aviation in much the same way as the National Youth Administration's college assistance program provided grants for college educations. The second was the air age education movement that gave youngsters a thorough grounding in matters related to aviation so they would be prepared for the coming age of the airplane.[4]

Because the program had existed for only a year when critics began to complain that it was not contributing to the "national defense," it is unfair to judge its effectiveness in producing civilian pilots. If, however, the three-year period from July 1, 1939 to June 30, 1942 is examined, we see that the CPTP trained 125,762 pilots, including 13,094 flight instructors and 3,565 commercial pilots. Regrettably, there is no adequate way of correlating these figures to determine how many pilots the CPTP added to the total number of private pilots in the United States. However, a CAA report determined that, largely as a result of the CPTP, the number of private pilots increased "101.9 percent from 1939 to 1940, and 59.7 percent from 1940 to 1941, compared with gains of 36.0 percent from 1938 to 1939, and 30.0 percent from 1937 to 1938."[5]

It is reasonable to assume that had the war not intervened, the CPTP would have continued to turn out private pilots successfully and provide a prolonged economic stimulus to private aviation. This assumption, however, largely misses the point. The program was not intended solely to train private pilots, but also to make them available to the military in an emergency. When the need for preparedness became critical in late 1940, the CPTP's success in training civilian pilots was of no consequence to the critics who complained that it failed to provide them in sufficient numbers to the armed forces. Thus, the program's dual nature was its strength and its undoing. Just as it began to demonstrate its effectiveness in accomplishing one of its primary goals, its mandate began to change from a civilian to a military one, and so did the criteria upon which it was judged.

The second focus of air conditioning, the air age education movement, which began in 1942 and reached an estimated quarter of a million American youths during the peak years of World War II, lost much of its immediacy once the war ended. Although some form of aviation education continued in American schools well into the 1960s, by 1949, the CAA's Aviation Education Division, the institutional umbrella for air age education, had been absorbed into the agency's Office of Aviation Development. This was a clear sign that the CAA had lost interest in air age education as a federally supported program after World War II.[6]

Moreover, as Joseph Corn has pointed out, the use of aviation to teach geography, social science, physics, and English, as well as the number of in-service training courses for teachers after the war, declined noticeably. Perhaps the most telling sign that air age education was no longer practical in American schools was that "in the three years after 1947," half as many articles on the subject were published in education journals as had appeared "during the three years from 1944 to 1947." From 1950 to 1953, "a third fewer still" were written.[7]

The second period of the CPTP ran from late 1940 until its termination in 1944. This era was marked by a gradual and unsystematic change in policy that attempted to tailor the program more strictly to military requirements. In the latter part of 1940, as the crisis in Europe worsened and American war preparations became more critical, the dichotomy between the program's New Deal agenda and its war preparedness became more pronounced. It was continually criticized for its alleged failure to produce sufficient candidates for military pilot training, and the program began to make subtle adjustments to bring itself into line with military needs. Robert Hinckley, however, who chafed at having to justify the CPTP's existence as a civilian-based program, argued that it did provide quantities of men for the armed forces and that these men were better equipped for military flight training than their counterparts who had not been trained by the CPTP.

The burgeoning conflict with the military about what the CPTP could reasonably be expected to do in its war-preparedness role and yet still maintain its civilian trappings would later pose more serious problems. As time went on and the United States entered World War II, the CPTP's conflict with the military widened into a jurisdictional dispute between the Army Air Forces and the Civil Aeronautics Administration over control of civil aeronautics. The CPTP was in a quandary. It was a civilian program that somehow had to demonstrate its worth to the military as a legitimate method of providing pilots to the armed forces. The Army Air Forces did not believe that the CPTP could or should be adapted to military use and continually procrastinated over how to integrate the program's nationwide network of facilities into the AAF's pilot training system. Complicating matters was the attitude of General Henry H. "Hap" Arnold, chief of the Army Air Forces, who adamantly defended the AAF's right not only to control civil aviation in wartime, but also to train its own pilots as it saw fit without outside interference.

Nevertheless, CAA officials and the Army Air Forces agreed in mid-1942 that the CPTP would train AAF enlisted reserve personnel as noncombat pilots for a variety of duties—as instructors, ferry, liaison, and glider pilots and as commercial pilots for Air Transport Command—but not for combat. In contrast, the navy did allow CPTP trainees to qualify as combat pilots and used the program effectively to screen those who were unfit for pilot duty.

Meanwhile, Robert Hinckley, who had laid the groundwork for the CPTP, ushered it through Congress, and seen it through its first two-and-three-quarters years of operation, resigned as assistant secretary of commerce for air in mid-1942 to join the Sperry Corporation. The last vestiges of New Deal influence in the program had disappeared. As a result, the military's hold over the CPTP became stronger. A new cast of characters—William A. M. Burden, R. McLean Stewart, and Robert Lovett—all with strong Wall Street banking backgrounds and equally strong ties to the business community, took over policymaking. Unlike Hinckley, who had resisted militarizing the CPTP, these men set about to ensure that the program would become more responsive to the need to turn out vast quantities of pilots for the armed forces. As if to mirror that transformation, the program's name was changed in late 1942 to the War Training Service.

Part of the drive to make the Civilian Pilot Training Program-War Training Service more compatible with military needs and more efficient was the tendency of the Army Air Forces to award training contracts to large aviation schools and consolidate training. This practice, which began in 1943, contributed to transforming the CPTP from a civilian to a military program. It is likely that, more than any other factor, the redirection of training resources altered the program's emphasis from Hinckley's original New Deal, educational conception that would provide economic stimulus to private aviation.

Despite these changes, the program continued to encounter difficulties: another agreement between the Army Air Forces and the Civil Aeronautics Administration in January 1943 that added further conditions and stipulations and institutionalized the military aspects of the program; subsequent disputes with the AAF over payment of men in enlisted reserve status; settlement of whether the CAA would continue to maintain administrative and budgetary control of the program; and, perhaps most serious, shortages of training aircraft and spare parts. These problems were eventually solved, and the program continued through 1943. Yet despite the fact that during fiscal years 1943 and 1944 the CPTP-WTS trained thousands of military pilots, the Army Air Forces decided that the program's results were insufficient and requested that it be evaluated. Requirements for trained pilots had lessened, and the AAF perceived that maintaining the CPTP-WTS was not in its best interest. Early in 1944, the navy ended its agreement with the CPTP-WTS, and shortly afterward the AAF followed suit.

How effective, then, was the CPTP-WTS during this phase of its existence? The nagging question of how many pilots were provided to the military before the war—a question that initially arose in late 1940 and was then raised repeatedly by critics—was never completely resolved. Despite the claims of the Civil Aeronautics Administration and the counterclaims of the Army Air Forces and the navy, authoritative figures were never made available on the number of men who enlisted that were trained by the CPTP. Even the CAA, in a postmortem on the wartime role of the CPTP, could only estimate that—of the 108,349 enrolled from fiscal year 1940 through fiscal year 1942 (July 1, 1939 to June 30, 1942)—42,026 "enlisted in either the Army Air Forces or the Naval Reserve for further flight training." If these statistics are accurate, the rate of enlistment was considerably less than 50 percent.[8]

To criticize the program for not providing sufficient numbers of military pilots is unjustified, however. After all, before Pearl Harbor the CPTP was entirely civilian, with no legally binding stipulation that trainees enlist in the armed forces. Moreover, it was intended to be a war-preparedness program, and in 1940, when the United States became increasingly conscious of the impending conflict, its failure to provide men in great numbers was the source of considerable friction between the CAA and the military.

The CPTP may not have provided the military with as many pilots as it could have in prewar days, yet according to the CAA's seemingly reliable statistics the men it did provide were better prepared for military aviation training than those who had not been through CPTP courses. Moreover, they were less likely to fail than individuals who had not taken CPTP training. One must inevitably conclude that before the war began, the CPTP was good preparation for military aviation. In the flurry of mobilization, however, quantity seemed to be more important than quality.

Yet during fiscal years 1943 and 1944, after the program had been redesigned to accommodate the needs of the military, statistics on the number of pilots that the CPTP-WTS produced are impressive. It trained 55,348 Army Air Corps enlisted reservists in a variety of pilot specialties. This figure was nearly doubled for the navy—105,000 officers, aviation cadets, and enlisted men. In contrast to the AAF, which spent $31,021,685 of its own funds on the program in fiscal years 1943 and 1944, the navy spent more than double that amount—$66,687,758—during the same period. The navy's favorable experience in using the CPTP-WTS to give preliminary training to its combat pilots suggests that the program might have been equally successful in training AAF combat pilots had the air force chosen to use it in such a way.[9]

The program grew at a remarkable pace during the war. From fiscal year 1942 to fiscal year 1943 (July 1, 1941 to June 30, 1943), the CPTP-WTS budget increased from $27 million to $108,229,423. The number of hours flown in CPTP-WTS programs nearly doubled, going from 1,857,860 to 3,648,950, and the number of trainees jumped 177 percent, from 40,096 to 111,140. From fiscal year 1943 to fiscal year 1944 (July 1, 1942 to June 30, 1944), as the program began to wind down, the WTS budget decreased from $108,229,423 to $97,125,802. The number of hours flown increased only slightly, from 3,648,950 to 3,842,970. During the same period, the number of trainees increased more than 94 percent, from 111,140 to 215,676.[10] From fiscal year 1940 to fiscal year 1944 (July 1, 1939 to June 30, 1944), the program consumed $273,355,255 in budget, accumulated 11,889,442 flight hours, and trained 435,165 men. This amounts to an average individual expenditure of $628.16 per person trained. In view of the 288 billion dollars expended by the United States during World War II, the approximately two-and-three-quarter million spent on the CPTP-WTS seems modest.[11]

The final period of the CPTP ran from early 1944 to mid 1946. Now, proponents grappled with the questions of how it could shift back to the older civilian goals that had led to its creation and whether it could survive demobilization. Early in 1944, active lobbying for the CPTP's continuation began by the Civil Aeronautics Administration, which had sponsored the program; the fixed-base operators, who had provided the training; the colleges and universities at which the program had been based; and congressional supporters of aviation, all of whom had seen the wartime economic benefits of the program.

Other considerations came into play, however. One of the most important stemmed from the postwar manifestation of the gospel of aviation. Despite the destruction wrought by the airplane in World War II, the gospel lingered; its adherents postulated that postwar prosperity would bring with it "an airplane in every garage." Although the war had interrupted the thrust of the CPTP's attempt to fulfill its New Deal mandate—training young Americans to be civilian pilots—individuals who promoted airplanes as a form of personal transportation hoped that the CPTP would resume such training after the war and thus breathe new life into private flying.[12]

Nevertheless, when pressed to provide a rationale for the CPTP's postwar existence, advocates turned away from its prewar goals:

widened public participation in aviation, air conditioning youth, and the economic stimulation of private flying. They again attempted to accommodate the CPTP to the military by promoting it as a postwar national defense measure. This crucial tactical error, coupled with the parochialism of the military in wanting to maintain its own flight training programs and the fiscal austerity of the immediate postwar period, made efforts of the program's backers only partially successful. The CPTP legislation was extended for a two-year period but failed to get an appropriation from Congress during that time.

The steady stream of private pilots provided by a postwar CPTP might indeed have increased the demand for private flying in the United States. Nevertheless, in *Postwar Outlook for Private Flying* Geisse and Williams suggest that the prewar CPTP tended to stimulate interest in non-CPTP flight training rather than detract from it. Had this trend continued after the war, even without a renewed CPTP, more than four hundred thousand former CPTP-WTS trainees could have provided a needed impetus for private flying by buying airplanes and getting other people interested in taking flying lessons and purchasing airplanes. This did not happen, however.

Thus, the residual effect of the CPTP was not a factor in producing a long-term stimulation of private flying in the United States. Although the number of certified private pilots did grow from 189,156 in 1946, to 244,270 in 1947, to 306,699 in 1948, the production of personal airplanes peaked at 34,568 in 1946 before dropping to 15,339 in 1947 and 7,039 in 1948. After 1948 and through the mid-1950s, production hovered at little more than three thousand personal airplanes a year. The increasing numbers of pilots did not stimulate a corresponding demand for aircraft.[13]

Moreover, one could argue that even a renewed postwar CPTP might not have been as significant an impetus as had been predicted given the other significant problems that confronted private flying. Unlike CAA promoters and prognosticators, the social scientist William Fielding Ogburn provided a less sanguine and more accurate view of the prospects for private flying in *The Social Effects of Aviation* (1946). Ogburn predicted correctly that, after the war, private flying would be done "by the professional and semi-professional pilot rather than the average citizen." Moreover, despite simplified controls, the piloting of small planes would require skill, and "the early helicopters will not be easy to fly or to handle in emergencies." Finally, Ogburn predicted that individuals likely to purchase light aircraft and helicopters would most probably be "businessmen, taxi and non-scheduled air firms, agricultural, mining, and fishery companies, and governments which will hire trained pilots." The use of light aircraft would be restricted to "dusting and spraying insecticides . . . patrolling forests, fighting fires, inspecting cattle ranges, transporting occasional passengers and sight-seers, Coast Guard work, emergency rescues, photographic mapping, ambulance work, deliveries by department stores, for gathering news, and for training pilots."[14] As Ogburn points out, the "growth in the number of planes from 1939 to 1941 was the result of the stimulation of the Civilian Pilot Training program." However, "the fourteen-year period between 1929 and 1942 shows an average increase of 7 per cent a year. In comparison, the growth of the number of automobiles for the thirteen years after the number had reached 8000 was at a rate of 47 per cent a year." These statistics suggest strongly that private airplanes would probably never have competed seriously with automobiles as a means of personal transportation.[15]

There are still other reasons for the failure of private aviation to live up to its postwar potential. Ogburn noted that, according to Geisse and Williams, a survey of private plane owners from 1931 to 1939 revealed that "the mean period of ownership of planes for 83 per cent of the owners was less than 2.5 years." This statistic would seem to suggest that airplane owners, for whatever reasons, tired of their craft after a short period. Unlike automobile owners, however, who trade their cars in periodically, aircraft owners simply gave up flying.[16]

Ogburn also observed that private flying was thought to be expensive, inconvenient, and less useful and pleasurable than anticipated. For example, 55 to 60 percent of respondents to a study done for the CAA in 1940 stated that they had given up flying "for financial reasons." Besides the purchase price of the aircraft, which Ogburn (according to figures provided by Geisse and Williams) placed at between $1,164 and $61,000 before the war, owners also had extensive operating costs. The annual cost for a $2,000 light airplane, for example, would range from $8.50 for two hundred hours of operation to $11.50 for a hundred hours. These expenditures included direct operating costs, hangar fees, depreciation, and insurance. Geisse and Williams, however, failed to take into account such other costs as fuel and oil, maintenance, overhaul, delay expense (weather, mechanical failure, refueling and inspection), and ground transportation expenses. Other respondents stated that the time spent in going to and from the airport "decreased the utility of the plane to too large an extent to make its use worth while" or that the pleasure derived from flying the plane "was less than anticipated."[17]

Moreover, Ogburn cited fear as a limiting factor in personal airplane operation. Although "the number of accidents per 1,000,000 miles of private flying decreased from 18.8 in 1930 to 13.1 in 1940, a 30 per cent decrease, the accident rate for private flying in 1940 was still higher than that in scheduled air operations; there were 13 accidents per 1,000,000 miles flown in private flying in 1940 as compared with .45 in scheduled operations." According to Civil Aeronautics Board statistics, 59 percent of these accidents took place during takeoff or landing, 13 percent during taxiing, and 3 percent while the aircraft was in a stall or spin.[18]

Ogburn also cited another survey taken in 1944 by Edward G. Doody for Parks Air College, one of the largest flight schools in the country. The survey attempted to get at "some of the reasons given for not planning to take up flying after the war." Nearly 28 percent of the respondents cited "indifference" as the primary reason; next came fear (24 percent), impracticality (18 percent), and age and physical fitness (13 percent). In contrast to the prewar survey, only a fraction of the respondents cited expense.[19] Doody's survey demonstrates a trend among the great numbers of pilots who were veterans. Twenty-four percent cited fear as a determining factor in not wanting to fly after the war.

The figure of 24 percent may have been modest considering studies conducted by Douglas D. Bond. An Army Air Forces psychiatrist in World War II and, later, a professor of psychiatry and head of the medical school at Western Reserve University, Bond investigated fear and anxiety among pilots and combat crews of the 8th Air Force. In *The Love and Fear of Flying*, Bond cited the example of a peacetime airline passenger, who upon seeing an airplane "crash and burn, and then, despite the availability of another aircraft, decide[s] to go by train." One would have to "commend him on his good sense." In wartime, however, "such a decision on the part of a flyer, no matter how recently he may have been a civilian, is capable of bringing down upon his head all kinds of unpleasantness and punishments. Such fears constituted the greatest single cause for the elimination of flyers following their training and before they entered combat, and were second only to battle wounds in necessitating long-term 'grounding' in the largest combat air force ever assembled."[20]

Bond's point is instructive. "Because civilian flying is very safe compared to service flying, those factors in the minds of flyers which are thrown into such sharp relief by the circumstances of combat will not be so clearly seen in civilian flight. There is little doubt, however, that the same factors are at work." Veterans of combat flying who had seen or experienced accidents were predisposed to be anxious about flying, and such a predisposition can cause accidents. From Bond's comments, it is reasonable to assume that returning airmen stayed away from private flying because of anxiety or fear based on wartime experiences. Moreover, it is likely that once these airmen were removed from circumstances in which they were forced to fly, many rejected the opportunity to fly voluntarily and for pleasure or recreation.[21]

The welter of restrictive and often irrational CAA regulations that had grown up in the interest of public and pilot safety also worked against private flying. Theodore P. Wright, a CAA administrator who sensed the need to uncomplicate licensing and registration procedures, took several steps to alleviate the problem and make it easier for average people to obtain pilot's licenses. One requirement that was set aside was that mandating pilot trainees to learn navigation and meteorology, information akin to learning how automobile engines worked in order to obtain a driver's license. Easing these strictures, however, was experimental and lasted only a few years.[22]

Another important factor was the shortage of landing places for private aircraft. In testimony before the Senate's Committee on Commerce in March 1945, William T. Piper, head of the largest lightplane manufacturer in the United States and executive committee member of the Personal Aircraft Council of the Aeronautical Chamber of Commerce, asserted that "the need . . . is for legislation that will permit the construction of the largest number of landing facilities possible quickly, cheaply, and in convenient or accessible locations. . . . Every community (in the land)—all 16,752 of them—should be encouraged to provide a convenient and economical landing facility immediately." Piper argued for airparks (airports with complete facilities for private aircraft with hangars as well as fuel and repair facilities); flightstops (abundant landing places along highways); and air harbors (landing facilities for float planes and amphibian aircraft).[23]

Although then-CAA administrator Wright was a promoter of private aviation, precious few airports of the type Piper described were ever built. The comprehensive $1.25 billion National Airport Plan, submitted to Congress by the CAA in November 1944, set aside 39 percent of its budget for new, small airports to serve private pilots. The CAA, however, sold the massive program to Congress as a public works project—to act as a hedge against a postwar economic downturn—and as a national defense measure. When the anticipated postwar recession did not take place, Congress's enthusiasm for the proposal waned because it appeared that its public works aspect was no longer unnecessary. Perhaps more important is that small, private airports lost funding to large commercial airports that had potential for military use during a national emergency.[24]

Perhaps the most critical limiting factor to the projected growth of private aviation after the war was the lack of an inexpensive, safe aircraft. Eugene Vidal's proposal for a $700 aircraft, for example, had run into trouble on many fronts. Fred Weick's Ercoupe, a two-place, simplified control aircraft developed before the war and designed with the average person in mind, did not attract sufficient attention, and the company that manufactured it, Engineering and Research Corporation, soon went out of business. Piper designed three aircraft—the Sky Coupe, the Skycycle, and the Sky Sedan—expressly for the hypothetical mass market, yet they never reached production. The manufacture of other mass-market aircraft such as the North American Navion and the Republic Seabee, built by larger aircraft companies attempting to break into private aviation, was discontinued after a few years of poor sales.[25]

Tied in with safety, strict regulation of private flying, and the lack of landing facilities and an affordable, safe airplane was the inadequacy of the air traffic control system. As John R. M. Wilson has accurately pointed out, before the war "there was enough space so that disputes were rare and easily settled, but the rapid development of military aviation and of the air industry in general began to crowd the skies by the mid-forties and increase friction between users." This crowding and friction continued well beyond the war, as the CAA and military aviation fought jurisdictional battles for control of the airways. One can only imagine the demands placed on the air traffic control system had the postwar boom, with its expected 450,000 private aircraft, come to pass. In view of the air traffic control problems that still plague the airways, it is doubtful that the system would have been capable of handling it or of growing to meet demands.

Finally, CAA prognosticators such as Geisse and Williams, whose optimistic report was published well before the conclusion of World

War II, failed to anticipate that public attitudes toward private flying might be negative after the war. Two significant polls taken in 1946 show a marked contrast to Edward G. Doody's low estimate of public indifference toward private flying after World War II (28 percent of those polled in Doody's survey cited indifference). The first, taken in January by *Fortune* magazine, asked, "Do you think you will ever want to learn to pilot a plane?" Overwhelmingly, 74.2 percent of respondents answered negatively. Even the majority (59.2 percent) of those from twenty-one to thirty-four answered no.[26]

The second poll, taken in April 1946 by the American Institute of Public Opinion, asked similar questions and yielded similar results. Sixty-nine percent of respondents replied negatively to "Would you like to learn to fly an airplane?" Of those queried in the twenty-one to twenty-nine-year-old age bracket, the vote was close: 50 percent yes and 47 percent no. Of people from thirty to forty-nine, however, negative answers outnumbered positive, 68 to 28 percent.[27] Thus, even if the CPTP had survived the war, it probably would not have been a significant factor in bringing about the expected postwar boom in private aviation.

More than forty years after the conclusion of the CPTP, interest groups such as the Aircraft Owners and Pilots Association (AOPA) began to argue that a CPTP-like clone, the National Pilot Training (NPT) Program, should be created. The NPT program would foster the growth of the pilot population in the United States, which AOPA contended was shrinking rapidly because of retirements and public indifference. Advocates of such a plan cited statistics showing that the pilot population in the United States rose from approximately 733,000 in 1970 to 827,000 in 1980, but declined to slightly more than 709,000 in 1985. The number of student pilots shrank in even greater numbers than the pilot population as a whole, with significant numbers of military pilots no longer making the transition to civilian aviation.[28]

Through flight training scholarships subsidized by the federal Aviation Trust Fund (collected through levies on airfares and the sale of fuel) the program would give college students the opportunity to progress from private pilot certificates to airline pilot ratings and thus increase the pilot population. The NPT program, at least in theory, would also stimulate the demand for private flying—general aviation—in the United States. Although such a demand has never been high, individuals who advocate general aviation are concerned about lack of interest in the industry and government's refusal to help subsidize the high costs connected with flying, including those of obtaining a private pilot's license. The ideas that gave birth to the CPTP have thus come full circle.[29]

In theory, a plan like the NPT program might work, at least on one level, in providing government-subsidized pilot training. Unlike the CPTP, its energies would not be diffused by the necessity of striving for two goals, but rather would concentrate on a single objective. In their eagerness to promote the training of additional pilots, however, advocates of the NPT program seem to have disregarded the problems surrounding the infrastructure of general aviation—safety versus overly strict federal regulation, inadequate airport and landing facilities, lack of affordable aircraft, failure of the government to provide up-to-date air traffic control facilities, and an already overcrowded sky. Some of these serious problems, particularly those related to control of the sky, plague all forms of air transportation. If the past is any indication, the creation of another full-scale program like the CPTP, although perhaps a successful means of adding to the pool of pilots, would not solve more urgent problems that beset aviation. The NPT might even contribute to such problems by creating more pilots to add to the already overburdened infrastructure.

In *The American Commonwealth* (1888), the British diplomat-scholar James Bryce wrote cogently about the American form of government. "There is an excessive friction in the American system," he said, "a waste of force in the strife of various bodies and persons created to check and balance one another. . . . Power is so much subdivided that it is hard at a given moment to concentrate it for prompt and effective action."[30]

Bryce's words might well define the essential political context in which the Civilian Pilot Training Program evolved. At the outset, the CPTP's power was fragmented by the dichotomy between its New Deal and war-preparedness goals. During the war, in its various encounters with the Army Air Forces, the CPTP's power was further diminished by the demands of war and military self-interest. After the war, as proponents wavered in deciding whether to redefine its goals in terms of the prewar agenda or fit it into another military context, the CPTP's power finally ran out.

For both the New Deal and the military, the CPTP was an experiment in the compatibility of a civilian-based program with the institutional requirements of the armed forces before, during, and after a war. The program seemed always to be in conflict with those requirements and, to make matters worse, was constantly being outstripped by events. In one sense, its foibles and idiosyncrasies are characteristic of the duality forced upon it by the Roosevelt administration's measured preparations for war and, in another sense, of the demands placed upon it by the need to adjust itself time and again to changing conditions.

The CPTP's legacy was mixed. During its seven-year span, the program, as conceived by Robert Hinckley, only partially lived up to its original New Deal goals to revive private flying and air condition young Americans for the burgeoning air age. Like Eugene Vidal before him, Hinckley failed to realize the limits of federal assistance to private aviation. Despite his good intentions, his vision of the CPTP and political reality were never in alignment. Although the CPTP successfully trained military pilots during the war, America's entry into World War II altered the program beyond recognition. For a variety of reasons, some budgetary, some political, some social and cultural, the CPTP faded after the war and was never revived.

If Robert Hinckley had stayed on to guide the CPTP during and after the war, it is doubtful that even his singleminded effort to maintain a civilian focus for the program could have stemmed the tide. Besides, Hinckley had other concerns. After his stint with the Sperry Corporation, he returned to Washington in 1944 to become director of the Office of Contract Settlement. In 1946, he became one of the founders and directors of the American Broadcasting Company. Yet, his belief in the Civilian Pilot Training Program did not falter. In 1949, in honor of the tenth anniversary of the beginning of the CPTP, he wrote to several colleges and universities that had participated to request information on it from their records. His purpose was to write the history of the program. Although a partially completed draft of the manuscript exists in the Hinckley Papers at the University of Utah, the project was never finished. Sadly, Hinckley's published autobiography, which appeared in 1977, merely touches upon the CPTP. It does not do justice to the program's constant struggle to redefine itself or to its many ambiguities.[31]

The Civilian Pilot Training Program was a unique and instructive reflection of the Roosevelt administration's New Deal policy toward aviation and its efforts toward war preparedness and mobilization. In attempting to fulfill some of the New Deal's most ambitious and optimistic ideas about aviation and provide for the country's war needs, the CPTP found itself in a untenable position. Like so much of the New Deal, it became a casualty of war.

Appendixes

Public—No. 153—76th Congress
Chapter 244—First Session

An Act
to provide for the training of civil aircraft pilots, and for other purposes

Be it enacted by the Senate and House of Representatives of the United States of America in Congress assembled, That this Act may be cited as the "Civilian Pilot Training Act of 1939."

SEC. 2. The Civil Aeronautics Authority is authorized, within the limits of available appropriations made by the Congress, to train civilian pilots or to conduct programs for such training, including studies and researches as to the most desirable qualifications for aircraft pilots. Such training or programs shall be conducted pursuant to such regulations as such Authority may from time to time prescribe, including regulations requiring students participating therein to maintain appropriate insurance and to pay such laboratory or other fees for ground-school training, not exceeding $40 per student, as the Authority may deem necessary or desirable;

Provided, That in the administration of this Act, none of the benefits of training or programs shall be denied on account of race, creed, or color. Such training or programs may be carried out either through the use of the facilities and personnel of the Authority or by contracts with educational institutions or other persons (as defined in section 1 (27) of the Civil Aeronautics Act of 1938).

SEC. 3. At least 5 per centum of the students selected for training under this Authority shall be selected from applicants other than college students.

SEC. 4. The Authority is authorized to lease or accept loans of such real property, and to purchase, lease, exchange, or accept loans of such personal property, as may be necessary or desirable for carrying out the provisions of this Act.

SEC. 5. For the purposes of carrying out its functions under this Act, the Authority is authorized to exercise all powers conferred upon it by the Civil Aeronautics Act of 1938 and to appoint and fix the compensation of experienced instructors, airmen, medical and other professional examiners and experts in training and research without regard to the provisions of other laws applicable to the employment and compensation of officers and employees of the United States. The provisions of section 3709 of the Revised Statutes shall not apply to contracts with educational institutions and other persons for the use of aircraft or other facilities or for the performance of services authorized by section 2 of this Act.

SEC. 6. Any executive department of independent establishment is hereby authorized to cooperate with the Authority in carrying out the purposes of this Act, and for such purposes may lend or transfer to the Authority, by contract or otherwise, or if so requested by the Authority, lend to educational institutions or other persons cooperating with the Authority in the conduct of any such training or program, civilian officials, or employees, aircraft and other property or equipment, and lands or buildings under its control and in excess of its own requirements.

SEC. 7. There is hereby authorized the sum of $5,675,000 for the purpose of carrying out the provisions of this Act during the fiscal years 1939 and 1940 and not to exceed the sum of $7,000,000 during each subsequent fiscal year. This Act shall expire on July 1, 1944, and all contracts, leases, or other obligations entered into under this Act shall expire on or prior to such date:

Provided, That no alien shall receive training under the provisions of this Act.

Approved, June 27, 1939.

Controlled Private Flying Course
CPTP Demonstration Program

(Source: *Air Commerce Bulletin*, March 15, 1939, 232–33.)

Preliminary Ground Instruction.

I. Thorough familiarization with functioning of airplane, controls and instruments:
   (a) Starting.
   (b) Warming up.
   (c) Stopping engines.
   (d) Warnings:
      1. Danger from propellers.
      2. Difference between ground and air speed.
      3. Parking plane during strong wind.
      4. Running engine with no one in the cockpit.
   NOTE.—The above is ground instruction given before the actual dual time is started.

Stage A. Dual Instruction—8 Hours.

II. Taxiing to proficiency:
   (a) Handling plane.
      1. Into wind.
      2. Cross wind.
      3. Down wind.
      4. Gusty air.
III. Take-offs:
   (a) Into wind.
   (b) Cross wind.
   (c) Down wind (demonstrate only on auxiliary field).
IV. Air Work:
   (a) Straight and level flight.
   (b) Gentle climbs and turns.
   (c) Gentle turns.
   (d) 70-degree turns.
   (e) Spirals and approaches for landings.

V. Landings:
  (a) Into wind.
  (b) Cross wind.
  (c) Down wind (demonstrate only on auxiliary field).
VI. Stalls and spins; stressing approach and recovery.
VII. Emergencies:
  (a) Simulated forced landings from—
    1. Take-off from less than 200 feet of altitude.
    2. 90 degrees from over 200 feet of altitude.
    3. 180 degrees from above 400 feet of altitude.
  NOTE.—Students should be permitted to solo at any time after 8 hours when in the opinion of their instructors they are qualified. The order of teaching and time spent on maneuvers is left to the instructor's judgment to suit his conditions and personnel. Instruction periods 30 minutes each. All landing practice without power.

Stage B. Primary Solo—5 Hours Solo—1 Hour Dual.

VIII. Solo flight—three landings recommended.
  IX. Practice Work of Stage A periods I, II, III, IV, and V only:
  (a) All take-offs and landings into wind only.
  (b) A 10-minute check by instructor preferably after first three solo flights of 30 minutes each.
  (c) 30-minute check after 3 hours.
  NOTE.—Total of stages A and B to be 14 hours flying time. All landings practiced without power.

Stage C. Advanced Solo—13 Hours Solo—8 Hours Dual.

  X. Instruction (1 hour):
  (a) Precision landing (180-degree U-type approach).
  (b) 30-degree eights around pylons
  Solo (2 hours)—practice above.
 XI. Instruction (1 hour):
  (a) Review period IX.
  (b) Precision landings (360-degree U-type final approach).
  (c) 70-degree power turns
  Solo (2 hours)—practice above.
XII. Instruction (1 hour):
  (a) Review period X.
  (b) Precision landings 720 degrees (minimum two turns).
  (c) 70-degree eights around pylons.
  Solo (2 hours)—practice above.
XIII. Instruction (1 hour):
  (a) Review period XI.
  (b) Stalls and spins.
  (c) Slips.

Solo (2 hours)—practice above. (Spins may be solo or with a certificated instructor.)

XIV. Instruction (1 hour):
(a) Power approaches and looking over fields.
(b) Power landings.
Solo (1 hour)—practice above.

XV. Instruction (1 hour):
(a) Cross country (second type of aircraft used.)
Solo (2 hours), cross country, 50 miles minimum and two full-stop landings at different airports.

XVI. Instruction (1 hour)
(a) Front seat indoctrination or opposite seat.
(b) Complete private flight test given.
Solo (2 hours)—goes through two complete tests alone and practice maneuvers as needed.

XVII. Check by instructor for private flight test.
Note.—In stage C, length of period should range from 30 minutes to 1 hour at discretion of instructor after judging student and his tendency to tire. Additional instruction to that prescribed should be given on any maneuvers the instructor deems necessary. Above is a minimum outline only. Simulated forced landings should be given on all dual periods.

Recapitulation

Stage	Number of Hours Dual	Solo
A. Dual	8	
B. Primary solo	1	5
C. Advanced solo	8	13
Total	17	18

Selected CAA Research Reports

Backstrom, Oscar, Jr., and Morris S. Viteles. *An Analysis of Graphic Records of Pilot Performance Obtained by Means of the R-S Ride Recorder.* Part 2. Philadelphia: University of Pennsylvania. January 1946.

Brimhall, Dean R., et al. *A Preliminary Study of Physical Standards in Relation to Success in Flight Training.* Washington, D.C.: National Research Council. February 1944.

Dorcus, Roy M. *The Influence of Physiologically Effective Doses of Epinephrine on Vestibularly Induced Nausea.* University of California at Los Angeles. November 1942.

Dunlap, Jack W., and Morey J. Wantman. *An Investigation of the Interview as a Technique for Selecting Aircraft Pilots.* The University of Rochester, Harvard University and The University of Michigan. August 1944.

Dunlap, Jack W., et al. *Tests of the "Ability to Take It."* Rochester, N.Y.: University of Rochester. February 1943.

Edgerton, Harold A., and Robert Y. Walker. *History and Development of the Ohio State Flight Inventory,* Part 1: *Early Versions and Basic Research.* Columbus: The Ohio State University. July 1945.

Festinger, Leon, and Seymour Wapner. *A Test of Decision Time: Reliability and "Generality."* Rochester, N.Y.: University of Rochester. September 1945.

Festinger, Leon, et al. *Comparison of Student Pilot Performance in Successive Check Flights as Measured by Photographic Records.* Rochester, N.Y.: University of Rochester. March 1946.

Forbes, Alexander, and Hallowell Davis. *Electroencephalography of Naval Aviators.* Pensacola, Fla.: Naval Air Station. April 1943.

Franzen, Raymond. *A Method for Selecting Combinations of Tests and Determining Their Best "Cut-Off Points" to Yield a Dichotomy Most Like a Categorical Criterion.* Washington, D.C.: National Research Council. March 1943.

Franzen, Raymond, and Louisa Blaine. *Evaluation of Respiratory Measures for Use in Pilot Selection.* Washington, D.C.: National Research Council. January 1944.

Franzen, Raymond, and Dean R. Brimhall. *Analysis of Physical Defects Found by the Armed Services in Pilots Certified to be without Disquali-*

fying Defect by CPT Examination. Washington, D.C.: CAA Division of Research. July 1942.

Franzen, Raymond, and Dean R. Brimhall. *Problems of Consistency Arising from CAA Medical Examinations.* Washington, D.C.: CAA Division of Research. February 1942.

Franzen, Raymond, and Dean R. Brimhall. *The Relation to Accident of Physical Defects Noted in Standard CAA Medical Examinations.* Washington, D.C.: CAA Division of Research. July 1942.

Franzen, Raymond, and Ross A. McFarland. *Detailed Statistical Analysis of Data Obtained in the Pensacola Study of Naval Aviators.* Pensacola, Fla.: Naval Air Station. January 1945.

Geldard, Frank A. *A Study of the Sleep Motility of Student Pilots.* Charlottesville: University of Virginia. April 1944.

Johnson, H. M., and Mary L. Boots. *Analysis of Ratings in the Preliminary Phase of the CAA Training Program.* New Orleans, La.: Tulane University. October 1943.

Johnson, H. M., et al. *On the Actual and Potential Value of Biographical Information as a Means of Predicting Success in Aeronautical Training.* Tulane University and the University of North Carolina. August 1944.

Kelly, E. L. *The Development of "A Scale for Rating Pilot Competency."* Lafayette, Ind.: Purdue University. July 1943.

———. *The Flight Instructor's Vocabulary.* Lafayette, Ind.: Purdue University. October 1943.

Kelly, E. L., and E. Ewart. *The Effectiveness of "Patter" and of "Fundamentals of Basic Flight Maneuvers" as Training Aids.* Lafayette, Ind.: Purdue University. December 1942.

Kelly, E. L., and E. Ewart. *A Preliminary Study of Certain Predictors of Success in Civilian Pilot Training.* Lafayette, Ind.: Purdue University. December 1942.

Kogan, L. S., M. J. Wantman, and J. W. Dunlap. *Analysis of the Desire to Fly (D-F) Inventory.* Rochester, N.Y.: University of Rochester. October 1945.

Kogan, L. S., M. J. Wantman, and J. W. Dunlap. *Analysis of the Personal History Inventory.* Rochester, N.Y.: University of Rochester. February 1945.

Larson, Leonard A. *A Factor Analysis of Some Cardiovascular-Respiratory Variables with Particular Reference to the Schneider and the McCurdy-Larson Tests.* Springfield, Mass.: Springfield College. July 1943.

Lewis, Don. *The Effect of Noise and Vibration on Certain Psychomotor Responses.* Iowa City: The State University of Iowa. January 1943.

McFarland, Ross A., and Ralph C. Channell. *A Revised Serial Reaction Time Apparatus for Use in Appraising Flying Aptitude.* Cambridge, Mass.: Graduate School of Business Administration, Harvard University. September 1944.

McFarland, Ross A., and Ralph C. Channell. *A Revised Two-Hand Coordination Test.* Cambridge, Mass.: Graduate School of Business Administration, Harvard University. October 1944.

McFarland, Ross A., and Raymond Franzen. *The Pensacola Study of Naval Aviators-Final Summary.* Pensacola, Fla.: Naval Air Station. November 1944.

McKay, Walter. *The Development of the CAA-NRC Flight Recorder.* Cambridge, Mass.: Massachusetts Institute of Technology. September 1944.

Miles, Walter R. *A Micro-recorder for Measuring Skin Temperature and Sweating in Airplane Pilots.* New Haven, Conn.: Yale University School of Medicine. December 1943.

Nance, Roy D., Claude E. Buxton, and Kenneth W. Spence. *The Effect of Distraction Lights Upon Performance on the Washburn Serial Coordination Test.* Iowa City: The State University of Iowa. April 1944.

National Research Council Committee on Selection and Training of Aircraft Pilots. *The Aircraft Pilot: 5 Years of Research: Summary of Outcomes.* Washington, D.C. June 1945.

———. *The CAA-National Testing Service.* Washington, D.C. November 1944.

———. *An Historical Introduction to Aviation Psychology.* Washington, D.C. October 1942.

———. *History and Development of the Ohio State Flight Inventory,* Part 2: *Recent Versions and Current Applications.* Washington, D.C. November 1945.

———. *Investigation of the Relative Amount of Time Spent on the Ground and in the Air by Civilian Pilot Training Students.* Washington, D.C. March 1945.

———. *The Psychology of Learning in Relation to Flight Instruction.* Washington, D.C. June 1943.

———. *Report on the Boston-Midwest Project.* Washington, D.C. November 1945.

———. *Report on CAA-National Testing Service (First Phase: June 20, 1942–August 2, 1942).* Washington, D.C. January 1943.

———. *Report on CAA-National Testing Service.* Washington, D.C. August 1943.

———. *Report on CAA-National Testing Service.* Washington, D.C. May 1944.

———. *The Role of Fatigue in Pilot Performance.* Washington, D.C. May 1946.

———. *Studies of Predictors of Achievement in Learning to Fly.* Washington, D.C. March 1944.

———. *A Study of Visual and Cardiovascular Standards in Relation to Success in Flight Training.* Washington, D.C. May 1946.

Odbert, Henry S., Leon Festinger, and Seymour Wapner. *"Ability-to-Take-It" Tests: Examiner Differences and Validation.* U.S. Navy, Bureau of Aeronautics, University of Rochester, Massachusetts General Hospital, Williams College. October 1945.

Spence, Kenneth W., Claude E. Buxton, and Arthur W. Melton. *The Effect of Massing and Distribution of Practice on Rotary Pursuit Test Scores.* Dept. of Psychology, Army Air Forces School of Aviation Medicine, Randolph Field, Tex. and Dept. of Psychology, State University of Iowa, Iowa City. March 1945.

Spence, Kenneth W., Claude E. Buxton, and Arthur W. Melton. *The Effect of Massing and Distribution of Practice on the S.A.M. Complex Coordination Test.* Army Air Forces School of Aviation Medicine, Randolph Field, Tex. and State University of Iowa, Iowa City. December 1945.

Taylor, Craig, and Raymond Franzen. *Measures of Exercise Tolerance.* Stanford University and New York University. February 1946.

Tiffin, Joseph, and John Bromer. *Analysis of Eye Fixations and Patterns of Eye Movements in Landing a Piper Cub J-3 Airplane.* Lafayette, Ind.: Purdue University.

Tinker, Miles, and William S. Carlson. *Sensitivity of Peripheral Vision in Relation to Skill in Landing an Airplane.* Minneapolis: University of Minnesota. April 1943.

Viteles, Morris S., and Albert S. Thompson. *An Analysis of Photographic Records of Aircraft Pilot Performance.* Philadelphia: University of Pennsylvania. July 1944.

Viteles, Morris S., and Albert S. Thompson. *The Use of Standard Flights and Motion Photography in the Analysis of Aircraft Pilot Performance.* Philadelphia: University of Pennsylvania. May 1943.

Viteles, Morris S., Oscar Backstrom, Jr., and Albert S. Thompson. *An Analysis of Graphic Records of Pilot Performance Obtained by Means of the R-S Ride Recorder.* Philadelphia: University of Pennsylvania. November 1943.

Viteles, Morris S., Raymond Franzen, and Robert C. Rogers. *The Association Between Ratings on Specific Maneuvers and Success or Failure in Flight Training of RAF Cadets.* Washington, D.C.: National Research Council. October 1944.

Viteles, Morris S., et al. *A Course in Training Methods for Pilot Instructors.* Washington, D.C.: National Research Council. September 1943.

Walker, R. Y., S. V. Bennett, and E. S. Ewart. *A Study of Individual Differences among Flight Instructors in Making Spot Landings.* Knoxville: Institute of Aviation Psychology, University of Tennessee. February 1946.

Wendt, G. R. *Studies in Motion Sickness.* Middletown, Conn.: Wesleyan University. December 1944.

Wendt, G. R., and A. D. Tuttle. *Studies in Motion Sickness.* Series B. Middletown, Conn.: Wesleyan University. April 1946.

Williams, A. C., Jr., J. W. Macmillan, and J. G. Jenkins. *Preliminary Experimental Investigation of "Tension" as a Determinant of Performance in Flight Training.* College Park: University of Maryland. January 1946.

Selected Air Age Education Series Titles

Arey, Charles K. *The Airport.* New York: Macmillan, 1942.

———. *Elementary School Science for the Air Age.* New York: Macmillan, 1942.

Aviation Education Research Group. Teachers College. Columbia University. *Science of Pre-Flight Aeronautics.* New York: Macmillan, 1942.

———. University of Nebraska. *Elements of Pre-Flight Aeronautics.* New York: Macmillan, 1942.

———. *Teachers Manual for Elements of Pre-Flight Aeronautics.* New York: Macmillan, 1942.

Bartlett, Hall. *Social Studies for the Air Age: A Text for High School Students.* New York: Macmillan, 1942.

Bauer, Hubert A. *Globes, Maps, and Skyways: A Text for High School Students.* New York: Macmillan, 1942.

Cartwright, Catherine, et al. *Bibliography of Aviation Education Materials: An Annotated List of Books and Visual Aids for the Use of Schools and Libraries.* New York: Macmillan, 1942.

Cohen, Rose N., ed. *Flying High: An Anthology of Aviation Literature for Junior High School Students.* New York: Macmillan, 1942.

Cross, E. A. *Wings for You: A Book about Aviation for Senior High School Students.* New York: Macmillan, 1942.

Engelhardt, N. L., Jr. *Education for the Air Age.* New York: Macmillan, 1942.

Fitzpatrick, Frederick L., and Karl A. Stiles. *The Biology of Flight.* New York: Macmillan, 1942.

———. *Teachers' Manual for the Biology of Flight.* New York: Macmillan, 1942.

Manzer, J. G., M. M. Peake, and J. M. Leps. *Physical Science in the Air Age: A Teachers' Guide.* New York: Macmillan, 1942.

Osteyee, George. *Mathematics in Aviation.* New York: Macmillan, 1942.

Renner, George T., and Hubert A. Bauer. *The Air We Live In.* New York: Macmillan, 1942.

Renner, George T. *Geographic Education for the Air Age: A Guide for Teachers and Administrators.* New York: Macmillan, 1942.

———. *Human Geography in the Air Age.* New York: Macmillan, 1942.

Stover, George F., ed. *Teachers Manual for Science of Pre-Flight Aeronautics.* New York: Macmillan, 1942.

Wilber, Gordon O., and Emerson E. Neuthardt. *Aeronautics in the Industrial Arts Program: A Handbook for Students and Teachers.* New York: Macmillan, 1942.

Memorandum of Agreement, Dated January 19, 1943, Covering Use of CAA War Training Service by the Army Air Forces

Part I
Training of Air Corps Enlisted Reservists under the Supervision of the CAA War Training Service

1. The CAA War Training Service (formerly known as CPT) states that as of January 9, 1943, approximately 9500 Air Corps enlisted reservists were receiving pilot training under the supervision of the CAA War Training Service pursuant to arrangements previously entered into with the Army Air Forces and that estimates indicated that approximately 4000 Air Corps enlisted reservists were awaiting assignment to such training.

2. For the purposes of the program outlined herein, the CAA War Training Service will continue its pilot training courses known as the Elementary, Secondary, Cross-Country, Link Instrument, Instructor, and Flight Officer courses, as described in Exhibit I herewith, which courses shall be subject to such modification as may be made from time to time with the concurrence of the Army Air Forces. With effect from the date hereof, it is agreed that all such Air Corps enlisted reservists are to be trained under the supervision of the CAA War Training Service in the numbers necessary to produce:

a. Graduates of cross-country course (who have also graduated from the elementary and secondary courses or who have had an equivalent number of certified flight hours) as follows:

250 each month, commencing April 30, 1943.

b. Graduates of the instructor course (who have also been graduated from the elementary, secondary, cross-country, and flight instrument courses, or who have had an equivalent number of certified flight hours and instrument instruction) as follows:

Each month, up to August 31, 1943, all such graduates as can be made available, and 350 such graduates each month thereafter.

3. Commencing March 1, 1943, assignment of men to training will be substantially in accordance with the following schedule:

Course	Monthly Input	Population in Training after April 1, 1943
Elementary course (8 weeks)	931	1,862
Secondary course (8 weeks)	791	1,582
Cross-country course (8 weeks; 250 to graduate each month)	672	1,344
Flight instrument course (8 weeks)	389	778
Instructor (350 to graduate each month)	369	738
Total	3,152	6,304

When the number of Air Corps enlisted reservists, as indicated under 1 above, available to the CAA War Training Service for assignment to training, falls below a figure which will produce sufficient graduates of the secondary course to provide the required monthly input of the cross-country course, as set forth above, the CAA will so advise the Army Air Forces, and a decision will be made by the Army Air Forces as to the steps, if any, to be taken to provide for further utilization of the unused facilities of the said course and of the courses senior thereto. It is intended that the facilities of the elementary and secondary courses which are released from employment for the purposes of Part I of this Memorandum of Agreement will be utilized for the purposes of the training provided for in Part II hereof.

4. Members of the Air Corps enlisted reserve in training, as provided above, will be under the supervision of the CAA War Training Service for training and discipline. They will remain on inactive status until instructions are issued to the contrary by the Commanding General, Army Air Forces. The cost of tuition, subsistence, commutations, and other necessary expenses of the training program, including the acquisition and maintenance of equipment and facilities, will be paid out of appropriations available to the CAA War Training Service.

5. Air Corps enlisted reservists who fail to report for training or to continue in training as directed by the CAA War Training Service will be reported by name to the Commanding General, Army Air Forces, who will take such further action as may be consistent with existing policies.

6. CAA War Training Service is now conducting Flight Officers courses at its standardization center at Houston, Texas, and under contract with certain private flight contractors. These courses have been undertaken to

provide 200 graduates to be available for the purposes of the Air Transport Command. It is agreed that CAA War Training Service will continue with such training until delivery has been made of the said 200 flight officer graduates, and of such other graduates of the said course as may subsequently be called for by specific request and authorization of the Commanding General, Army Air Forces.

7. CAA War Training Service will continue to provide pilot training for Negro members of the Air Corps enlisted reserve as per request dated August 10, 1942, by the Commanding General, Army Air Forces.

8. Lists of graduates and pertinent records and information relating thereto will be supplied by the CAA War Training Service each month to the Army Air Forces Flying Training Command, or as the Commanding General, Army Air Forces, may otherwise direct.

9. Existing facilities, including accommodations, airplanes, link trainers, and other equipment will be used to the extent available. Also, CAA War Training Service may purchase required planes and equipment now in the hands of private owners which are not being utilized in the war effort.

10. The CAA War Training Service reports that the training program contemplated by 2 b, above, cannot be carried out unless the following deficiencies in the number of airplanes and link trainers available for the advanced courses can be purchased:

71 instrument equipped airplanes of not less than 120 horsepower.

33 link trainers equipped with the required instruments.

It is agreed that if said planes and link trainers cannot be obtained by CAA War Training Service from private owners, this agreement will be re-opened and the program outlined in paragraphs 2 and 3 above subject to revision consistent with equipment available.

11. Materials and parts necessary to maintain the existing facilities in efficient and safe operation will be made available by scheduling the production of necessary parts and materials, where the production of such parts and materials does not interfere with the manufacture of combat aircraft. The Army Air Forces will support such minimum requests as may be necessary in this connection to the War Production Board, Joint Aircraft Committee, or other agencies having control of the allocation of the use of materials and production facilities. However, every possible effort will be made by the CAA War Training Service to obtain airplanes and spare parts, not necessary in the war effort, from civilian agencies. Where necessary airplanes will be cannibalized to maintain operating aircraft in safe and serviceable condition.

Part II
Provision of Elementary Flight Instruction by CAA War Training Service in Conjunction with Army Air Forces College Program

1. The Army Air Forces is to call to active duty 70,000 enlisted reservists, hereinafter called trainees, who will be assigned to training in such colleges as may be selected for this purpose, subject to coordination with the CAA War Training Service as to availability of pilot training facilities in conjunction with such colleges. The Commanding General, Army Air Forces, will advise the CAA War Training Service of the number to be assigned to each college. It is contemplated that throughout the remainder of 1943 the population in each college will remain constant.

2. Commencing March 31, 1943, or at the beginning of any thirty-day period thereafter as designated by the Commanding General, Army Air Forces, one-fifth of the number of trainees at each of the colleges selected will be given elementary flight instruction each month, or during aforesaid designated thirty-day period, by CAA War Training Service in light planes of the types certified for use in the CAA War Training Service elementary course. (Two passenger airplanes, 50 horsepower and up are specified. Tandem seating airplanes are preferred, but not required. Piper Cub, Aeronca, Taylorcraft, and Interstate planes are the leading makes used.)

3. The CAA War Training Service will have full responsibility for the provision of such elementary flight instruction, which will be given in accordance with the outline attached, marked Exhibit II. This calls for a minimum of ten hours flight instruction, including two hours solo.

4. The Army Air Forces officer in command at each college will have responsibility for the delivery of trainees to CAA War Training Service for such elementary flight instruction at designated airports in accordance with schedules to be established by the CAA War Training Service. The CAA school concerned will, however, be responsible for the provision of transportation to and from the airport. The Army Air Forces will support applications for necessary priorities in this connection. Otherwise, the responsibility of the CAA War Training Service will extend only to the provision of flight instruction and to the control and supervision of trainees while at the designated airport or while undergoing flight instruction.

5. Ground school instruction will be provided by the Army Air Forces.

6. Army Air Forces contracts with colleges will provide for the employment of CAA War Training Service coordinators to coordinate the activities of flight contractors or will permit supplemental contracts to be made by CAA with such colleges to provide for the continued availability to CAA War Training Service of the services of such coordinators.

7. The making of contracts with flight instruction contractors will be a function of the CAA War Training Service.

8. The existing stock of qualified airplanes owned by, or available to flight contractors, over and above those required for the purposes of the training

to be provided under Part I, will be used for the purpose of providing the flight instruction contemplated in paragraph 3 above; provided, however, that qualified planes now constituting the pool of privately owned small planes in the hands of the public which are not otherwise required for use in the war program, may, to the extent available, be acquired by such flight contractors or by CAA War Training Service for the purpose of providing such flight instruction or maintaining the existing stock of planes in efficient operation.

9. Arrangements will be made to schedule the manufacture and supply of the minimum requirements for parts and materials necessary to maintain in efficient and safe flying condition, for the purposes of the instruction contemplated in paragraph 3 above, the 2500 light planes which the CAA War Training Service estimates to be available for such purposes, where the production of such parts and materials does not interfere with the manufacture of combat aircraft. The Army Air Forces will make appropriate recommendations in this connection to the War Production Board, Joint Aircraft Committee, and the Army and Navy Munitions Board. However, every possible effort will be made by the CAA War Training Service to obtain airplanes and spare parts, not necessary in the war effort, from civilian agencies. Where necessary airplanes wil be cannibalized to maintain operating aircraft in a safe and serviceable condition.

FOR THE COMMANDING GENERAL, ARMY AIR FORCES

ROBERT W. HARPER
Colonel, G. S. C.
Ass't. Chief of Air Staff, A-3

FOR THE CIVIL AERONAUTICS ADMINISTRATION

R. McLEAN STEWART
Executive Asst. to the Administrator

January 19, 1943

Notes

Introduction

1. Quoted in Gerald D. Nash, *The Great Depression and World War II: Organizing America, 1933–1945,* St. Martin's Series in Twentieth Century United States History (New York: St. Martin's Press, 1939), 101.

2. Robert A. Divine, *Roosevelt and World War II* (Baltimore: Penguin Books, 1969), 16.

3. Wesley Frank Craven and James Lea Cate, eds., *Plans and Early Operations,* vol. 1, The Army Air Forces in World War II (Chicago: University of Chicago Press, 1948), 104.

4. Eliot Janeway, *The Struggle for Survival: A Chronicle of Economic Mobilization in World War II,* Chronicles of America Series, ed. Allan Nevins (New Haven: Yale University Press, 1951), 53:24.

5. Janeway, *The Struggle for Survival,* 24–25.

6. Wesley Frank Craven and James Lea Cate, eds., *Men and Planes,* the Army Air Forces in World War II (Chicago: University of Chicago Press, 1955), 6:431.

7. William E. Leuchtenburg, "The New Deal and the Analogue of War," in *Change and Continuity in Twentieth Century America,* ed. John Braeman, Robert H. Bremner, and Everett Walters (Columbus: Ohio State University Press, 1964), 109–10.

8. Quoted in Leuchtenburg, "The New Deal and the Analogue of War," 127; see Edwin C. Johnson, *Mars in Civilian Disguise: An Exposure of the Military Purposes Underlying the Student Pilot Training Program Being Administered by the Civil Aeronautics Authority,* Foreword by John Dewey, Committee on Militarism in Education, 2929 Broadway, New York City.

9. Nash, *The Great Depression and World War II,* 103; David Brody, "The New Deal and World War II," in *The New Deal,* vol. 1, *The National Level,* ed. John Braeman, Robert H. Bremner, and David Brody (Columbus: Ohio State University Press, 1975), 274.

10. Janeway, *The Struggle for Survival,* 9, 11–12.

11. Richard Polenberg, *War and Society: The United States, 1941–1945* (Philadelphia: J.B. Lippincott, 1972), 80–82.

Chapter 1. The CPTP, the New Deal, and War Preparedness

1. Robert H. Hinckley and JoAnn Wells, *"I'd Rather Be Born Lucky than Rich": The Autobiography of Robert H. Hinckley,* Charles Redd Monographs in Western History, no. 7 (Provo, Utah: Brigham Young University Press, 1977, 71). Hereafter cited as Hinckley and Wells.

2. Hinckley and Wells, 1–98; Samuel Milner, "Hinckley's Miracle," [FAA] *World,* May 1983, 6–9, 17; *Who's Who in America, 1942–1943* (Chicago: A. N. Marquis, 1942), 1077.

3. Hinckley and Wells, 58–61.

4. Ibid., 68–71.

5. Ibid., 73ff; John R. M. Wilson, *Turbulence Aloft: The Civil Aeronautics Administration amid Wars and Rumors of Wars, 1938–1953* (Washington, D.C.: U.S. Department of Transportation, Federal Aviation Administration, 1979), 14, 34–41; *Handbook of Airline Statistics,* 1971 ed. (Washington, D.C.: Civil Aeronautics Board, Bureau of Accounts and Statistics, Accounting, Costs and Statistics Division, 1972), 453.

6. Milner, "Hinckley's Miracle," 7; Hinckley and Wells, 79–80; Robert H. Hinckley, *Adventures in Democracy: The Story of the Civilian Pilot Training Program,* unpublished ms., 26, box 80, fd. 1, Papers of Robert H. Hinckley, Special Collections Department, University of Utah Libraries, Salt Lake City.

7. Hinckley, *Adventures in Democracy,* 44.

8. Hinckley and Wells, 79.

9. Arthur M. Schlesinger, Jr., "The Broad Accomplishments of the New Deal," in *The New Deal: Revolution or Evolution?* Problems in American Civilization, ed. Edwin C. Rozwenc (Boston: D.C. Heath, 1959), 29–30.

10. Richard Polenberg, "The Decline of the New Deal," in *The New Deal,* vol. 1, *The National Level,* ed. John Braeman, Robert H. Bremner, and David Brody (Columbus: Ohio State University Press, 1975), 262–63.

11. Hinckley, *Adventures in Democracy,* 18, 28; Polenberg, "The Decline of the New Deal," 262.

12. Hinckley, *Adventures in Democracy,* 18, 28.

13. Albert U. Romasco, *The Politics of Recovery: Roosevelt's New Deal* (New York: Oxford University Press, 1983), 243.

14. Nick A. Komons, *Bonfires to Beacons: Federal Civil Aviation Policy under the Air Commerce Act, 1926–1938* (Washington, D.C.: U.S. Department of Transportation, Federal Aviation Administration, 1978), 88, 84, 210; Elsbeth E. Freudenthal, *The Aviation Business from Kitty Hawk to Wall Street* (New York: Vanguard Press, 1940), 88, 120. For a good description of this period in American aviation, see Komons, "The Chaos of Laissez Faire in the Air," in *Bonfires to Beacons,* 7–33, and Richard P. Hallion, "American Aviation in the Mid-1920s," in *Legacy of Flight: The Guggenheim Contribution to American Aviation* (Seattle: University of Washington Press, 1977), 3–19.

15. For a detailed look at the Roosevelt administration's attitudes toward aviation, the events that led up to the Black Committee hearings, and the hearings themselves, see Nick A. Komons, *The Cutting Air Crash: A Case Study in Early Federal Aviation Policy* (Washington, D.C.: U.S. Department of Transportation, Federal Aviation Administration, 1973), 1–12; Komons, *Bonfires to Beacons,* 219–379; Henry Ladd Smith, *Airways: The History of Commercial Aviation in the United States* (New York: Alfred Knopf, 1942), 156–310; U.S. Congress, Senate, Special Committee on Investigation of Air Mail and Ocean Contracts, *Investigation of Air Mail and Ocean Contracts,* 73d Cong., 2d sess., pts. 1–9; and Arthur M. Schlesinger, Jr., *The Coming of the New Deal: The Age of Roosevelt* (Boston: Houghton Mifflin, 1958), 449–50.

16. From Black Committee Hearings, "Testimony of D. M. Sheaffer," Special Committee on the Investigation of Air Mail and Ocean Mail Contracts, U.S. Senate, 73d Cong., 2d sess., 1550, as quoted in Smith, *Airways,* 168.

17. Smith, *Airways,* 167–70.

18. Quoted in Schlesinger, *The Coming of the New Deal,* 450–51.

19. "To Right a Wrong," *Business Week,* April 20, 1935, 36.

20. John F. Shiner, *Foulois and the U.S. Army Air Corps, 1931–1935* (Washington, D.C.: Office of Air Force History, U.S. Air Force, 1983), 125–37; Benjamin D. Foulois and Carroll V. Glines, *From the Wright Brothers to the Astronauts: The Memoirs of Major General Benjamin D. Foulois* (New York: Arno Press, 1980), 235–61.

21. Shiner, *Foulois,* 131; Eldon W. Downs, "Army and the Air Mail—1934," *Airpower Historian,* January 1962, 41.

22. Shiner, *Foulois,* 135, 138.

23. Kenneth S. Davis, *The Hero: Charles A. Lindbergh and the American Dream* (Garden City: Doubleday, 1959), 333.

24. Quoted in Komons, *Bonfires to Beacons,* 261; *Los Angeles Times,* February 24, 1934, 4.

25. Foulois and Glines, *From the Wright Brothers to the Astronauts,* 255.

26. Quoted in Shiner, *Foulois,* 144.

27. Ibid., 148.

28. See Arnold E. Briddon, Ellmore A. Champie, and Peter A. Marraine, *FAA Historical Fact Book: A Chronology, 1926–1971* (Washington, D.C.: U.S. Department of Transportation, Federal Aviation Administration, Office of Information Services, 1974), 4–5; "National Transportation Policy," *Journal of Air Law,* 1936, 170–71 (this article [178–86] also contains an excellent synopsis of the recommendations of the Federal Aviation Commission).

29. Tom D. Crouch, "An Airplane for Everyman: The Department of Commerce and the Light Plane Industry, 1933–1937," unpublished ms., National Air and Space Museum History Project Files, Smithsonian Institution, Washington, D.C., 2; Gore Vidal, "Love of Flying," *New York Review of Books,* January 17, 1985, 16.

30. Vidal, "Love of Flying," 17; Crouch, "An Airplane for Everyman," 2.

31. Crouch, "An Airplane for Everyman," 7, 10.

32. Ibid., 8–9, 10.

33. Eugene L. Vidal, Address to Michigan Aeronautical Activities Association, and the Detroit Section, Society of Automotive Engineers, April 16, 1934, quoted in ibid., 3–4.

34. Ibid., 9.

35. Ibid., 9–10.

36. "This Light Plane Business," *Aviation,* December 1935, 25–28.

37. "$700 Airplane," *Time,* January 6, 1934, 46; *Aircraft Year Book for 1934* (New York: Aeronautical Chamber of Commerce of America, 1934), 81–84.

38. Crouch, "An Airplane for Everyman," 14.

39. Harold L. Ickes, *The Secret Diary of Harold L. Ickes* (New York: Simon and Schuster, 1953), 1:142–43; Minutes of the Special Board for Public Works, February 1, 1934, R.G. 135, National Archives, Washington, D.C., cited in Crouch, "An Airplane for Everyman," 16–17, 36; ibid., 14–15.

40. Ibid., 17–18, 23.

41. Cy Caldwell, "Vidal Statistics," *Aero Digest,* June 1936, 25.

42. Komons, *Cutting Air Crash,* 15; Komons, *Bonfires to Beacons,* 280.

43. Komons, *Cutting Air Crash,* 14, 24; Komons, *Bonfires to Beacons,* 280.

44. Komons, *Bonfires to Beacons,* 25.

45. Komons, *Cutting Air Crash,* 278–79.

46. Ibid., 27.

47. For a full text of the Copeland Committee hearings, see U.S. Congress, Senate, Subcommittee of the Committee on Commerce, *Safety in Air: Hearings Before a Subcommittee of the Committee on Commerce* (A Resolution to Investigate Certain Airplane Accidents and Interstate Air Commerce), 74th Cong., 2d sess., 1936–37, pts. 1–3.

48. Komons, *Bonfires to Beacons,* 281–82.

49. Ibid., 282.

50. Ibid., 283.

51. Ibid., 280.

52. Ibid., 294–95.

53. Quoted in ibid., 295.

54. Ibid., 295.

55. Komons, *Cutting Air Crash,* 74–75.

56. Komons, *Bonfires to Beacons,* 349–50.

57. Ibid., 363–66, 370–78.

58. Briddon, Champie, and Marraine, *FAA Historical Fact Book,* 34–35; Clinton M. Hester, "The Civil Aeronautics Act of 1938," *Journal of Air Law,* July 1938, 459.

59. "The Appoint-mints with the HOle," *Aviation,* August 1938, 19.

60. Komons, *Bonfires to Beacons,* 267, 246.

61. Arthur M. Schlesinger, Jr., ed., *The Almanac of American History* (Greenwich, Conn.: Bison Books, 1983), 469, 471, 473.

62. Samuel Eliot Morison, *The Oxford History of the American People*

(New York: The New American Library, 1972), 3:345. See also, Morison, *History of United States Naval Operations in World War II*, vol. 3, *The Rising Sun in the Pacific, 1931–April 1942* (Boston: Little, Brown, 1975), 3–18.

63. William A. Manchester, *The Glory and the Dream: A Narrative History of America, 1932–1972* (New York: Bantam Books, 1980), 189.

64. Forrest C. Pogue, *George C. Marshall: Education of a General, 1880–1939* (New York: Viking Press, 1963), 321–22.

65. F. Robert van der Linden, "The Struggle for the Long-Range Heavy Bomber: The United States Army Air Corps, 1934–1939," master's thesis, George Washington University, 1981, 139–40.

66. "Transcript of 500th Press Conference (November 15, 1938)," in *The Public Papers and Addresses of Franklin D. Roosevelt*, ed. Samuel I. Rosenman (New York: Macmillan, 1941), 7:599.

67. U.S. Congress, House, Committee on Interstate and Foreign Commerce, *Training of Civil Aircraft Pilots: Hearings on H.R. 50[9]3*, 76th Cong., 1st sess., March 20 and 27, 1939, 2.

68. Hinckley, *Adventures in Democracy*, 29.

69. Ibid., 31.

70. "Press Conference no. 512 (December 27, 1938)," *Complete Presidential Press Conferences of Franklin D. Roosevelt* (New York: Da Capo Press, 1972), 12:319–24.

71. "The President Urges the Congress to Pass Additional Appropriations for National Defense, January 12, 1939," in *The Public Papers and Addresses of Franklin D. Roosevelt*, ed. Rosenman, 8:73.

72. *New York Times*, March 19, 1939, 3:1.

73. David O. Levine, *The American College and the Culture of Aspiration, 1915–1940* (Ithaca, N.Y.: Cornell University Press, 1986), 196, 97–98.

74. Press Release, Civil Aeronautics Authority, June 24, 1939, box 62, fd. 4, The Papers of Robert H. Hinckley, Special Collections Department, University of Utah Libraries, Salt Lake City.

75. Hinckley, *Adventures in Democracy*, 34–36; *American Aviation Daily*, January 9, 1939, 21; Press Release, Civil Aeronautics Authority, June 24, 1939, box 62, fd. 4, The Papers of Robert H. Hinckley, Special Collections Department, University of Utah Libraries, Salt Lake City.

76. William R. Enyart, "What's Ahead for Private Flying," *National Aeronautics*, May 1938, 11.

77. "Wanted: Fewer Rules, More Airports," *American Aviation*, November 1, 1938, 8.

78. George Gallup, "The Gallup Poll," *Washington Post*, January 20, 1939, n.p., box 62, fd. 1, The Papers of Robert H. Hinckley, Special Collections Department, University of Utah Libraries, Salt Lake City.

Chapter 2. "Baptism of Fire"

1. Robert H. Hinckley, *Adventures in Democracy: The Story of the Civilian Pilot Training Program*, unpublished ms., 46, box 80, fd. 1, The Papers

of Robert H. Hinckley, Special Collections Department, University of Utah Libraries, Salt Lake City.

2. *American Aviation Daily,* May 4, 1939, 17; John R. M. Wilson, *Turbulence Aloft: The Civil Aeronautics Administration Amid Wars and Rumors of Wars, 1938–1953* (Washington, D.C.: U.S. Department of Transportation, Federal Aviation Administration, 1979), 16–17.

3. Wilson, *Turbulence Aloft,* 19.

4. David L. Porter, *The Seventy-Sixth Congress and World War II, 1939–1940* (Columbia: University of Missouri Press, 1979), 12, 17, 19.

5. Hinckley, *Adventures in Democracy,* 46–47.

6. See Nick A. Komons, *Bonfires to Beacons: Federal Civil Aviation Policy under the Air Commerce Act, 1926–1938* (Washington, D.C.: U.S. Department of Transportation, Federal Aviation Administration, 1978), 370–72, for a description of Lea's involvement in the Civil Aeronautics Act; see also, 76th Cong., 1st sess., "H.R. 5093, A Bill to Provide for the Training of Civil Aircraft Pilots, and for Other Purposes," March 16, 1939, 1–4, box 62, fd. 1, The Papers of Robert H. Hinckley, Special Collections Department, University of Utah Libraries, Salt Lake City.

7. U.S. Congress, House, Committee on Interstate and Foreign Commerce, *Training of Civil Aircraft Pilots: Hearings on H.R. 50[9]3,* 76th Cong., 1st sess., March 20 and 27, 1939, title page. Although the hearings were held on two separate dates, the published version is paginated consecutively. The H.R. (House of Representatives) number on the hearings was erroneously printed as H.R. 5073. Hinckley's expectation that the CPTP would train twenty thousand pilots in its first year was not part of the legislation.

8. Ibid., 2–3.

9. Ibid., 3.

10. Ibid., 3–4.

11. Ibid., 6, 9.

12. Ibid., 26.

13. Ibid., 13–15.

14. Bulwinkle was a long-time Democratic congressman and North Carolina National Guard officer who had commanded an American Expeditionary Forces infantry unit in World War I; see *Who's Who in America, 1938–39,* ed. A. N. Marquis (Chicago: A. N. Marquis, 1938), 449; *Training of Civil Aircraft Pilots: Hearings on H.R. 50[9]3,* March 20, 1939, 21–22.

15. *Training of Civil Aircraft Pilots,* 28.

16. Ibid., 29.

17. Ibid., 30.

18. Ibid., 31.

19. Ibid., 32–33.

20. Cook had had a brief but distinguished career in naval aviation. An energetic, even fiery, naval officer, he strongly advocated an expanded naval air weapon and did not hesitate to speak out for more money and resources. After an early stint in command of surface vessels (in addition to administrative and staff positions), Cook had learned to fly in 1928. In September of

that year, he assumed command of the carrier U.S.S. *Langley.* In 1933, after the untimely death of Admiral William A. Moffett aboard the airship *Akron,* Cook was given temporary command of the navy's Bureau of Aeronautics. In June 1936, after holding various positions in the naval air hierarchy, including command of the carrier U.S.S. *Lexington,* he was named chief of the bureau. See Arthur B. Cook, Biographical File, National Air and Space Museum Archives, Smithsonian Institution, Washington, D.C.; Archibald D. Turnbull and Clifford L. Lord, *History of United States Naval Aviation* (New Haven, Conn.: Yale University Press, 1949), 296; *Training of Civil Aircraft Pilots: Hearings on H.R. 50[9]3,* March 27, 1939, 35–36.

21. *Training of Civil Aircraft Pilots,* 38–40.

22. Ibid., 41.

23. Yount was the Army Air Corps' expert on training. In the fall of 1938, he had been called to Washington from his post at Randolph Field, Texas, as commander of the Air Corps Training Center to become leader of a small group of officers responsible for planning a new AAC training program. See Wesley Frank Craven and James Lea Cate, eds., *Men and Planes,* the Army Air Forces in World War II (Chicago: University of Chicago Press, 1955), 6:430; *Training of Civil Aircraft Pilots: Hearings on H.R. 50[9]3,* March 27, 1939, 42–43.

24. Ibid., 44–45.

25. Ibid., 47–48.

26. Ibid., 48.

27. Ibid., 49.

28. Ibid., 55–56.

29. Ibid., 56.

30. Ibid., 56.

31. Ibid., 56.

32. Ibid., 64.

33. Ibid., 65.

34. Minutes, Committee on Interstate and Foreign Commerce, House of Representatives, 76th Cong., 1st sess., April 5, 1939, 24–25, *Digest of Public General Bills with Index,* 76th Cong., 1st sess., Final Issue, 288.

35. 76th Cong., 1st sess., House, "Training of Civil Aircraft Pilots" [Report no. 393], April 10, 1939, 2.

36. Ibid.

37. U.S. Congress, House, *Congressional Record,* 76th Cong., 1st sess., 1939, 84, pt. 4: 4476–92.

38. Ibid.

39. Ibid.

40. Ibid., 4481.

41. Ibid., 4482.

42. Ibid.

43. Ibid., 4483.

44. Ibid., 4480, 4486.

45. Ibid., 4487.

46. Ibid., 4488.

47. Ibid., 4490.

48. Ibid., 4490; Janet W. Bragg, unpublished and untitled ms. [48]; Ltr., Jill D. Snider to author, undated.

49. U.S. Congress, House, *Congressional Record,* 76th Cong., 1st sess., 1939, 84, pt. 4: 4490.

50. See Robert J. Jakeman, "America's Black Air Pioneers, 1909–1939," Air Command and Staff College Student Report (Maxwell AFB, Ala.: Air University, 1988), 15–19, for a well-thought-out delineation of the periods of black involvement in American aviation from 1900 to 1939.

51. Jakeman, "America's Black Air Pioneers," 4490–91.

52. Ibid., 4491–92.

53. 76th Cong., 1st sess., "H.R. 5619, an Act to Provide for the Training of Civil Aircraft Pilots and for other Purposes," April 20, 1939, 1–3, box 62, fd. 1, The Papers of Robert H. Hinckley, Special Collections Department, University of Utah Libraries, Salt Lake City.

54. Quoted in Komons, *Bonfires to Beacons,* 268–69, 368, 375–78, 439.

55. 76th Cong., 1st sess., "S. 2119, a Bill to Provide for the Training of Civil Aircraft Pilots, and for Other Purposes," April 8, 1939, 1–3.

56. U.S. Congress, Senate, Subcommittee of the Committee on Commerce, *Training of Civil Aircraft Pilots: Hearings on S. 2119,* 76th Cong., 1st sess., April 20, 1939, contents page.

57. Ibid., 68–69.

58. Ibid., 70–71.

59. Ibid., 71–72.

60. Ibid., 77–78.

61. Ibid., 80.

62. Ibid., 82–83.

63. Ibid., 84–86.

64. Ibid., 87–88.

65. See John H. Towers Biographical File, National Air and Space Museum Archives, Smithsonian Institution, Washington, D.C., 89.

66. Ibid., 89–90.

67. Ibid., 91. This statistic, like the 7,400 figure (i.e., licensed pilots between the ages of eighteen and thirty) cited by Hinckley in the first round of House hearings, is difficult to verify. Why Hinckley would have cited two different statistics is open to speculation.

68. Ibid., 94.

69. *American Aviation Daily,* May 26, 1939, 97; 76th Cong., 1st sess., Senate, "Training of Civil Aircraft Pilots" [Report no. 580] June 7, 1939, 1–3, box 62, fd. 1, The Papers of Robert H. Hinckley, Special Collections Department, University of Utah Libraries, Salt Lake City.

70. *American Aviation Daily,* June 20, 1939, 185; Public—no. 153—76th Congress, Chapter 244—First Session, "An Act to Provide for the Training of Civil Aircraft Pilots, and for Other Purposes," 1–2.

71. *American Aviation Daily,* July 10, 1939, 22; August 2, 1939, 107; Au-

gust 3, 1939, 114; August 5, 1939, 121; August 7, 1939, 126; August 8, 1939, 130–31; August 9, 1939, 140.

72. Hinckley, *Adventures in Democracy,* 50.

Chapter 3. The Uneasy Transition from Peace to War

1. *Air Commerce Bulletin,* February 15, 1939, 227–28; March 15, 1939, 231. The original thirteen schools were Purdue University, the Universities of Alabama, Minnesota, Washington, New York, Michigan, North Carolina, and Kansas, the Massachusetts Institute of Technology, Texas A&M College (Arlington, Texas, branch), Georgia School of Technology, San Jose State College, and Pomona Junior College. According to the March 15, 1939, issue of *Air Commerce Bulletin* (231), Purdue University in Lafayette, Indiana, became the first school to begin the demonstration program in February 1939. Emmet F. Hamer of West Liberty, Ohio, was the first college student to begin training at Purdue.

2. *Air Commerce Bulletin,* February 15, 1939, 228; March 15, 1939, 232.

3. *Air Commerce Bulletin,* February 15, 1939, 228.

4. *Air Commerce Bulletin,* March 15, 1939, 231.

5. Ibid., 231; *American Aviation Daily,* June 17, 1939, 174.

6. *American Aviation Daily,* June 26, 1939, 207–8.

7. *American Aviation Daily,* August 9, 1939, 140.

8. Robert H. Hinckley and JoAnn Wells, *"I'd Rather Be Born Lucky than Rich": The Autobiography of Robert H. Hinckley,* Charles Redd Monographs in Western History, no. 7 (Provo, Utah: Brigham Young University Press, 1977), 81. Hereafter cited as Hinckley and Wells.

9. Address by Mr. Robert H. Hinckley . . . at the Annual Membership Meeting of the Rocky Mount, North Carolina, Chamber of Commerce, March 5, 1940, 17, Robert H. Hinckley Institute of Politics Files, University of Utah, Salt Lake City; *Air Commerce Bulletin,* September 15, 1939, 59–63.

10. Ibid., 61–62.

11. James H. Farmer, *Celluloid Wings: The Impact of Movies on Aviation* (Blue Ridge Summit, Pa.: TAB Books, 1984), 333.

12. Frank S. Nugent [review of *20,000 Men a Year*], *New York Times Film Reviews, 1913–1968,* vol. 3, *1939–1948* (New York: Arno Press, 1970), 1648; Anon. Review of *20,000 Men a Year, Variety Film Reviews, 1938–1942* (New York: Garland Publishing, 1983), n.p. [October 25, 1939]; Farmer, *Celluloid Wings,* 333.

13. *Civil Aeronautics Journal,* January 1, 1940, 3.

14. Ibid., 4.

15. *Civil Aeronautics Journal,* June 1, 1940, 229.

16. Ibid.

17. John R. M. Wilson, *Turbulence Aloft: The Civil Aeronautics Administration amid Wars and Rumors of Wars* (Washington, D.C.: U.S. Department of Transportation, Federal Aviation Administration, 1979), 99–100.

18. Patricia Strickland, *The Putt-Putt Air Force: The Story of the Civilian Pilot Training Program and The War Training Service [1939–1944]* (Washington, D.C.: U.S. Department of Transportation, Federal Aviation Administration, n.d.), 73–74; Wilson, *Turbulence Aloft*, 99; Civil Aeronautics Administration, *Wartime History of the Civil Aeronautics Administration*, unpublished report, U.S. Department of Transportation, FAA Library, Washington, D.C., Research 1–10. See also, Dean R. Brimhall, "Applied Research: Men," *Flying and Popular Aviation*, February 1942, 56.

19. Wilson, *Turbulence Aloft*, 99 (cites Brimhall, "Applied Research," 56).

20. Ibid., 99–100; Strickland, *The Putt-Putt Air Force*, 74.

21. Strickland, *The Putt-Putt Air Force*, 75; Wilson, *Turbulence Aloft*, 100.

22. Wilson, *Turbulence Aloft*, 100; Strickland, *The Putt-Putt Air Force*, 75–76.

23. Morris S. Viteles and Albert S. Thompson, *The Use of Standard Flights and Motion Photography in the Analysis of Aircraft Pilot Performance*, Report no. 15 (Washington, D.C.: Civil Aeronautics Administration, Division of Research, May 1943), ix.

24. Viteles and Thompson, *The Use of Standard Flights*, x.

25. Wilson, *Turbulence Aloft*, 99–100 (cites Brimhall, "Applied Research," 56).

26. Morris S. Viteles et al., *A Course in Training Methods for Pilot Instructors*, Report no. 20 (Washington, D.C.: Civil Aeronautics Administration, Division of Research, September 1943), viii. Emphasis in original.

27. Viteles et al., *A Course in Training Methods*, ix; Strickland, *The Putt-Putt Air Force*, 77.

28. Morris S. Viteles, *The Aircraft Pilot: Five Years of Research, a Summary of Outcomes* (Washington, D.C.: National Research Council, June 15, 1945), 2.

29. *Wartime History*, CPT-23; *Civil Aeronautics Journal*, January 1, 1940, 3.

30. "Domestic Civil Aircraft Production by Types for the Year 1938 and Comparison with 1936 and 1937," and "Domestic Civil Aircraft Production for the Years 1938, 1939 and January-August 15, 1940," box 60, fd. 1, The Papers of Robert H. Hinckley, Special Collections Department, University of Utah Libraries, Salt Lake City.

31. "Domestic Civil Aircraft Production for the Years 1938, 1939 and January-August 15, 1940"; "Cub Congratulates CAA" [advertisement], *Aviation*, August 1939, 3. A forty-horsepower-engine Cub Trainer cost $1,098, nearly $400 more than Eugene Vidal's ideal "airplane for everyman."

32. "Domestic Civil Aircraft Production for the Years 1938, 1939 and January-August 15, 1940."

33. Joseph S. Edgerton, "11,000 Students Wanting to Fly Train for Peace or War Duty," *Washington Star*, October 8, 1939, n.p., box 76, fd. 4, The Papers of Robert H. Hinckley, Special Collections Department, University of Utah Libraries, Salt Lake City.

34. "Comments on the Civilian Pilot Training Program . . . from Whom Unsolicited Statements about the CPTP Have Been Received," 8–20, box 80, fd. 8, The Papers of Robert H. Hinckley, Special Collections Department, University of Utah Libraries, Salt Lake City.

35. "Comments on the Civilian Pilot Training Program . . . from Whom Unsolicited Statements about the CPTP Have Been Received."

36. David O. Levine, *The American College and the Culture of Aspiration, 1915–1940* (Ithaca, N.Y.: Cornell University Press, 1986), 196–98.

37. William F. Ogburn, Jean L. Adams, and S. C. Gilfillan, *The Social Effects of Aviation* (Boston: Houghton Mifflin, 1946), 444.

38. John W. Studebaker, "Air Youth's Place in the Schools," *Air Youth Horizons,* January 1940, 3.

39. Lyle W. Ashby, "Education for the Air Age: A Brief Survey of Aviation Education Today," *Journal of the National Education Association,* March 1943, 74; Joseph J. Corn, *The Winged Gospel: America's Romance with Aviation, 1900–1950* (New York: Oxford University Press, 1983), 123, 116. For a fuller discussion of the antecedents of air age education, see "Adults and the 'Winged Superchildren of Tomorrow,'" in Corn, *The Winged Gospel,* 113–33.

40. "Minutes on Meeting of Advisory Committee on Aviation Education," December 18, 1941, 1–2, box 61, fd. 14, The Papers of Robert H. Hinckley, Special Collections Department, University of Utah Libraries, Salt Lake City; see also, Robert H. Hinckley, "Fly for Your Lives," *Collier's,* April 25, 1942, 14, 61.

41. Strickland, *The Putt-Putt Air Force,* 89–90.

42. Ibid., 90–93; Catherine Cartwright et al., *Bibliography of Aviation Education Materials: An Annotated List of Books and Visual Aids for the Use of Schools and Libraries* (New York: Macmillan, 1942), v–vi.

43. Rose N. Cohen, ed. *Flying High: An Anthology of Aviation Literature for Junior High School Students* (New York: Macmillan, 1942), 40–48; George T. Renner, *Human Geography in the Air Age* (New York: Macmillan, 1942), ix, 1–6; Hall Bartlett, *Social Studies for the Air Age: A Text for High School Students* (New York: Macmillan, 1942), vii-viii.

44. Corn, *The Winged Gospel,* 124; Geoffrey Perrett, *Days of Sadness, Years of Triumph: The American People, 1939–1945* (Madison: University of Wisconsin Press, 1985), 369.

45. Cyril C. Trubey, "When It Comes to 'Pre-Flight' Instruction—a Little Learning Is a Dangerous Thing," *Nation's Schools,* September 1942, 23–24.

46. Richard Wright, *Native Son* (New York: Harper & Row, 1966), 19–20.

47. "The Negro in the Air," letter from William J. Powell, *Craftsmen Aero News,* July 1937, 12.

48. "The Negro in the Air," 12.

49. "History and Future Plans of the Craftsmen of Black Wings, Inc.," *Craftsmen Aero News,* January 1937, 4–5.

50. "History and Future Plans."

51. Floyd C. Covington, foreword to William J. Powell, *Black Wings* (Los Angeles: Ivan Deach, Jr., 1934), iii.

52. Miscellaneous clippings and correspondence, "Anderson-Forsythe," Black Wings Files, Aeronautics Department, National Air and Space Museum, Smithsonian Institution, Washington, D.C.

53. Ibid.

54. Albert Forsythe to Von Hardesty, Black Wings Files, Aeronautics Department, National Air and Space Museum, Smithsonian Institution, Washington, D.C.; Von Hardesty and Dominick Pisano, *Black Wings: The American Black in Aviation* (Washington, D.C.: Smithsonian Institution Press, 1984), 17.

55. Hardesty and Pisano, *Black Wings,* 19–20; Jill D. Snider, "A Race Soars Upward: Aviation and the Black American, 1900–1942," dissertation proposal, University of North Carolina, 1987, 31.

56. B. Joyce Ross, "Mary McLeod Bethune and the National Youth Administration: A Case Study of Power Relationships in the Black Cabinet of Franklin D. Roosevelt," in *Black Leaders of the Twentieth Century,* ed. John Hope Franklin and August Meier (Urbana: University of Illinois Press, 1982), 192–93.

57. Memorandum, Brimhall to Hinckley, September 27, 1939, 2, box 22, fd. 8, The Papers of Robert H. Hinckley, Special Collections Department, University of Utah Libraries, Salt Lake City. Italics mine.

58. Memorandum, "Civilian Pilot Training for Colored Students," December 14, 1939, box 64, book 3, The Papers of Robert H. Hinckley, Special Collections Department, University of Utah Libraries, Salt Lake City; Roscoe Wright to Thomas C. Hennings, Jr., October 21, 1940, "Negro Pilot Training," CAA Central Files, R.G. 237, box 378, National Archives and Records Agency, Washington, D.C.; Hardesty and Pisano, *Black Wings,* 2–3. An excellent account of the CPTP at Tuskegee Institute appears in Robert J. Jakeman, *The Divided Skies: Establishing Segregated Flight Training at Tuskegee, Alabama, 1934–1942* (Tuscaloosa: University of Alabama Press, 1992).

59. John W. Davis to John P. Morris, October 12, 1942, "Negro Pilot Training," CAA Central Files, R.G. 237, box 378, National Archives and Records Agency, Washington, D.C.

60. Roscoe Wright to Thomas C. Hennings, Jr., October 21, 1940; Robert Hinckley to Eleanor Roosevelt, February 20, 1941, "Negro Pilot Training," CAA Central Files, R.G. 237, box 378, National Archives and Records Agency, Washington, D.C.

61. Charles I. Stanton, acting administrator CAA, to Major General George E. Stratemeyer, chief of staff, Army Air Forces, June 30, 1942, CPT Memoranda and Reports, FAA Historical Files, FAA Library, Washington, D.C.; Alan L. Gropman, *The Air Force Integrates, 1945–1964* (Washington, D.C.: U.S. Office of Air Force History, 1978), 6.

62. Charles E. Planck, "Enter Mars, Exit Girls," in *Women with Wings* (New York: Harper & Bros., 1942), 150. Although the literature on women's participation in the CPTP is sketchy, see also, Stephen Bates, "Lady with Wings," *Popular Aviation,* May 1940, 55–56; 88; George R. Reiss, "The Gals

Are Flying," *Popular Aviation,* March 1940, 46–48; and Strickland, *The Putt-Putt Air Force,* 55–67.

63. *American Aviation Daily,* January 24, 1942, 105; May 15, 1943, 66; Strickland, *The Putt-Putt Air Force,* 56.

64. Wesley Frank Craven and James Lea Cate, eds., *Men and Planes,* the Army Air Forces in World War II (Chicago: University of Chicago Press, 1955), 6:263–64.

65. *Civil Aeronautics Journal,* June 15, 1940, 241; *Wartime History,* CPT-23.

66. "Plans Announced for 45,000 New Pilots," *Civil Aeronautics Journal,* June 15, 1940, 241–42; *Wartime History,* CPT-23.

67. *American Aviation,* September 15, 1940, 1, 20–21.

68. "Press Conference no. 707 (January 7, 1941)," *Complete Presidential Press Conferences of Franklin D. Roosevelt* (New York: Da Capo Press, 1972), [17: 19–20].

69. "Press Conference no. 707."

70. *American Aviation Daily,* April 3, 1941, 151; May 20, 1941, 89.

71. "Analysis of the Editorial Entitled 'Mr. Hinckley's Great Boondoggle' from the September 15 Issue of *American Aviation,*" 10, Robert H. Hinckley Institute of Politics Files, University of Utah, Salt Lake City.

72. Tables 1, 2, and 3 are adapted from information in D. Brimhall to Administrator, Civil Aeronautics, "Solution of the Air Corps Washout Problem," November 4, 1941, 3, 4, 2, 1, box 64, book 3, The Papers of Robert H. Hinckley, Special Collections Department, University of Utah Libraries, Salt Lake City.

73. D. Brimhall to Administrator, Civil Aeronautics, "Solution of the Air Corps Washout Problem."

74. Donald S. Lopez, interview by author, January 19, 1988, Washington, D.C., tape recording, National Air and Space Museum, Smithsonian Institution, Washington, D.C. See also, Donald S. Lopez, *Into the Teeth of the Tiger* (New York: Bantam, 1986), 16–17.

75. Robert H. Hinckley, "Aviation—Not as Usual," speech before the National Aviation Training Association Annual Convention, Kansas City, Missouri, December 1, 1941, Robert H. Hinckley Institute of Politics Files, University of Utah, Salt Lake City.

Chapter 4. The CPTP Goes to War

1. C. B. Allen, "C.A.A. Is Facing Loss of Its Pilot Training Set-Up," newspaper clipping, National Air and Space Museum History Project Files, Smithsonian Institution, Washington, D.C.

2. "A Brief Chronology of CAA Pilot Training Programs for the Armed Forces," box 51, fd. 11, The Papers of Dean R. Brimhall, Special Collections Department, University of Utah Libraries, Salt Lake City; Eliot Janeway, *The Struggle for Survival: A Chronicle of Economic Mobilization in World War*

II, the Chronicles of America Series, ed. Allan Nevins (New Haven, Conn.: Yale University Press, 1951), 53:52.

3. John R. M. Wilson, *Turbulence Aloft: The Civil Aeronautics Administration amid Wars and Rumors of Wars* (Washington, D.C.: U.S. Department of Transportation, Federal Aviation Administration, 1979), 102; quoted in Wilson, 102.

4. Civil Aeronautics Administration, *Wartime History of the Civil Aeronautics Administration,* unpublished report, U.S. Department of Transportation, FAA Library, Washington, D.C., 7.

5. Quoted in Wilson, *Turbulence Aloft,* 89–90.

6. Ibid., 90; *American Aviation Daily,* January 10, 1942, 40.

7. Snodgrass to Arnold, January 6, 1942, Henry H. Arnold Collection, box 41, Manuscript Division, Library of Congress, Washington, D.C.

8. Major E. F. Gillespie, Plans Division, to Commanding General Army Air Forces Arnold, with copy Executive Order 8974 attached, December 16, 1941, Henry H. Arnold Collection, box 41, Manuscript Division, Library of Congress, Washington, D.C.; Commanding General Army Air Forces Arnold to Assistant Secretary of War for Air Lovett, "Use of CAA Organization in Connection with the War Effort," n.d., Henry H. Arnold Collection, box 41, Manuscript Division, Library of Congress, Washington, D.C.

9. Arnold E. Briddon, Ellmore A. Champie, and Peter A. Marraine, *FAA Historical Fact Book: A Chronology, 1926–1971* (Washington, D.C.: U.S. Department of Transportation, Federal Aviation Administration, Office of Information Services, 1974), 45.

10. U.S. Congress, Senate, Committee on Military Affairs, *National Defense: Hearings on H.R. 3791,* 76th Cong., 1st sess., January 17–February 22, 1939, 40.

11. Commanding General Army Air Forces Arnold to General Johnson, "C.A.A. Training System," January 17, 1941, Henry H. Arnold Collection, box 41, Manuscript Division, Library of Congress, Washington, D.C.

12. Arnold to Yount, April 13, 1942, Henry H. Arnold Collection, box 41, Manuscript Division, Library of Congress, Washington, D.C.

13. See confidential memo, Chief of Air Staff Stratemeyer to Assistant Secretary of War for Air Lovett, "The Utilization of the CPT by the Navy," December 22, 1942, Henry H. Arnold Collection, box 98, Manuscript Division, Library of Congress, Washington, D.C.

14. Arthur W. Radford, "CPT and the Navy," *Flying,* January 1943, 20–21, 132; Wilson, *Turbulence Aloft,* 99; Chief of Air Staff Stratemeyer to Assistant Secretary of War for Air Lovett, "Use of CPT Schools and Facilities," December 22, 1942, Henry H. Arnold Collection, box 98, Manuscript Division, Library of Congress, Washington, D.C.

15. For a good description of Arnold's efforts to make the air force an independent service, see Herman S. Wolk, *Planning and Organizing the Postwar Air Force, 1943–1947* (Washington, D.C.: Office of Air Force History, 1984).

16. David Shawe, "Protests Mount over Army's Failure to Use CPTP Facilities," *American Aviation,* July 1, 1942, 1, 15; "CPT Runs at 25% Capacity as U.S. Dawdles," *American Aviation,* September 15, 1942, 25; Robert H. Hinckley and JoAnn Wells, *"I'd Rather Be Born Lucky than Rich": The Autobiography of Robert H. Hinckley,* Charles Redd Monographs in Western History, no. 7 (Provo, Utah: Brigham Young University Press, 1977), 94. Hereafter cited as Hinckley and Wells.

17. Quoted in Hinckley and Wells, 94–95.

18. "Notes on Conversation between Mr. Hinckley, Richard Stokes, and Dr. Brimhall, July 8, 1942, Regarding Mr. Stokes' visit with General Arnold," box 20, The Papers of Robert H. Hinckley, Special Collections Department, University of Utah Libraries.

19. *American Aviation Daily,* March 31, 1942, 129; April 3, 1942, 152; Shawe, "Protests Mount," 15.

20. Hinckley and Wells, 95.

21. James Forrestal, Secretary of the Navy, to Jesse Jones, Secretary of Commerce, May 7, 1942, FAA Historical Files, FAA Library, Washington, D.C.

22. Stanton to Lovett, ["Chronology and documentation of the Army-CAA working-out of a program of Civilian Pilot Training to be coordinated with Army requirements"], hereafter cited as Stanton Chronology, June 11, 1942, Assistant Secretary of War for Air, box 130, R.G. 107, National Archives and Records Agency, Washington, D.C.; *American Aviation Daily,* February 18, 1942, 204.

23. Wesley Frank Craven and James Lea Cate, eds., *Men and Planes,* Army Air Forces in World War II (Chicago: University of Chicago Press, 1955), 6:494–97; Stimson to the Secretary of Commerce [Jesse Jones], February 21, 1942, box 130, R.G. 107, National Archives and Records Agency, Washington, D.C.

24. Stanton Chronology.

25. Ibid.

26. Ibid.

27. Ibid.

28. Memo, Commanding General Army Air Forces Arnold to Colonel Ennis, "C.A.A. Press Releases Concerning Flying Training," March 29, 1942, Henry H. Arnold Collection, box 41, Manuscript Division, Library of Congress, Washington, D.C.

29. Stanton Chronology; Craven and Cate, eds., *Men and Planes,* 496.

30. Stanton Chronology.

31. Ibid.

32. *Wartime History,* 8, CPT-12; *American Aviation Daily,* June 27, 1942, 272; [U.S.] Department of Commerce, "Report of Pilot Training Programs, July 1939–February 1944, Conducted by Civil Aeronautics Administration Under Civilian Pilot Training Act of 1939 and Supplemental Reports to September 1944," 2, unpublished report, U.S. Department of Transportation, FAA Library, Washington, D.C.

33. "Bureaucracy Seen Brake on Aviation," *New York Times,* June 20, 1942, 28.

34. "Hinckley Resigns Washington Post," *New York Times,* July 8, 1942, 31.

35. Roosevelt to Hinckley, June 29, 1942, box 16, fd. 24, The Papers of Dean R. Brimhall, Special Collections Department, University of Utah, Salt Lake City; *New York Times,* July 15, 1942, 18.

36. *Aero Digest,* August 1942, 62.

37. Richard Polenberg, *War and Society: The United States, 1941–1945* (Philadelphia: J.B. Lippincott, 1972), 90.

38. *American Aviation Daily,* July 7, 1942, 23; William A. M. Burden Biographical File, National Air and Space Museum Archives, Smithsonian Institution, Washington, D.C.

39. Burden to Lovett, January 29, 1943, Assistant Secretary of War for Air, box 130, R.G. 107, National Archives and Records Agency, Washington, D.C.; *American Aviation,* February 1, 1943, 8; Wilson, *Turbulence Aloft,* 140.

40. Jonathan Foster Fanton, "Robert A. Lovett: The War Years," Ph.D. diss., Yale University, 1978, 12, 16, 6–7, 23.

41. Eric Larabee, *Commander-in-Chief: Franklin Delano Roosevelt, His Lieutenants, and Their War* (New York: Harper and Row), 215.

42. Fanton, "Robert A. Lovett," 85.

43. Shawe, "Protests Mount," 1, 15; "CPT Runs at 25% Capacity as U.S. Dawdles," 25.

44. "CAA-CPT Pilot Training for Army and Navy Air Forces," October 10, 1942, Tuskegee Archives, Patterson Papers, series 2, box 1, fd. 7, Tuskegee Institute, Tuskegee, Alabama.

45. "CAA-CPT Pilot Training."

46. Ibid.

47. Figures derived from statistics on CAA pilot training in *Wartime History,* CPT-23–24.

48. Lovett to Burden, September 9, 1942, Assistant Secretary of War for Air, box 130, R.G. 107, National Archives and Records Agency, Washington, D.C.

49. Lovett to Taylor, September 12, 1942, Assistant Secretary of War for Air, box 130, R.G. 107, National Archives and Records Agency, Washington, D.C.; Burden to Lovett, October 2, 1942, Assistant Secretary of War for Air, box 130, R.G. 107, National Archives and Records Agency, Washington, D.C.

50. Burden to Lovett, "Development of a Program for Continuing the Training of Pilots by CAA for the Army Air Forces: Additional Uses for Training Facilities," December 21, 1942, box 130, R.G. 107, National Archives and Records Agency, Washington, D.C., 16.

51. Craven and Cate, eds., *Men and Planes,* 516; *Wartime History,* CPT-8.

52. Lovett to Stratemeyer, December 15, 1942, Assistant Secretary of War for Air, box 130, R.G. 107, National Archives and Records Agency, Washington, D.C.

53. Ibid.

54. Ibid.

55. Stratemeyer to Assistant Secretary of War for Air Lovett, "Use of CPT Schools and Facilities."

56. Ibid.

57. Ibid.

58. Ibid.

59. Ibid.

60. *American Aviation Daily,* December 21, 1942, 238.

61. *American Aviation Daily,* January 2, 1943, 6; January 20, 1943, 91.

62. "Memorandum of Agreement, January 19, 1943, Covering Use of CAA War Training Service by the Army Air Forces," Assistant Secretary of War for Air, box 130, R.G. 107, National Archives and Records Agency, Washington, D.C.

63. Brimhall to Hinckley, January 21, 1943, The Papers of Robert H. Hinckley, Special Collections Department, University of Utah Libraries, Salt Lake City.

64. Stewart to Mooney, February 11, 1943, Assistant Secretary of War for Air, box 130, R.G. 107, National Archives and Records Agency, Washington, D.C. Phase 1 of the CPTP was from its origins to July 1, 1942; phase 2 was from July 1, to December 15, 1942.

65. *American Aviation Daily,* February 13, 1943, 213; March 13, 1943, 65; April 14, 1943, 219–20.

66. Although the exact figures on the number of contractors who were terminated are not available in journalistic accounts, the papers of the Assistant Secretary of War for Air, or the Hinckley Papers, they were extrapolated from information in Civil Aeronautics Administration, "Pilot Training Centers Elementary Course Summer 1942," June 22, 1942, box 62, fd. 16, The Papers of Robert H. Hinckley, Special Collections Department, University of Utah Libraries, Salt Lake City, and *American Aviation Daily,* April 20, 1943, 247–48, and April 21, 1943, 255–56; Wilson, *Turbulence Aloft,* 104.

67. Ibid., 104.

68. U.S. Congress, Senate, Subcommittee of the Committee on Appropriations, *Urgent Deficiencies in Certain Appropriations for Fiscal Year 1943: Hearings on H.J. Res. 115,* 78th Cong., 1st sess., April 19 and 20, 1943, 7.

69. Quoted in a letter from Senator O'Daniel to Josh Lee, April 19, 1943, Assistant Secretary of War for Air, box 130, R.G. 107, National Archives and Records Agency, Washington, D.C.

70. Ibid.

71. U.S. Congress, Senate, *Urgent Deficiencies in Certain Appropriations for Fiscal Year 1943,* 1–53, 69–80.

72. AFPMP-7-1M, June 1, 1943, Assistant Secretary of War for Air, box 130, R.G. 107, National Archives and Records Agency, Washington, D.C.; *American Aviation Daily,* July 2, 1943, 8.

73. *American Aviation Daily,* April 14, 1943, 219–20; U.S. Congress, Senate, Subcommittee of the Committee on Commerce, *Training of Pilots under the Civil Aeronautics Administration War Training Service: Hearing on S. 1037 and H.R. 1670,* 78th Cong., 1st sess., May 4, 1943, 5.

74. U.S. Congress, Senate, *Congressional Record,* Senate, 78th Cong., 1st

sess., 1943, 89, pt. 4:5058; see also, U.S. Congress, Senate, *Training of Pilots under the Civil Aeronautics Administration War Training Service,* 1–7.

75. *American Aviation Daily,* January 16, 1943, 28.

76. Wesley Frank Craven and James Lea Cate, eds., *Plans and Early Operations,* Army Air Forces in World War II (Chicago: University of Chicago, 1948), 1: 129; Joint Aircraft Committee Memo, January 5, 1943, Henry H. Arnold Collection, box 99, Manuscript Division, Library of Congress, Washington, D.C.

77. Hanley to Joint Aircraft Committee, January 10, 1943, Henry H. Arnold Collection, box 99, Manuscript Division, Library of Congress, Washington, D.C.

78. Ibid.

79. "Memorandum of Agreement, January 19, 1943"; Stewart to Harper, May 24, 1943, Assistant Secretary of War for Air, box 130, R.G. 107, National Archives and Records Agency, Washington, D.C.

80. Stewart to Smith, March 11, 1943, Assistant Secretary of War for Air, box 130, R.G. 107, National Archives and Records Agency, Washington, D.C.

81. *American Aviation Daily,* January 20, 1943, 123; *American Aviation,* November 11, 1943, 39.

82. *American Aviation,* November 15, 1943, 54–55; Stewart to Harper, May 22, 1943, Assistant Secretary of War for Air, box 130, R.G. 107, National Archives and Records Agency, Washington, D.C.

83. Brownell to Assistant Chief of Air Staff, Training, November 8, 1943, Assistant Secretary of War for Air, box 130, R.G. 107, National Archives and Records Agency, Washington, D.C.; Burden to Lovett, November 3, 1943, Assistant Secretary of War for Air, box 130, R.G. 107, National Archives and Records Agency, Washington, D.C.

84. Brownell to Harper, November 8, 1943, Assistant Secretary of War for Air, box 130, R.G. 107, National Archives and Records Agency, Washington, D.C.

85. Harper to Lovett, November 12, 1943, Assistant Secretary of War for Air, box 130, R.G. 107, National Archives and Records Agency, Washington, D.C.

86. Ibid.

87. *American Aviation Daily,* January 12, 1944, 45; January 15, 1944, 63.

88. Future Release, War Department Bureau of Public Relations, n.d., Assistant Secretary of War for Air, box 130, R.G. 107, National Archives and Records Agency, Washington, D.C.

Chapter 5. The CPTP and Postwar Aviation

1. War Department Press Release, March 16, 1944, Assistant Secretary of War for Air, box 130, R.G. 107, National Archives and Records Agency, Washington, D.C.

2. Undated excerpt from the *Congressional Record,* A3049–A3050, box 64, book 3, The Papers of Robert H. Hinckley, Special Collections Department, University of Utah Libraries, Salt Lake City.

3. *American Aviation,* December 15, 1943, 15; NATA's name was later changed to the National Aviation Trades Association.

4. *N.A.T.A. Dispatch,* February 8, 1944, 2.

5. Civil Aeronautics Administration, *Wartime History of the Civil Aeronautics Administration,* unpublished report, U.S. Department of Transportation, FAA Library, Washington, D.C., Research, CPT-23–CPT-24; David O. Levine, *The American College and the Culture of Aspiration, 1915–1940* (Ithaca, N.Y.: Cornell University Press, 1986), 197–98.

6. Joseph J. Corn, *The Winged Gospel: America's Romance with Aviation, 1900–1950* (New York: Oxford University Press, 1983), 108. Emphasis in original.

7. John H. Geisse and Samuel C. Williams, *Postwar Outlook for Private Flying* (Report to W. A. M. Burden, Esq., special aviation assistant to the secretary of commerce), September 30, 1943, National Air and Space Museum Archives, Smithsonian Institution, Washington, D.C., 44. For other wartime and postwar predictions about private flying in the United States, see John H. Geisse, "Suggestions for Furthering Private Flying," unpub. paper, April 27, 1944, National Air and Space Museum Archives, Smithsonian Institution, Washington, D.C.; Geisse, "Post-War Private Flying," National Air and Space Museum Archives, Smithsonian Institution, Washington, D.C., n.d.; *Civil Aviation and the National Economy* (Washington, D.C.: U.S. Department of Commerce, Civil Aeronautics Administration, September 1945); *Tomorrow's Customers for Aviation* (New York: Crowell-Collier Publishing Company, August 1944); and William F. Ogburn, Jean L. Adams, and S. C. Gilfillan, *The Social Effects of Aviation* (Boston: Houghton Mifflin, 1946), esp. 242–68. Ogburn's bibliography (725–37) also contains a wealth of information on topics related to postwar private flying and the CPTP.

8. Geisse and Williams, *Postwar Outlook,* 44, 18.

9. *Civil Aviation and the National Economy* (Washington, D.C.: U.S. Department of Commerce, Civil Aeronautics Administration, 1945), 30.

10. R. McLean Stewart, "The Work of Civilian Aviation in the Training of Pilots," address to the National Aviation Training Association, St. Louis, Missouri, December 3, 1943, FAA Historical Files, Federal Aviation Administration Library, Washington, D.C.

11. U.S. Congress, Senate, Subcommittee of the Committee on Commerce, *A Bill to Extend the Civilian Pilot Training Act of 1939,* Hearings on S. 1432, 78th Cong., 2d sess., February 2–3, 1944, 1.

12. Ibid., 3.

13. Ibid., 4.

14. Ibid., 4–5.

15. Ibid., 8–10.

16. Ibid., 12.

17. U.S. Congress, House, *Congressional Record,* 78th Cong., 2d sess., June 19, 1944, 90, pt. 5:6211.

18. U.S. Congress, House, *Congressional Record,* 78th Cong., 2d sess., January 27, 1944, 90, pt. 4:856, 962, 1631; *American Aviation,* March 15, 1944, 24; *N.A.T.A. Dispatch,* March 9, 1944, 3, March 17, 1944, 1, April

11, 1944, 1; John R. M. Wilson, *Turbulence Aloft: The Civil Aeronautics Administration amid Wars and Rumors of Wars* (Washington, D.C.: U.S. Department of Transportation, Federal Aviation Administration, 1979), 79–81; *American Aviation,* June 15, 1944, 18.

19. *American Aviation,* June 15, 1944, 18; 78th Cong., 2d sess., House of Representatives Report no. 1622, "Extending the Civilian Pilot Training Act," June 10, 1944, 1; U.S. Congress, House, *Congressional Record,* 78th Cong., 2d sess., June 19, 1944, 90, pt. 5:211.

20. *Congressional Record,* June 19, 1944, 6211–21.

21. Ibid., 6213–14.

22. Ibid., 6212, 6214.

23. U.S. Congress, House, *Congressional Record,* 78th Cong., 2d sess., 1944, 90, pt. 5:6650; "An Act to Extend the Civilian Pilot Training Act of 1939," Public Law 391, June 30, 1944, *U.S. Statutes at Large,* 1944, vol. 58, pt. 1:648.

24. *American Aviation Daily,* July 5, 1944, 12.

25. *American Aviation Daily,* July 13, 1944, 52; July 29, 1944, 132.

26. U.S. Congress, House, Subcommittee of the Committee on Appropriations, *Department of Commerce Appropriation Bill for 1946: Hearings,* 79th Cong., 1st sess., January 26, 1945, 104; Fred Hamlin, "Train or Not to Train?" *Flying,* April 1944, 67; *American Aviation Daily,* April 5, 1944, 178; Memo, Secretary of War to Senator Josiah W. Bailey, March 16, 1944, Assistant Secretary of War for Air, box 130, R.G. 107, National Archives; Memo, Acting Director, Bureau of Budget to Secretary of Commerce, February 2, 1944, box 63, The Papers of Robert H. Hinckley, Special Collections Department, University of Utah Libraries; U.S. Congress, House, Subcommittee of the Committee on Appropriations, *Department of Commerce Appropriation Bill for 1947,* Hearings, 79th Cong., 2d sess., February 8, 1946, 668; *Congressional Record,* May 22, 1946, 5405.

27. Arthur Schlesinger, Jr., ed., *The Almanac of American History* (Greenwich, Conn.: Bison Books, 1983), 502, 514; William L. O'Neill, *American High: The Years of Confidence, 1945–1960* (New York: Free Press, 1986), 87.

28. *N.A.T.A. Dispatch,* May 5, 1944, 3.

29. See chapter 3, "Unification and a Separate Air Force," in Herman S. Wolk, *Planning and Organizing the Postwar Air Force, 1943–1947* (Washington, D.C.: Office of Air Force History, 1984), 80–112.

30. "Summary of War-Time Training, Notes on Expansion," Carl A. Spaatz Collection, Chief of Staff Files, 1946–48, Air Force Training, box 255, Manuscript Division, Library of Congress, Washington, D.C.

31. "Extending the Civilian Pilot Training Act," 2; 78th Cong., 2d sess., Senate Report no. 782, "Extending the Civilian Pilot Training Act of 1939," March 29, 1944, 1–2.

32. *American Aviation Daily,* April 5, 1944, 178; *American Aviation,* June 15, 1944, 18.

33. Alfred Goldberg, ed., *A History of the United States Air Force, 1907–1957* (Princeton, N.J.: Van Nostrand, 1957, repr. New York: Arno, 1972), 171.

34. Spaatz to Arnold, July 10, 1946, Henry H. Arnold Papers, Library of Congress, Personal Files, ca. 1946–50, box 283, Manuscript Division, Library of Congress, Washington, D.C.

35. Wilson, *Turbulence Aloft,* 164; *National Aeronatics,* October 1945, 49.

36. 79th Cong., 2d sess., House of Representatives Report no. 1890, "State, Justice, Commerce, and the Judiciary Appropriation Bill Fiscal Year 1947," 3.

37. *National Aeronautics,* January 1947, 1–5.

Conclusion

1. John H. Geisse and Samuel C. Williams, *Postwar Outlook for Private Flying* (Report to W.A.M. Burden, Esq., special aviation assistant to the secretary of commerce), September 30, 1943, National Air and Space Museum Archives, Smithsonian Institution, Washington, D.C., 11.

2. Devon Francis, *Mr. Piper and His Cubs* (Ames: Iowa State University Press, 1973), 87.

3. See Joseph J. Corn, *The Winged Gospel: America's Romance with Aviation, 1900–1950* (New York: Oxford University Press, 1983), 113–33.

4. Corn, *The Winged Gospel,* 121.

5. Civil Aeronautics Administration, *Wartime History of the Civil Aeronautics Administration,* unpublished report, U.S. Department of Transportation, FAA Library, Washington, D.C., CPT-23–CPT-24; *Civil Aviation and the National Economy* (Washington, D.C.: U.S. Department of Commerce, Civil Aeronautics Administration, 1945), 30.

6. *Statistical Handbook of Civil Aviation, 1949* (Washington, D.C.: U.S. Department of Commerce, Civil Aeronautics Administration, n.d.), 31–32.

7. Corn, *The Winged Gospel,* 132.

8. *Wartime History,* CPT-25.

9. Ibid., CPT-23–24.

10. Ibid.

11. Robert Goralski, *World War II Almanac, 1931–1945: A Political and Military Record* (New York: G. P. Putnam, 1981), 421.

12. Corn, *The Winged Gospel,* 91–111.

13. *Statistical Handbook of Civil Aviation, 1949,* 25, 51; *Statistical Handbook of Civil Aviation, 1955* (Washington, D.C.: U.S. Department of Commerce, Civil Aeronautics Administration, n.d.), 49.

14. William F. Ogburn, Jean L. Adams, and S. C. Gilfillan, *The Social Effects of Aviation* (Boston: Houghton Mifflin, 1946), 263–64.

15. Ogburn, Adams, and Gilfillan, *Social Effects of Aviation,* 264–65.

16. Ibid., 244.

17. Ibid., 244; W. J. Skinner, *Economics of Personal Airplane Operation,* Circular Series no. 10 (Corvallis: Oregon State College, 1947), 6; Ogburn, Adams, and Gilfillan, *Social Effects of Aviation,* 246–47.

18. Ogburn, Adams, and Gilfillan, *Social Effects of Aviation,* 245.

19. Ibid., 244–45.

20. Douglas D. Bond, *The Love and Fear of Flying* (New York: International Universities Press, 1952), 9.

21. Bond, *Love and Fear of Flying,* 13.

22. John R. M. Wilson, *Turbulence Aloft: The Civil Aeronautics Administration Amid Wars and Rumors of Wars* (Washington, D.C.: U.S. Department of Transportation, Federal Aviation Administration, 1979), 165.

23. Francis, *Mr. Piper and His Cubs,* 120.

24. Wilson, *Turbulence Aloft,* 173.

25. Francis, *Mr. Piper and His Cubs,* 121–23; Daniel R. Zuck, *An Airplane in Every Garage* (New York: Vantage, 1958), 37.

26. *Public Opinion Quarterly,* Spring 1946, 138.

27. *Public Opinion Quarterly,* Summer 1946, 246.

28. Steven Thompson, "The Great Pilot Shortage," *Air and Space Smithsonian,* October-November 1986, 62–63.

29. Thompson, "The Great Pilot Shortage," 62–63; Steven Thompson, "Hard Times in Hangar Town," *Air and Space Smithsonian,* April-May 1986, 76–78, 83–84.

30. Quoted in Alan Brinkley, review of *The Power Game: How Washington Works,* by Hedrick Smith, *New York Times,* March 27, 1988, 1.

31. Robert H. Hinckley and JoAnn Wells, *"I'd Rather Be Born Lucky than Rich": The Autobiography of Robert H. Hinckley,* Charles Redd Monographs in Western History, no. 7 (Provo, Utah: Brigham Young University Press, 1977), 106–7, 123–28.

Bibliography

Primary Material

The most important source of primary material for this study was the Papers of Robert H. Hinckley in the Special Collections Department of the University of Utah Library in Salt Lake City. The Hinckley Papers, which I visited on two occasions in 1986 and 1987, contain a wealth of information, particularly about the early days of the CPTP (1939–41) and about Hinckley. Among the many papers, reports, items of correspondence, and newspaper clippings was Hinckley's unpublished and uncompleted manuscript *Adventures in Democracy: The Story of the Civilian Pilot Training Program,* upon which I drew for the first two chapters of this book. I also found a great many of Hinckley's speeches for the Civil Aeronautics Administration and some postwar biographical information at the Robert H. Hinckley Institute of Politics at the University of Utah.

Another important source of information on the CPTP and WTS was the Papers of Dean R. Brimhall, Hinckley's longtime business and professional associate and director of research at the CAA, also in the Special Collections Department of the University of Utah Library. The Brimhall Collection often duplicates material contained in the Hinckley Papers, but I discovered on my second visit that Brimhall often had an insider's view of the agency and of the CPTP, especially during the war years. This was largely because he stayed on with the CAA after Hinckley departed for the Sperry Corporation in 1942.

For the history of the CPTP during the war, I found that the Assistant Secretary of War for Air Files (R.G. 107) in the National Archives and Records Agency, Washington, D.C., were critical to my research. The files not only included material from the Assistant Secretary of War for Air Robert A. Lovett, but also contained valuable information unavailable in the Robert Hinckley Papers. Likewise, the Henry H. Arnold Papers in the Library of Congress, Manuscript Division, Washington, D.C., contain material that relates to the U.S. Army Air Corps' and, later, the Army Air Forces' interaction with the Civil Aeronautics Administration on the CPTP and WTS programs. The Arnold Papers also shed valuable light on the nature of the jurisdictional battle between the AAF and the CAA during the war.

Of limited usefulness were the Federal Aviation Administration Historical Files in Washington, D.C., which contain some information on the administration of the CPTP and the WTS. These files, however, did include an unpublished report from the Civil Aeronautics Administration, *Wartime History of the Civil Aeronautics Administration,* that was especially helpful in providing statistical and financial information. The Federal Aviation Administration records (R.G. 237), National Archives and Records Agency, Washington, D.C., contain correspondence, reports, and other primary material on the CPTP and WTS programs. The most important was correspondence that illuminated aspects of the experience of blacks in relation to the CPTP.

The National Air and Space Museum Archives Research Files and the Aeronautics Department History Project Files contain miscellaneous research materials (both primary and secondary), unpublished information, and photographs that relate to the CPTP and WTS. Of marginal importance to this study were the Harry Hopkins Papers in the Franklin Delano Roosevelt Library, Hyde Park, N.Y., which contain some information on Hinckley's years as an official of the Works Progress Administration.

In most instances, the published hearings on the CPTP were the only way to cover the legislative proceedings in detail. Among the most helpful were: U.S. Congress, House, Committee on Interstate and Foreign Commerce, *Training of Civil Aircraft Pilots: Hearings on H.R. 50[9]3,* 76th Cong., 1st sess., March 20 and 27, 1939; U.S. Congress, Senate, Subcommittee of the Committee on Commerce, *Training of Civil Aircraft Pilots: Hearings on S. 2119,* 76th Cong., 1st sess., April 20, 1939; and U.S. Congress, Senate, Subcommittee of the Committee on Commerce, *A Bill to Extend the Civilian Pilot Training Act of 1939,* Hearings on S.1432, 78th Cong., 2d sess., February 2–3, 1944.

Secondary Material

There is little secondary material on the Roosevelt administration's aviation policy in the New Deal years. Two notable exceptions are: Nick A. Komons, *Bonfires to Beacons: Federal Civil Aviation Policy under the Air Commerce Act 1926–1938* (Washington, D.C.: U.S. Department of Transportation, Federal Aviation Administration, 1978), and John R. M. Wilson, *Turbulence Aloft: The Civil Aeronautics Administration amid Wars and Rumors of Wars, 1938–1953* (Washington, D.C.: U.S. Department of Transportation, Federal Aviation Administration, 1979), on which I have relied for contextual information. I have also used two unpublished manuscripts that shed considerable light on New Deal aviation policy: Tom D. Crouch, "An Airplane for Everyman: The Department of Commerce and the Light Plane Industry, 1933–1937," and Von D. Hardesty, "Aviation and the New Deal," in the National Air and Space Museum History Project Files, Smithsonian Institution, Washington, D.C.

For general contextual information on F.D.R. and the New Deal, I relied upon William E. Leuchtenburg, *Franklin D. Roosevelt and the New Deal, 1932–1940* (New York: Harper and Row, 1963); Frank Freidel, *Franklin D. Roosevelt: Launching the New Deal* (Boston: Little, Brown, 1973); and James MacGregor Burns, *Roosevelt: The Lion and the Fox* (San Diego: Harcourt Brace Jovanovich, 1956) and *Roosevelt: The Soldier of Freedom* (San Diego: Harcourt Brace Jovanovich, 1970).

I found the following secondary sources to be especially useful on aspects of the New Deal that relate to this study: David Brody, "The New Deal and World War II," in *The New Deal*, vol. 1, *The National Level*, ed. John Braeman, Robert H. Bremner, and David Brody (Columbus: Ohio State University Press, 1975), 267–309; William E. Leuchtenburg, "The New Deal and the Analogue of War," in *Change and Continuity in Twentieth Century America*, ed. John Braeman, Robert H. Bremner, and Everett Walters (Columbus: Ohio State University Press, 1964), 81–143; Richard Polenberg, "The Decline of the New Deal," in *The New Deal*, vol. 1, *The National Level*, ed. John Braeman, Robert H. Bremner, and David Brody (Columbus: Ohio State University Press, 1975), 262–63; B. Joyce. Ross, "Mary McLeod Bethune and the National Youth Administration: A Case Study of Power Relationships in the Black Cabinet of Franklin D. Roosevelt," in *Black Leaders of the Twentieth Century*, ed. John Hope Franklin and August Meier (Urbana: University of Illinois Press, 1982), 191–219; and Arthur M. Schlesinger, Jr., *The Coming of the New Deal*, in *The Age of Roosevelt* (Boston, 1959), and "The Broad Accomplishments of the New Deal," in *The New Deal: Revolution or Evolution? Problems in American Civilization* (Boston: D. C. Heath, 1959), 29–34.

For contextual information on the transition from New Deal to war preparedness-mobilization, I found the following useful: Robert A. Divine, *Roosevelt and World War II* (Baltimore: Penguin Books, 1970); Eliot Janeway, *The Struggle for Survival: A Chronicle of Economic Mobilization in World War II*, vol. 53, the Chronicles of America Series (New Haven: Yale University Press, 1951); Gerald D. Nash, *The Great Depression and World War II: Organizing America, 1933–1945*, St. Martin's Series in Twentieth Century United States History (New York: St. Martin's Press, 1939); Richard Polenberg, *War and Society: The United States, 1941–1945* (Philadelphia: J. B. Lippincott, 1972); and David L. Porter, *The Seventy-Sixth Congress and World War II, 1939–1940* (Columbia: University of Missouri Press, 1979).

For contextual information on the postwar environment for the CPTP, I found the following useful: Joseph J. Corn, *The Winged Gospel: America's Romance with Aviation, 1900–1950* (New York: Oxford University Press, 1983); William F. Ogburn, Jean L. Adams, and S. C. Gilfillan, *The Social Effects of Aviation* (Boston: Houghton Mifflin, 1946); and Herman S. Wolk, *Planning and Organizing the Postwar Air Force, 1943–1947* (Washington, D.C.: Office of Air Force History, 1984).

The most comprehensive newspaper coverage of the CPTP-WTS was contained in the pages of the *New York Times*. Among the periodicals I consulted were *Air Commerce Bulletin* and its successor, *Civil Aeronautics Journal*, which provide often biased institutional reportage of events, and *The*

Aircraft Year Book, which presents the annual industry view, again biased. Most useful for day-to-day comprehensive reporting of the news on the CPTP was *American Aviation Daily,* upon which I drew heavily, and, for interpretive journalism on the subject, *American Aviation,* published bi-weekly. Invaluable for its coverage of the legislative proceedings is the *Congressional Record.*

Published Public Records and Documents

U.S. Congress. Senate. Special Committee on Investigation of Air Mail and Ocean Contracts. *Investigation of Air Mail and Ocean Contracts.* 73d Cong., 2d sess., pts. 1–9.

U.S. Congress. Senate. Subcommittee of the Committee on Commerce. *Safety in Air: Hearings Before a Subcommittee of the Committee on Commerce.* (A Resolution to Investigate Certain Airplane Accidents and Interstate Air Commerce). 74th Cong., 2d sess., 1936–37, pts. 1–3.

U.S. Congress. Senate. Committee on Military Affairs. *National Defense: Hearings.* 76th Cong., 1st sess., January 17 to February 22, 1939.

U.S. Congress. House. Committee on Interstate and Foreign Commerce. *Training of Civil Aircraft Pilots: Hearings on H.R. 50[9]3.* 76th Cong., 1st sess., March 20 and 27, 1939.

U.S. Congress. Senate. Subcommittee of the Committee on Commerce. *Training of Civil Aircraft Pilots: Hearings on S. 2119.* 76th Cong., 1st sess., April 20, 1939.

U.S. Congress. Senate. Subcommittee of the Committee on Appropriations. *Urgent Deficiencies in Certain Appropriations for Fiscal Year 1943: Hearings on H.J. Res. 115.* 78th Cong., 1st sess., April 19 and 20, 1943.

U.S. Congress. Senate. Subcommittee of the Committee on Commerce. *Training of Pilots under the Civil Aeronautics Administration War Training Service: Hearing on S. 1037 and H.R. 1670.* 78th Cong., 1st sess., May 4, 1943.

U.S. Congress. Senate. Subcommittee of the Committee on Commerce. *A Bill to Extend the Civilian Pilot Training Act of 1939, Hearings on S. 1432.* 78th Cong., 2d sess., February 2–3, 1944.

U.S. Congress. House. Subcommittee of the Committee on Appropriations. *Department of Commerce Appropriation Bill for 1946: Hearings.* 79th Cong., 1st sess., January 26, 1945.

U.S. Congress. House. Subcommittee of the Committee on Appropriations, *Department of Commerce Appropriation Bill for 1947, Hearings.* 79th Cong., 2d sess., February 8, 1946.

U.S. Civil Aeronautics Administration. *War Training Service Standard Practice Manual for Procedure, 1943.*

Unpublished Manuscripts and Reports

Burden, William A. M. *Latin American Air Transportation* (Preliminary), confidential report prepared for the Coordinator of Commercial and

Cultural Relations between the American Republics, June 1941. National Air and Space Museum Archives, Smithsonian Institution, Washington, D.C.

Crouch, Tom D. "An Airplane for Everyman: The Department of Commerce and the Light Plane Industry, 1933–1937," unpublished ms., National Air and Space Museum History Project Files, Smithsonian Institution, Washington, D.C.

Emme, Eugene M. "German Air Power: 1919–1939," Ph.D. diss., University of Iowa, 1949.

Fanton, Jonathan Foster. "Robert A. Lovett: The War Years," Ph.D. diss., Yale University, 1978.

Geisse, John H., and Samuel C. Williams. *Postwar Outlook for Private Flying.* Report to W. A. M. Burden, Esq., Special Aviation Assistant to the Secretary of Commerce. September 30, 1943. National Air and Space Museum Archives, Smithsonian Institution, Washington, D.C.

———. "Post-War Private Flying." Preprint of paper presented at War Engineering Annual Meeting of the Society of Automotive Engineers, Detroit. January 10–14, 1944. National Air and Space Museum Archives, Smithsonian Institution, Washington, D.C.

———. "Suggestions for Furthering Private Flying." Preprint of paper presented to National Light Aircraft Meeting of the Institute of the Aeronautical Sciences, Detroit. April 27, 1944. National Air and Space Museum Archives, Smithsonian Institution, Washington, D.C.

Hardesty, Von D. "Aviation and the New Deal," unpublished ms., National Air and Space Museum History Project Files, Smithsonian Institution, Washington, D.C.

Stewart, R. M. "The Work of Civilian Aviation in the Training of Pilots." FAA Historical Files. U.S. Department of Transportation. FAA Library. Washington, D.C.

U.S. Civil Aeronautics Administration. *Wartime History of the Civil Aeronautics Administration.* Unpublished report. FAA Historical Files. U.S. Department of Transportation. FAA Library. Washington, D.C.

van der Linden, F. Robert. "The Struggle for the Long-Range Heavy Bomber: The United States Army Air Corps, 1934–1939," master's thesis, George Washington University, 1981.

Vidal, Eugene L. Address to Michigan Aeronautical Activities Association, and the Detroit Section, Society of Automotive Engineers, April 16, 1934.

Books and Published Reports

Bender, Marylin, and Selig Altschul. *The Chosen Instrument.* New York: Simon and Schuster, 1982.

Bilstein, Roger. *Flight in America, 1900–1983.* Baltimore: Johns Hopkins University Press, 1984.

Briddon, Arnold, et al. *FAA Historical Fact Book: A Chronology, 1926–1971.*

Washington, D.C.: U.S. Department of Transportation, Federal Aviation Administration, 1974.

Burden, William A. M. *The Struggle for Airways in Latin America.* New York: Council on Foreign Relations, 1943.

Burns, James MacGregor. *Roosevelt: The Lion and the Fox.* San Diego: Harcourt Brace Jovanovich, 1956.

———. *Roosevelt: The Soldier of Freedom.* San Diego: Harcourt Brace Jovanovich, 1970.

Cartwright, Catherine, et al. *Bibliography of Aviation Education Materials: An Annotated List of Books and Visual Aids for the Use of Schools and Libraries.* New York: Macmillan, 1942.

Civil Aviation and the National Economy. [Washington, D.C.]: U.S. Department of Commerce. Civil Aeronautics Administration. September 1945.

Corn, Joseph J. *The Winged Gospel: America's Romance with Aviation, 1900–1950.* New York: Oxford University Press, 1983.

Cozzens, James Gould. *A Time of War: Air Force Diaries and Pentagon Memos, 1943–45.* Edited by Matthew J. Bruccoli. Columbia, S.C.: Bruccoli Clark, 1984.

Craven, Wesley Frank, and James Lea Cate, eds. *Plans and Early Operations.* Vol. 1. The Army Air Forces in World War II. Chicago: University of Chicago Press, 1948.

———. *Men and Planes.* Vol. 6. The Army Air Forces in World War II. Chicago: University of Chicago Press, 1955.

Davis, Kenneth S. *The Hero: Charles A. Lindbergh and the American Dream.* Garden City, N.Y.: Doubleday, 1959.

Divine, Robert A. *Roosevelt and World War II.* Baltimore: Penguin Books, 1970.

Farmer, James H. *Celluloid Wings: The Impact of Movies on Aviation.* Blue Ridge Summit, Pa.: TAB Books 1984.

Foulois, Benjamin D., and Carroll V. Glines. *From the Wright Brothers to the Astronauts: The Memoirs of Major General Benjamin D. Foulois.* New York: Arno Press, 1980.

Francillon, Rene J. *McDonnell Douglas Aircraft since 1920.* London: G. P. Putnam's Sons, 1979.

Freidel, Frank. *Franklin D. Roosevelt: Launching the New Deal.* Boston: Little, Brown, 1973.

Freudenthal, Elsbeth E. *The Aviation Business: From Kitty Hawk to Wall Street.* New York: Vanguard, 1940.

Goldberg, Alfred, ed. *A History of the United States Air Force, 1907–1957.* Princeton, N.J.: Van Nostrand, 1957. Reprint. New York: Arno Press, 1972.

Goralski, Robert. *World War II Almanac, 1931–1945: A Political and Military Record.* New York: G. P. Putnam's Sons, 1981.

Gropman, Alan L. *The Air Force Integrates, 1945–1964.* Washington, D.C.: U.S. Office of Air Force History, 1978.

Hardesty, Von, and Dominick Pisano. *Black Wings: The American Black in Aviation.* Washington, D.C.: Smithsonian Institution Press, 1984.

Hinckley, Robert H., and JoAnn J. Wells. *"I'd Rather Be Born Lucky than Rich": The Autobiography of Robert H. Hinckley.* Charles Redd Monographs in Western History, no. 7. Provo, Utah: Brigham Young University Press, 1977.

Holley, Irving B., Jr. *Buying Aircraft: Materiel Procurement for the Army Air Forces.* United States Army in World War II. Washington, D.C.: Office of the Chief of Military History, 1964.

Ickes, Harold L. *The Secret Diary of Harold L. Ickes.* Vol. 1. New York: Simon and Schuster, 1953.

Jakeman, Robert J. "America's Black Air Pioneers, 1909–1939." Air Command and Staff College Student Report. Maxwell AFB, Ala.: Air University, 1988.

———. *The Divided Skies: Establishing Segregated Flight Training at Tuskegee Alabama, 1934–1942.* Tuscaloosa: University of Alabama Press, 1992.

Janeway, Eliot. *The Struggle for Survival: A Chronicle of Economic Mobilization in World War II.* Vol. 53. The Chronicles of America Series. New Haven: Yale University Press, 1951.

Johnson, Edwin C. *Mars in Civilian Disguise: An Exposure of the Military Purposes Underlying the Student Pilot Training Program Being Administered by the Civil Aeronautics Authority.* Foreword by John Dewey. Committee on Militarism in Education. 2929 Broadway, New York City.

Komons, Nick A. *Bonfires to Beacons: Federal Civil Aviation Policy under the Air Commerce Act 1926–1938.* Washington, D.C.: U.S. Department of Transportation, Federal Aviation Administration, 1978.

———. *The Cutting Air Crash: A Case Study in Early Federal Aviation Policy.* Washington, D.C.: U.S. Department of Transportation, Federal Aviation Administration, 1973.

Langer, William L., ed. *Encyclopedia of World History.* Boston: Houghton Mifflin, 1948.

Larabee, Eric. *Commander-in-Chief: Franklin Delano Roosevelt, His Lieutenants, and Their War.* New York: Harper and Row, 1987.

Leuchtenburg, William E. *Franklin D. Roosevelt and the New Deal, 1932–1940.* The New American Nation Series. New York: Harper and Row, 1963.

Levine, David O. *The American College and the Culture of Aspiration, 1915–1940.* Ithaca, N.Y.: Cornell University Press, 1986.

Lopez, Donald S. *Into the Teeth of the Tiger.* New York: Bantam Books, 1986.

Manchester, William A. *The Glory and the Dream: A Narrative History of America, 1932–1972.* New York: Bantam Books, 1980.

Morison, Samuel Eliot. *History of United States Naval Operations in World War II.* Vol. 3: *The Rising Sun in the Pacific, 1931–April 1942.* Boston: Little, Brown, 1975.

———. *The Oxford History of the American People.* Vol. 3. New York: New American Library, 1972.

Nash, Gerald D. *The Great Depression and World War II: Organizing America, 1933–1945.* The St. Martin's Series in Twentieth Century United States History. New York: St. Martin's Press, 1939.

Ogburn, William F., Jean L. Adams, and S. C. Gilfillan. *The Social Effects of Aviation.* Boston: Houghton Mifflin, 1946.

O'Neill, William L. *American High: The Years of Confidence, 1945–1960.* New York: Free Press, 1986.

Perrett, Geoffrey. *Days of Sadness, Years of Triumph: The American People, 1939–1945.* Madison: University of Wisconsin Press, 1985.

Pogue, Forrest C. *George C. Marshall: Education of a General, 1880–1939.* New York: Viking Press, 1963.

Polenberg, Richard. *War and Society: The United States, 1941–1945.* Philadelphia: J. B. Lippincott, 1972.

Porter, David L. *The Seventy-Sixth Congress and World War II, 1939–1940.* Columbia: University of Missouri Press, 1979.

Powell, William J. *Black Wings.* Los Angeles: Ivan Deach, Jr., 1934.

Rosenman, Samuel I. *The Public Papers and Addresses of Franklin D. Roosevelt.* Vols. 7 and 8. New York: Macmillan, 1941.

Schlesinger, Arthur M., Jr., ed. *The Almanac of American History.* Greenwich, Conn., Bison Books, 1983.

———. *The Coming of the New Deal.* In *The Age of Roosevelt.* Boston: Houghton Mifflin, 1959.

———. *The Crisis of the Old Order: 1919–1933.* In *The Age of Roosevelt.* Boston: Houghton Mifflin, 1957.

Shiner, John F. *Foulois and the U.S. Army Air Corps, 1931–1935.* Washington, D.C.: Office of Air Force History, 1983.

Smith, Henry Ladd. *Airways: The History of Commercial Aviation in the United States.* New York: Alfred A. Knopf, 1942.

Statistical Handbook of Civil Aviation. Washington, D.C.: U.S. Department of Commerce. Civil Aeronautics Administration, n.d.

Strickland, Patricia. *The Putt-Putt Air Force: The Story of the Civilian Pilot Training Program and the War Training Service [1939–1944].* Washington, D.C.: U.S. Department of Transportation, Federal Aviation Administration, n.d.

Tomorrow's Customers for Aviation. New York: Research Department, Crowell-Collier Publishing. August 1944.

Turnbull, Archibald D., and Clifford L. Lord. *History of United States Naval Aviation.* New Haven, Conn.: Yale University Press, 1949.

Viteles, Morris S., et al. *A Course in Training Methods for Pilot Instructors.* Report no. 20. Washington, D.C.: Civil Aeronautics Administration, Division of Research, September 1943.

Viteles, Morris S., and Albert S. Thompson. *The Use of Standard Flights and Motion Photography in the Analysis of Aircraft Pilot Performance.*

Report no. 15. Washington, D.C.: Civil Aeronautics Administration, Division of Research, May 1943.
Whitnah, Donald R. *Safer Skyways: Federal Control of Aviation, 1926–1966.* Ames: Iowa State University Press, 1966.
Wilson, John R. M. *Turbulence Aloft: The Civil Aeronautics Administration amid Wars and Rumors of Wars, 1938–1953.* Washington, D.C.: U.S. Department of Transportation, Federal Aviation Administration, 1979.
Wolk, Herman S. *Planning and Organizing the Postwar Air Force, 1943–1947.* Washington, D.C.: Office of Air Force History, 1984.
Wright, Richard. *Native Son.* New York: Harper and Row, 1966.

Articles and Book Chapters

"American Scene; Civil Aeronautics Authority Trains College Pilots at Purdue." *American Magazine,* November 1939, 69–71.
Anon. Review of *20,000 Men a Year.* In *Variety Film Reviews, 1938–1942.* New York: Garland Publishing, 1983, n.p. [October 25, 1939].
"The Appoint-mints with the HOle." *Aviation,* August 1938, 19.
Ashby, Lyle W. "Education for the Air Age: A Brief Survey of Aviation Education Today." *Journal of the National Education Association,* March 1943, 73–76.
Barry, W. "All-American Air Team; Inter-American Aviation Training Program." *Flying,* February 1944, 24–25.
Bates, Stephen. "Lady with Wings." *Popular Aviation,* May 1940, 55–56, 88.
"Better Patter; Technique for Basic Flight Instruction." *Time,* April 26, 1943, 39.
Bingham, Hiram. "An Open Letter to Postmaster General Farley." *National Aeronautic Magazine,* Special Air Mail Issue, March 1934.
Brimhall, Dean R. "Applied Research: Men." *Flying and Popular Aviation,* February 1942, 56.
Brody, David. "The New Deal and World War II." In *The New Deal,* vol. 1, *The National Level,* edited by John Braeman, Robert H. Bremner, and David Brody, 267–309. Columbus: Ohio State University Press, 1975.
"CAA Civilian Pilot Training Program." *Monthly Labor Review,* July 1940, 80–84.
"CAA's Non-College Training Program." *Aviation,* January 1940, 62.
Caldwell, Cy. "Vidal Statistics." *Aero Digest,* June 1936, 25.
"Civil Flyers, at Own Expense, Create Pilot Reserve for U.S." *Newsweek,* April 15, 1940, 60.
Corn, Joseph J. "Adults and the 'Winged Superchildren of Tomorrow.'" In *The Winged Gospel: America's Romance with Aviation, 1900–1950.* 113–33. New York: Oxford University Press, 1983.
"CPT Operator Gives Scholarships." *Aviation,* September 1942, 239.
Downs, Eldon W. "Army and the Airmail—1934." *Airpower Historian,* January 1962, 41.

"Dual or Duel?" *Aviation*, September 1938, 19.

Green, J. C. "New Jobs for 300,000 Pilots?" *Science Digest*, January 1946, 59–63.

Guyton, B. T. "Making of a Pilot; How the Navy Trains Its Airmen." *New York Times Magazine*, January 12, 1941, 6–7.

Hallion, Richard P. "American Aviation in the Mid-1920s." In *Legacy of Flight: The Guggenheim Contribution to American Aviation*, 3–19. Seattle: University of Washington Press, 1977.

Hamlin, F. "Train or not to Train? Surplus of Military Pilots Threatens to Curtail the Civilian Pilot Training Program." *Flying*, April 1944, 67–68.

———. "World Civilian Pilot Training Program? Plans to Train in the United States Flyers and Aviation Mechanics from All over the World." *Flying*, September 1944, 28.

Hester, Clinton M. "The Civil Aeronautics Act of 1938." *Journal of Air Law*, July 1938, 459.

Hinckley, Robert H. "Fly for Your Lives." *Collier's*, April 25, 1942, 14, 61.

Johnston, S. Paul. "Open Letter to a Senator." *Aviation*, July 1936, 31.

Kerr, F. "Spanish for U.S. Airmen to Aid Latin American Relations." *Education*, December 1941, 248–50.

"Latin Americans Receive Aviation Training by CAA." *Science News Letter*, November 4, 1944, 297.

Leuchtenburg, William E. "The New Deal and the Analogue of War." In *Change and Continuity in Twentieth Century America*, edited by John Braeman, Robert H. Bremner, and Everett Walters, 81–143. Columbus: Ohio State University Press, 1964.

Lodge, J. E. "Flyers by the Ten Thousand; CAA Courses Give Ground and Primary Flying Training." *Popular Science*, September 1940, 46–49.

Milner, Samuel. "Hinckley's Miracle." *[FAA] World*, May 1983, 6–9.

"Money Well Spent; a Few Millions to Train Airplane Pilots." *Saturday Evening Post*, February 4, 1939, 22.

Morris, J. P. "Civilian Pilot Training." *Scholastic*, March 8, 1943, 23.

"National Transportation Policy." *Journal of Air Law*, 1936, 166–67.

"Nazi Youth Are Trained for Aviation." *Aviation*, September 1940, 37.

Neville, L. E. "Keeping Them Aloft; Maintenance under the CAA Flight Training Program." *Aviation*, April 1940, 42–43.

Nugent, Frank S. Review of *20,000 Men a Year.* In *The New York Times Film Reviews, 1913–1968*, vol. 3, *1939–1948*, 1648. New York: Arno Press, 1970.

"Output of New Pilots Pushed as Nation's Air Demands Grow." *Newsweek*, May 5, 1941, 34–35.

Peck, J. "Civilian Jobs for Airmen." *Flying*, January 1946, 23–25.

"Pilot Increase: 100% in Year." *Aviation*, September 1941, 112.

Planck, Charles E. "Enter Mars, Exit Girls." In *Women with Wings*, 139–53. New York: Harper and Bros., 1942.

Polenberg, Richard. "The Decline of the New Deal." In *The New Deal,* vol. 1, *The National Level,* edited by John Braeman, Robert H. Bremner, and David Brody, 246–66. Columbus: Ohio State University Press, 1975.

"The President Urges the Congress to Pass Additional Appropriations for National Defense, January 12, 1939." In *The Public Papers and Addresses of Franklin D. Roosevelt,* edited by Samuel I. Rosenman, 8:73. New York: Macmillan, 1941.

"Press Conference No. 512 (December 27, 1938)." *Complete Presidential Press Conferences of Franklin D. Roosevelt.* Vols. 11–12. New York: Da Capo Press, 1972. [Vol. 12: 319–24].

"Press Conference No. 707 (January 7, 1941)." *Complete Presidential Press Conferences of Franklin D. Roosevelt.* Vols. 17–18. New York: Da Capo Press, 1972. [Vol. 17:19–20].

Radford, A. W. "CPT and the Navy." *Flying,* January 1943, 20–21.

Reiss, George R. "The Gals Are Flying." *Popular Aviation,* March 1940, 46–48.

Ross, B. Joyce. "Mary McLeod Bethune and the National Youth Administration: A Case Study of Power Relationships in the Black Cabinet of Franklin D. Roosevelt." In *Black Leaders of the Twentieth Century,* edited by Leon Litwack and August Meier, 191–219. Urbana: University of Illinois Press, 1982.

Ryan, T. C. "Training Flying Cadets at Civilian Schools." *Aviation,* October 1940, 53.

Schlesinger, Arthur M., Jr. "The Broad Accomplishments of the New Deal." In *The New Deal: Revolution or Evolution?* Problems in American Civilization, 29–34. Boston: D. C. Heath, 1959.

"Scholar's Wings; Civil Aeronautics Board's Nationwide Pilot-Training Program. *Time,* July 29, 1940, 43.

"Selection of Military Pilots." *Fortune,* September 1940, 77–81.

"$700 Airplane." *Time,* January 6, 1934, 46.

Shawe, David. "Protests Mount over Army's Failure to Use CPTP Facilities." *American Aviation,* July 1, 1942, 1, 15.

Stuart, J. "Armed Forces Pilot Pool; War Training Service, Military Version of the former CPTP." *Flying,* July 1943, 48–49.

Stubblefield, B. "How to Get CAA Training." *Aviation,* August 1940, 58.

Studebaker, John W. "Air Youth's Place in the Schools." *Air Youth Horizons,* January 1940, 3.

"This Light Plane Business." *Aviation,* December 1935, 25.

"To Right a Wrong." *Business Week,* April 20, 1935, 36.

"Training the Pilots." *Fortune,* March 1941, 140.

"Transcript of 500th Press Conference (November 15, 1938)." In *The Public Papers and Addresses of Franklin D. Roosevelt,* edited by Samuel I. Rosenman, 7:599. New York: Macmillan, 1941.

Trubey, Cyril C. "When it Comes to 'Pre-Flight' Instruction—A Little Learning Is a Dangerous Thing." *Nation's Schools,* September 1942, 23–24.

Vidal, Gore. "Love of Flying." *New York Review of Books,* January 17, 1985, 16.

Wood, H., and H. L. Pearlman. "Postwar Employment Outlook in Aviation Occupations." *Monthly Labor Review,* June 1945, 1186–1204.

Wright, Richard. "How 'Bigger' Was Born." In *Native Son,* xii. New York: Harper and Row, 1966.

Index